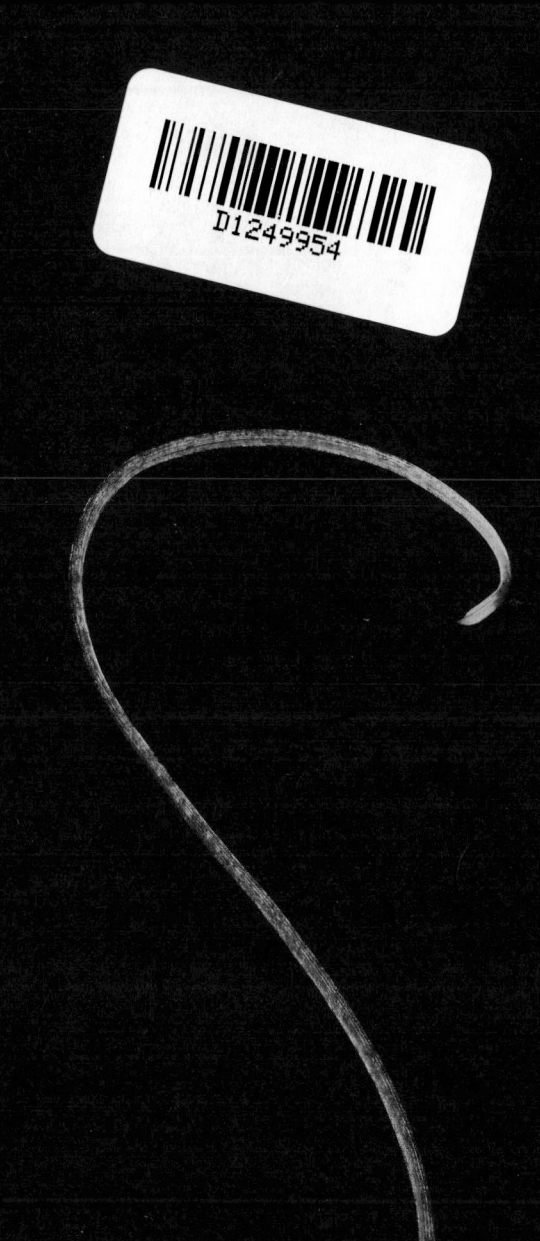

D1249954

THE NEW

L

LEXINGTON
PRESS

ORGANIZATIONAL WISDOM AND EXECUTIVE COURAGE

ORGANIZATIONAL WISDOM AND EXECUTIVE COURAGE

Edited by

Suresh Srivastva

David L. Cooperrider

The New Lexington Press
San Francisco

Copyright © 1998 by The New Lexington Press, 350 Sansome Street, San Francisco, California 94104.

The New Lexington Press is an imprint of Jossey-Bass Inc., Publishers.

All rights reserved. No part of this publication may be reproduced, stored in a retrieval system, or transmitted, in any form or by any means, electronic, mechanical, photocopying, recording, or otherwise, without the prior written permission of the publisher.

Substantial discounts on bulk quantities of The New Lexington Press books are available to corporations, professional associations, and other organizations. For details and discount information, contact the special sales department at (415) 433-1740; Fax (800) 605– 2665.

For sales outside the United States, please contact your local Simon & Schuster International Office.

The New Lexington Press Web address: http://www.newlex.com

Manufactured in the United States of America on Lyons Falls D'Anthology paper, which is a special blend of nontree fibers and totally chlorine-free wood pulp.

Library of Congress Cataloging-in-Publication Data
Organizational wisdom and executive courage / edited by Suresh
   Srivastva, David L. Cooperrider and associates.
     p.   cm.—(The New Lexington Press management and
organization sciences series)
Based on the papers prepared for a symposium held at Case
   Western Reserve University in October, 1996.
   Includes bibliographical references and index.
   ISBN 0-7879-1094-5 (hc : alk. paper)
   1. Management. 2. Organization. 3. Wisdom. 4. Courage.
    I. Srivastva, Suresh, date. II. Cooperrider, David L.
    III. Series.
   HD31. 0766 1997
   658—dc21   97-35883

FIRST EDITION

HB Printing 10 9 8 7 6 5 4 3 2 1

The New Lexington Press
Management and
Organization Sciences Series

CONTENTS

PART THREE
Aiming Higher: Disciplines for the Development of Wisdom and Courage

PREFACE

Many people believe that the best way to overcome uncertainties and complexities, such as those facing organizations today, is through wisdom. Although wisdom is conventionally conceived of as a rational and cognitive attribute, it is rarely independent of human passion and emotion. In many ways, some of them rather mysterious, wisdom is dependent on the state of our hearts at least as much as on the state of our minds. Exploring organizational wisdom and courage can enlighten us about the ways in which organizations can and do rely on the prerational or nonrational foundations of knowledge in managing an uncertain future. This book is about the place of wisdom and courage in organizations and the possibilities they offer.

Wisdom comes from the root word meaning "to know." *Courage* is derived from the French word for "heart." What if organizations functioned with a knowing heart? How would they then shape their future and that of others? It is our opinion that, whether viewed separately or together, organizational wisdom and courage have life-giving power. They reveal the primacy of passion, hope, joy, and several other affective dimensions of knowledge as they relate to the management of organizational complexity. The more confusing, surprising, and (according to some) threatening organizational domains become, the more wisdom and courage can enable the actors within them to thrive despite the insufficiencies of rationality and cognition.

The major contributors to organizational theory have made various assumptions about imagination, wisdom, courage, realities yet to come, and so on. When philosophers made a distinction between tacit knowledge (defined as that which is not accessible to our bare eyes) and explicit knowledge, they were hinting at the foundations of knowing. The notion of tacit knowledge is what comes into focus when we consider organizational theory dealing with the limits of rationality, task environments, authority of the situation, cooperation, and ideas such as "acting thinkingly" and "mindfulness." Most of our scholars have dealt with the role of accumulated, rationalized knowledge and its use in decision making. How to work simultaneously with the tacit aspects of knowledge and make it explicit through wisdom and courage is an exciting area for exploration. The questions begging to be answered (and reinforcing our continuing curiosity) include the following.

ABOUT WISDOM

- What would an organization purposefully designed to seek and uphold wisdom look like?
- Is knowledge wisdom? Is wisdom knowledge?
- Of what value is wisdom, anyway?
- Who are the keepers of wisdom?
- Are there cultural differences in wisdom? Is wisdom universal?

ABOUT COURAGE

- Do our organizations promote or discourage courage?
- Of what value is courage? What can it bring to an organization?
- How can organizational design enhance and embrace the display of courage, and who would dare join in that display? Is courage only a trait of individuals, or can it thrive organizationally?

ABOUT BRINGING WISDOM AND COURAGE TOGETHER

- What can be built from the bringing together of wisdom and courage?
- What type of communication is needed to foster a pairing of the two?
- What would the offspring of such a union be? What systems (old and new) would be necessary to keep the union alive and bearing?
- Are there any organizations out there that are already successfully combining wisdom and courage? Is it even possible? What would it look like? How can it be done?

These questions, and this book, are aimed to pique your ongoing curiosity and kindle your imagination about wisdom and courage in organizations. Both bring humanity and character to the field of organizational theory and practice. Whether considered separately or together, organizational wisdom and courage merit deep thought and cooperative exploration and discussion. It was with this goal in mind that the contributors to this volume assembled at Case Western Reserve University in October 1996 for a symposium on organizational wisdom and courage. The following chapters are the culmination of the multiple dialogues in which they engaged.

This book should appeal both to academics and to executives. It provides suitable material for graduate courses in organizational theory, including important new concepts and new ways to think about designing and conducting research. Perhaps most importantly, it invites academics to question some of the conventional epistemologies in the field of organizational behavior. Given the unquantifiable, nonpositivistic nature of wisdom and courage, studying them demands a value-driven epistemology and personal involvement.

Executives will find fresh ideas for dealing with the complex realities of contemporary management. Rather than offering specific guidelines for action, the book invites executives to reflect on their customary ways of understanding and managing organizational issues. It describes how wisdom and courage can provide a way for executives to intervene in organizational processes and bring about novel change.

Many of the ideas discussed in this book grew out of an advanced graduate seminar. They represent the culmination of a collective discourse among budding scholars and seasoned practitioners. The authors would like to thank the seminar participants, including Ilma Barros, Carla Carten, Thomas Conklin, Russel Griffin, Leonard McKendrick, Nancy Moleski, Beatriz Rivera, Argun Saatçioğlu, Param Srikantia, Robert Wright, Esther Wyss, and Danielle Zandee for their insights and input. We are also grateful for the thoughtful contributions of a recent graduate of our doctoral program, Charleyse Pratt. The trail of thought-provoking questions our student colleagues have left behind is a testament to their immense talent.

Our faculty colleagues—Diana Bilimoria, Richard Boyatzis, Susan Case, Vanessa Druskat, Ronald Fry, David Kolb, Eric Neilsen, William Pasmore, Peter Whitehouse, and Donald Wolfe—were also most gracious with their help and support. The symposium was assisted by a grant from the Weatherhead School of Management's Research Committee; we are indebted to its chairperson, Professor Bo Carlsson, for his expedient and caring response to our request. Dean Scott Cowen has always been a great supporter of ideas that are off the mainstream but relevant for the future of management thinking. His support for our work, as always, is greatly appreciated.

Finally, we would also like to thank Bonnie Copes and Retta Holdorf for their administrative support. They were a great asset in the staging of the symposium. Retta's exemplary dependability and her efforts to provide administrative supervision and support for our work was a cornerstone in completing this important task.

Cleveland, Ohio   SURESH SRIVASTVA
September 1997   DAVID L. COOPERRIDER

THE EDITORS

Suresh Srivastva is professor of organizational behavior at Case Western Reserve University's Weatherhead School of Management. Dr. Srivastva received his Ph.D. (1960) in social psychology from the University of Michigan. His present interests are in teaching professional managers in the field of social and managerial policy and consulting with organizations developing policies in the context of environmental and social change. He has consulted for numerous organizations, including Xerox Corporation, Polaroid, Arthur D. Little, Searle Pharmaceuticals, Kaiser Permanente, and GE. Dr. Srivastva is the author of numerous articles in the area of psychology and management. His major books include *Behavioral Science in Management, Anatomy of a Strike* (with T. Dayal and T. Alfred), *Job Satisfaction and Productivity* (with P. Salipante and others), *Management of Work* (with T. Cummings), *The Executive Mind* (with Associates), *Executive Power* (with Associates), *Executive Integrity* (with Associates), *Appreciative Management and Leadership* (with D. Cooperrider and Associates), and *Executive and Organizational Continuity* (with R. Fry and Associates).

David L. Cooperrider is associate professor of organizational behavior and cochair of the Program for Social Innovation in Global Management at Case Western Reserve University's Weatherhead School of Management. He is also chairman of the National Academy of Management's Division of Organization Development and Change. Dr. Cooperrider has consulted to a wide variety of organizations, including BP America, GTE, Touche Ross Canada, US AID, World Vision, the Nature Conservancy, and the American Hospital Association. Currently Dr. Cooperrider and his colleagues have ongoing organizational learning projects in place in fifty-seven organizations in over one hundred countries. Dr. Cooperrider received the Best Paper of the Year Award from the National Academy of Management, Division of Organization Development and Change (with Frank Barrett). He has been widely published, including articles in *Human*

Relations, Administrative Science Quarterly, the *Journal of Applied Behavioral Science,* and *Contemporary Psychology.* His most recent books include *Appreciative Leadership and Management* (with Suresh Srivastva and Associates), *International and Global Organization Development* (with Peter Sorenson and Associates), and *The Organization Dimensions of Global Change: No Limits to Cooperation* (with Jane Dutton and Associates).

THE CONTRIBUTORS

Nancy J. Adler is professor of organizational behavior and cross-cultural management at McGill University in Montreal, Quebec. She received her B.A. in economics, her M.B.A., and her Ph.D. in management from the University of California at Los Angeles. Dr. Adler conducts research and consults on strategic international human resource management, expatriation, global women leaders and managers, international negotiation, culturally synergistic problem solving, and global organizational development. She has published numerous articles and authored three books: *International Dimensions of Organizational Behavior, Women in Management Worldwide,* and *Competitive Frontiers: Women Managers in a Global Economy.*

Janice M. Beyer is the Harkins and Company Centennial Chair in Business Administration and professor of sociology at the University of Texas at Austin. She holds a Ph.D. in organizational behavior from Cornell University. Dr. Beyer's current research interests focus on organizational culture, socialization, and total quality management. She has coauthored two books, *Implementing Change* and *The Cultures of Work Organizations,* and published over seventy articles on such topics as organizational design, interorganizational relations, and human resources policies and practices.

Kenneth J. Gergen is the Gil and Frank Mustin Professor of Psychology at Swarthmore College, Pennsylvania, where he also directs the interpretation theory program. He has been active in introducing social constructionist ideas within various domains and is currently developing a "relational theory" approach to psychological issues. Among his most recent writings are *Realities and Relationships: Soundings in Social Construction, The Saturated Self,* and *Therapy as Social Construction* (coedited with Sheila McNamee).

Mary M. Gergen is associate professor of psychology and a member of the women's studies program at Pennsylvania State University, Delaware

County Campus, in Philadelphia. Dr. Gergen has written extensively on gender issues in psychology from a postmodern perspective. She has edited two books in feminist psychology, *Feminist Thought and the Structure of Knowledge* and *Toward a New Psychology of Gender* (with Sara Davis).

Pradip N. Khandwalla is professor of management at the Indian Institute of Management, Ahmedabad, India. He received his B.Com degree from Bombay University, his M.B.A. from the University of Pennsylvania's Wharton School of Management, and his Ph.D. from Carnegie-Mellon University. His research interests include organizational theory and design, effective management of public enterprises and strategic organizations, and social and economic development through management. His book *Excellent Management in the Public Sector* received the Escorts Award for the best management book of 1990. His latest book, *Management Styles,* is a study of ten archetypal management styles and defective versions of them.

Sheila McNamee is Communication Department chair and professor of communication at the University of New Hampshire. She writes and lectures extensively on research innovations, meanings in organizational life, and social construction in therapeutic processes. Her current work focuses on crafting a concept of relational responsibility. She was coeditor (with Kenneth J. Gergen) of *Therapy as Social Construction.*

David Niño is an organization development consultant and trainer with the City of Austin, Texas, where he specializes in adapting and implementing Total Quality Management in the public sector. He is a doctoral student in the Department of Management at the University of Texas at Austin, where he earned undergraduate and graduate degrees in philosophy, finance, and Latin American studies. During his professional career he has trained and consulted with public and private sector organizations in both the United States and Mexico.

Argun Saatçioğlu is a Ph.D. student in organizational behavior at Case Western Reserve University. He received his B.S. in management from Bilkent University, Ankara, Turkey, and his M.S. in organizational behavior from the University of Hartford, Connecticut. His current research interests include ways of generating knowledge in organizations, dialogue and authenticity in groups, diffusion of cultural innovations, and organization theory.

Edward E. Sampson is professor of psychology at California State University in Northridge, California, and a scholar with the Center for Critical Studies in Berkeley. He has published about a dozen books, including *Celebrating the Other,* and many major articles, including a series for *American Psychologist* that developed a social constructionist analysis of psychology.

William R. Torbert is professor in the Wallace E. Carroll School of Management at Boston College. He received his B.A. (1965) and Ph.D. (1971) from Yale University. He has consulted for numerous organizations, including Volvo, Lego, Citizens US HomeCare, Energy Corporation, and Digital Equipment Corporation. Professor Torbert is the author of several books, including *Personal and Organizational Transformations: The True Challenge of Generating Continual Quality Improvement* (with D. Fisher) and *Managing the Corporate Dream: Restructuring for Long-Term Success.*

Karl E. Weick is the Rensis Likert Collegiate Professor of Organizational Behavior and Psychology at the University of Michigan. Dr. Weick received his Ph.D. (1962) from Ohio State University. His research interests include social psychology, the effects of stress on thinking and imagination, social commitment, and links between theory and practice. In 1990 Dr. Weick received the Academy of Management's Irwin Award for distinguished lifetime scholarly achievement. His books include *The Social Psychology of Organizing* and *Managerial Behavior, Performance and Effectiveness,* which won the 1972 Book of the Year award from the American College of Hospital Administration.

Peter B. Vaill is professor of human systems at the School of Government and Business Administration, George Washington University, and former dean of the school. He has also served on the faculties of the Graduate School of Management, University of California, Los Angeles, the University of Connecticut School of Business Administration, and the Stanford Graduate School of Business. He holds a B.A. degree (1958) in psychology from the University of Minnesota and M.B.A. (1960) and D.B.A. (1964) degrees from Harvard Business School. His research and writing have chiefly been in the fields of organizational excellence, strategic management, organizational development, and the philosophy of social science. He has been consultant to corporations, government agencies, health systems, and educational institutions. He is the author of many books, including a book of essays on management, *Managing as a Performing Art* (1989).

1

AN INVITATION TO ORGANIZATIONAL WISDOM AND EXECUTIVE COURAGE

David L. Cooperrider and Suresh Srivastva

AN INCIDENT recounted by Huston Smith (1991) in his classic work on our "great wisdom traditions" provides a profound symbol for this chapter's opening:

> On July 16, 1945, in the deep privacy of a New Mexico desert, an event occurred that may prove to be the most important single happening of the twentieth century. A chain reaction of scientific discoveries that began at the University of Chicago and centered at "site Y" at Los Alamos was culminated. The first atomic bomb was, as we say, a success.
>
> No one had been more instrumental in this achievement than Robert Oppenheimer, director of the Los Alamos project. An observer who was watching him closely that morning has given us the following account: "He grew tenser as the last seconds ticked off. He scarcely breathed. He held on to a post to steady himself. . . . When the announcer shouted "Now!" and there came this tremendous burst of light, followed . . . by the deep-growing roar of the explosion, his face relaxed in an expression of tremendous relief." This much from the outside. But what flashed through Oppenheimer's own mind during those moments, he recalled later, were two lines from the *Bhagavad Gita* in which the speaker is God:
>
> "I am become death, the shatterer of worlds;
> Waiting for that hour that ripens to their doom."

There are at least three things that this story does for us. First, it is a classic commentary on the *big* context—something so big it scarcely needs mentioning. With the invention of the bomb, humankind indeed entered into a totally new era of history, perhaps even of evolution, marked simultaneously by the continued march of scientific knowledge, extraordinary technical and economic accomplishments, and the creation of a long list of global and local, linked threats. The issues of this era are especially noteworthy because of their many side effects, unclear cause-effect structures, worldwide reach, long lead times, and often irreversible consequences that are chronic and insidious rather than acute and dramatic—the discovery of a continent-sized hole in the ozone layer, toxic substance concentrations, debt-ridden economies whose instabilities are intensified by growing gaps between rich and poor, man-made climate change, and so on. When Oppenheimer "grew tenser as the last seconds ticked off" and "scarcely breathed," his mind instantly gravitated to a source of ancient wisdom. It was a signal moment: the scientist, the person, the Los Alamos project executive, searching not just for knowledge but for the *right knowledge*. A metaphor for our times?

A second thing the story does is to begin linking courage and wisdom together. Could it be that courage is a prerequisite for the pursuit of wisdom? Ultimately, isn't wisdom necessary to understanding the awesome and fragile fabric of life, and does it not take courage to open our hearts as fully as this understanding implies?

The third thing the anecdote does, for better or for worse, is to instantly elevate the stakes. All of a sudden, with our first mention of wisdom, we are talking about world affairs and dramatic choices of historic proportions. We are also reciting ancient texts (such as the *Bhagavad Gita*). Who are *we*, then, to speak of wisdom? Yes, we know our times are crying out for wisdom—but we back away. As we shall see next, the silence surrounding the subject of wisdom in the management literature is conspicuous. Is it indifference? No, we do not think so. Obviously there are many factors contributing to that silence, but the one thing that stands out is simply this: it is not easy to talk about wisdom without sounding pretentious. Discourses on wisdom and courage are often embedded in individualistic, "great man" stories. Historically they have been content-focused debates, the seeking (for possession) of a set of permanent principles. Indeed, one hope for this book is that we can begin to democratize our notions of wisdom and courage, to go beyond the individualism and gender bias of "great man" stories and begin discovering wisdom and courage within the everyday, mundane activities of our organizations and institutions—precisely where they matter most.

WHAT IS ORGANIZATIONAL WISDOM?

Precisely at a time when we sense that the need for wisdom is higher than ever, it appears, paradoxically, to be less and less available. In fact, there may be no aspect of organizational life about which the management field is more confused than the role of wisdom and courage in good management and effective executive leadership.

A quick case in point. Very recently two of the field's top researchers completed a much-needed review of the topics of wisdom and courage in the management literature (see Chapter Four). What turned up was totally surprising, even disturbing: they located not one study, not one index entry, in the literature on organizational behavior for either wisdom or courage. As if this was not enough, the scholars had already examined results from one of the largest pieces of research ever done on the fit between organizational cultures and individual values; it was a search for the "central values" that align people and organizations. Of 54 items culled from an initial list of 110, *none* included either courage or wisdom.

The only notable exceptions appear to be when business leaders themselves—people such as Walter Haas, Jr., Anita Roddick, J. Irwin Miller, Karen N. Horn, and others—explain their impressive careers in autobiographies. For example, when Robert Hass of Levi Strauss and Co. was asked in 1995 why his company had shown such courageous social leadership, he demonstrated an executive-level linkage of wisdom and courage. He replied that they had done it "by sticking with conventional wisdom and conventional practice—and not daring to take the lead in social practices as well as business practices . . . you're dooming yourself to extinction" (Bollier, 1996, p. 2). James E. Burke, the former chairman of the board and chief executive officer of Johnson & Johnson, was even more explicit about organizational wisdom. The key to his company's success, he said, was "the *wisdom of serving* the public. . . . We were faced by the Tylenol tragedy. Overnight one of our Tylenol products went from being a thriving business to becoming a murder weapon that killed seven people. But our response was . . . to serve the public interest—regardless of the cost. The critical difference was the social and ethical commitment we shared with our customers. . . . We too often fail to see the impressive results that can be achieved when buyer and seller honor their best impulses" (p. 6).

But seizing the moment like Johnson & Johnson did requires an organization that is courageous and visionary. The organization must be willing to stretch itself in new ways; it must be able to create conditions, conversations, and learning settings conducive to the generation of wise action. Under James Burke's leadership, Johnson & Johnson's sales grew from $2.5 billion to $9 billion over a twelve-year period. Building on precisely this example, Norman Lear's words amplify the importance of inquiry into organizational wisdom:

> Not so long ago, the church, the family, schools, and civil authority were the preeminent institutions of our culture. They were respected sources of moral authority. They transmitted the wisdom of one generation to the next. Now, for many complex economic and social reasons, these institutions have become less influential. And whether it likes it or not ... business has stepped into the breach. Business leaders have become role models. Their decisions set a moral benchmark for the nation. ... As the old ancestral order wanes, we are presented with an unprecedented challenge. In a culture that yearns for hope and constructive change—yet seems overwhelmed by cynicism, fear, and resentment—we urgently need new leadership [p. ix].

The hopeful message of this book is that contemporary society is not only profoundly shaped by organizations but also can be shaped for the better by them, through the leadership of great organizations. To an extent unimaginable a decade ago, the ideals of building a healthy, prosperous, and sustainable future for the world are taking on form and substance. Obstacles to cooperation and human enterprise that long seemed immovable have collapsed. With economic globalization and changing local conditions, organizations are increasingly stepping forward to wrestle with complex issues that affect not only their shareholders, employees, and customers but also the quality of life in the world's communities and cities, the world's ecosystems, and people in countries around the globe (Cooperrider and Dutton, forthcoming). The best path to the good society, we believe, is the construction of great organizations. We need to seek out and tell the stories of these organizations as a way of accelerating a new vocabulary of courage and wisdom (Srivastva and Cooperrider, 1990). Human systems often move in the direction of what they ask questions about.

This volume is based on the beliefs that wisdom is the pivotal force behind organizational greatness, that there can be no such greatness without the courage that sustains the search for wisdom's guidance, and that once they are combined into one single and powerful unity, our wiser and more courageous organizations will indeed begin to realize their potential as agents of change for world betterment.

OVERVIEW OF THE CONTENTS

The remaining ten chapters of this book were written for a symposium at Case Western Reserve University, in response to a call to the field to begin a new dialogue on questions exactly like these. The book is divided conceptually into three parts: "Evolutionary Wisdom: A Sensemaking Perspective," "Into the Relational Heart of Organization: The Social Construction of Wisdom and Courage," and "Aiming Higher: Disciplines for the Development of Wisdom and Courage." As we turn to a brief overview of each chapter, we hope to show that this collection has succeeded, at least in some small way, in starting a new conversation and perhaps even a new vocabulary of understanding.

EVOLUTIONARY WISDOM: A SENSEMAKING PERSPECTIVE

The chapters by Peter Vaill (Chapter Two), Karl Weick (Chapter Three), and Janice M. Beyer and David Niño (Chapter Four) share the conviction that organizational wisdom is not a transcendent attribute but rather a sensemaking response to temporality, to emergent processes, to specific conditions and opportunities, and to organizational culture. Sensemaking, in cognitive and cultural terms, is about sizing up a situation when one is faced with an imperative to act. Sensemaking, the authors contend, is the birthplace of both wisdom and courage because it sets the frame for decision making, becomes the basis for envisioning possible futures, creates the context for communicating and linking with others, and is itself transformed by the designs and processes of organizing. Wisdom is not a permanent trait but a dynamic process of subtle judging and knowing that must always be readjusted, restructured, and rebuilt. The chapters in Part One all locate the possibilities for accomplishing wisdom through the processes by which knowledge is created, shared, and acted on—all in temporally complex settings where timing, rhythms, and subtle crosscurrents are often everything. All three chapters examine organizational forces— management cultures, organizational designs, and the sheer velocity of change in organizations—that get in the way of wise sensemaking as well as courageous action. And all three are rich with examples to help us see how a sensemaking lens identifies important new ways to both think about and organize for increases in wisdom. A powerful common theme, or metaphor, involves the notion of management as a performing art, as improvisation. Sensemaking is thus an improvisational way of learning that makes action more intelligent and adaptive. It recapitulates the wisdom, say the authors, inherent in all evolutionary processes.

Peter B. Vaill, in "The Unspeakable Texture of Process Wisdom" (Chapter Two), begins by placing the whole theme of this book into the context of contemporary managerial and organizational life. In particular, he begins with his colorful metaphor of organizing as a performing art in the midst of permanent white water. What can we possibly mean by the transcendent, timeless notion of wisdom in a context in which novelty, surprise, chaos, unexpected emergencies, unclear cause-effect relationships, multiple meanings, and endless uncertainties all coexist with immediate demands for knowledgeable action, in the face of fallible knowledge? Could it be, he asks, that clues to organizational wisdom can be found in commonplace expressions such as "playing it by ear," "feeling your way around," or "nursing something along"? Is there possibly an epistemology or an understanding of managerial leadership and wisdom inherent in the expression "flying by the seat of your pants"?

Vaill's sensitivity to the messiness and complexity of contemporary managerial life, as well as to the "process wisdom" he later describes, grew from his own experiences in the late 1970s as a "midlevel general manager" (the dean) of a rapidly growing business school. The best one can do in such circumstances, Vaill says, is to feel your way along. Reflecting further, Vaill singles out the one thing that no formal management education could have ever prepared him for—temporality. To be "in possession" of all the management competencies and research-based truths taught in business schools would ensure very little in situ in the absence of an artful relationship with contingencies, unique rhythms and pacing, disjointed time streams, the evanescent flows of human relationships, and so on. "Sometimes I had a little bit of influence over the pace and sequence of things in one of these streams," acknowledges Vaill, "but as often I was 'playing catch-up,' 'dodging someone else's bullets,' 'being overtaken by events,' or 'trying to get ahead' of a situation. . . . The calendar was filled with contingencies." The point: everything in organizational life is interactive, and everything interactive exists in a spatiotemporal field of relationships. In Vaill's philosophy of temporality it is not just that managerial life is complex and fast-paced. Temporality is not so much something that managerial work has or has become (that is, it is not time-driven and time-obsessed), it is something managerial work *is*. As Vaill says, "It is temporal before it is anything else!"

Vaill introduces the term *process wisdom* to capture the feeling of moving through situations and problems and yet somehow acting "wisely" in relation to them. To the extent that managerial leadership is a performing art, it is perhaps best understood as street theater, where the script, the characters, the props, and the drama itself are all unfolding in real time. Drawing on Chester Barnard's early work (1938), Vaill highlights words like *feeling, judgment, balance,* and *appropriateness*. Wisdom, therefore, is a way of thinking and being in relation to motion and change, the spatiotemporal swirl. While struggling for an adequate way to talk about process wisdom, Vaill submits that it combines the qualities of mind and character we have always meant by wisdom with the ability to dance with change and instability without losing one's sense of purpose and direction. In this sense managerial leadership is not learned, it *is* learning. Much needed, the author concludes, is a learning process of process wisdom: "There can hardly be a more important quality for managerial leadership than process wisdom."

Almost seamlessly, Karl E. Weick's "The Attitude of Wisdom: Ambivalence as the Optimal Compromise" (Chapter Three) puts words to the kind of process wisdom signaled in the previous chapter and links it with forms of evolutionary adaptation. "Knowledge and ignorance balance on the pivot of improvisation," concludes Weick, and "this configuration exhibits the ambivalence of wisdom and celebrates the wisdom of ambivalence."

As Weick sees it, an attitude of wisdom is one way people in complex systems deal with fallible knowledge and remain adaptive in a world of permanent white water. The challenge of wisdom lies in the ways people approach situations: "When people create maps of an unknowable, unpredictable world, they face strong temptations toward either overconfident knowing or overly cautious doubt." Wisdom rises above the pull of both. Overconfident knowing is often unwise in the context of the temporal swirl because overconfidence ("we know everything there is to know") blocks the discernment of facts or conditions that are not obvious. It often blinds us to subtleties, deters other people from challenging our apparent knowledge, and ignores novelties that do not fit confident conclusions. At the other extreme is overly cautious doubt, which undermines wisdom in organizations in other, less obvious ways. Moving from wisdom to overcaution involves forgetting or dismissing what one knows and inflating the amount of knowledge that remains to be known. In the process, bold action is held at bay—and many times in organizational life it is only through action itself that better understandings unfold. The essence of wisdom is knowing that one does not know everything and appreciating that all knowledge is fallible; thus wisdom is found in the balance between knowing and doubting. Wisdom is about "successful simultaneity"—the need both to keep asking questions and to act like one has most of the answers. This is what will make action more intelligent and adaptive, because it recapitulates the wisdom inherent in all evolutionary processes.

To the extent to which wisdom is the capacity to judge rightly in matters relating to life and conduct, it is the attitude of wisdom, argues Weick, that needs cultivation in organizational life. We can take lessons, for example from the wise physician who modifies the traditional sequence symptom-diagnosis-treatment to symptom-treatment-diagnosis. Physicians who make this modification postpone the diagnosis to keep alive their questioning attitude, but they still act: they treat symptoms in order to be able to make the diagnosis, not the other way around. In this frame, a hunch held lightly is a direction to be followed, not a decision to be defended. It is easier to change directions than to reverse decisions. Less is at stake. Similar lessons can be drawn from the flexible treatment of preplanned material in jazz improvisation. What improvisation accomplishes, says Weick, is that it enables people to wade into situations with fallible knowledge, secure in the belief that they can recombine that knowledge by shifting fallibilities around. To be aware that one is ignorant but to act anyway is made possible when people trust that a combination of attentiveness, resilience, and improvisation can substitute for omniscience.

In Chapter Four, "Facing the Future: Backing Courage with Wisdom," Janice M. Beyer and David Niño build directly on Weick's notion of wisdom as a balance between knowing and doubting, but they conclude that business organizations are tough places to act with wisdom. Their chapter delves into the question, Exactly how do our corporate cultures support or undermine both courageous and wise action?

The chapter setup is interesting. First, as noted previously, Beyer and Niño surveyed the literature on organizational behavior and found *not one* study on courage or wisdom. They also examined the results from the largest study ever done on the fit between organizational cultures and individual values and there too found no reference to either courage or wisdom. The neglect of both terms in all of these sources raises important questions: What is it about these subjects that has led to their neglect specifically in writings about management? (They have been examined in some detail in other social science fields.) Could it be that courage and wisdom describe something exceptional, something not expected to happen very often, and are therefore peripheral to management concerns? (But charismatic leadership is likewise exceptional, and it is frequently discussed in the management literature.) Or could it be that these terms represent qualities to which managers do not aspire? Could it be that it is taboo to connect the ideals behind courage and wisdom with those underlying management?

To explore these issues, Beyer and Niño examine the courage and wisdom evidenced by whistle-blowers. The two studies they draw upon illustrate the isolation faced by people who publicly expose serious wrongdoing on the part of their organization. In the cases Beyer and Niño recount in their chapter, managers ignored or denied allegations of wrongdoing until the employees making them felt that they personally had to go public. Of course they experienced fear, and their fears were well-founded. The organizations retaliated in horrendous ways against them, in classic win-lose fashion. Sometimes the whistle-blowers received support from their coworkers, but by definition, never from management. People lost jobs and relationships, not to mention the impact on their families and communities. The managers also lost, because they ended up being exposed anyway and often had to pay major sums in damages. If wisdom is defined as an intellectual grasp of the means and ends of practical life, and if it involves reflection, judgment, and recognition of one's limitations and possibilities, then were the managers involved wise? More important, how do the cultures of work organizations support or undermine courageous and wise action?

Beyer and Niño's analysis is powerful. To help the reader better understand the relationship between courage and culture, for example, they contrast the cultures of dangerous occupations with managerial cultures. Cultures are explained as repositories of beliefs and practices that people use to cope with life's uncertainties. Police, soldiers, pilots, firefighters, high steel ironworkers, demolition workers, and underground miners are all cited by the authors as people whose occupational cultures help build courage in the face of dangers and risks. Police work is indeed dangerous, and to help justify taking the risks, police have cultivated an "ideology of absolute morality." According to this ideology, what the police do as agents of the state is by definition good and proper, because they are protecting the public in the name of the common good. Through this kind of ideology and other cultural forms like rites of passage, story telling, and taboos, the social significance of the work is elevated in the eyes of those performing it. Where there is no culture emphasizing the work's moral purpose, suggest the authors, there is little chance for acts of courage or wisdom.

And this is where managerial cultures are brought into question: no professional codes of ethics, bureaucratic mazes, a pragmatism that reinforces agility in avoiding blame, opportunism and shifting alliances, myths of rationality that diffuse the emotions that undergird moral convictions, deficit-oriented vocabularies (everything framed in terms of problems) that serve to continuously devalue the past, precious few stories about managerial work as a noble profession serving the common good, and so on. In such an occupational culture, conclude the authors, managers cannot act with courage or wisdom. Indeed, "their relative, situational morality is not anchored in sustained moral convictions and thus precludes their acting with true courage." But could it be, ask Beyer and Niño, that approaches to management research have also made us myopic and blinded us to courageous and wise behavior in organizations? Perhaps it is time to look for more that is admirable in management practice? Looking for courage and wisdom, they conclude, is perhaps a good place to start.

THE SOCIAL CONSTRUCTION OF WISDOM AND COURAGE

All that is wise or courageous grows from relationships. This is the keystone of all three chapters in Part Two. Wisdom and courage, the authors of Part Two contend, are not qualities or inner traits that some individuals possess or do not possess. More radically, wisdom and courage do not even exist as "things." They are not, for example, competencies or features of the natural world that are available for scientific exploration. Nor are they shared "ideals" that transcend cultures. What one group might define as courageous or wise another might label as heartless genocide or cowardly terrorism. Indeed, there is not one single act in the world, the authors of Part Two would contend, that can be claimed to be *inherently* wise or courageous. Rather, these authors agree, wisdom and courage are first and foremost words or elements in a discourse. Each of the authors writes from a social constructionist stance, which is interested not in wisdom and courage per se but in the ways the language and meanings surrounding wisdom and

courage are constructed and how those constructions function in ɪ.
tionship-enhancing or relationship-canceling ways.

More broadly, social constructionism is an approach to human science and practice that replaces the individual (or any single entity) with
the relationship as the locus of knowledge and wisdom. Philosophically
it involves a decisive shift in the Western intellectual tradition, from
cogito ergo sum, to *communicamus ergo sum.* The common thread in
most constructionist writing is a concern with the processes by which
human beings, their values, and commonsense and scientific knowledge
are both produced in, and reproduce, human communities. Constructionism replaces absolutist claims ("the final word") with the never-
ending collaborative quest to understand and construct options for
better living. (For the principal statement on this topic, see Gergen,
1994.)

One of the prominent strengths of the constructionist perspective,
from the vantage point of the exploration inaugurated by this volume,
is that it is always seeking to open the door to a fuller interweaving of
disparate communities of meaning. One will not find frozen definitions
of wisdom or courage in Part Two. While descriptions of social constructionism vary widely and are subject to an enormous and rapidly
expanding body of scholarship, there are at least three exciting ways
social constructionism can expand the scope and significance of organizational scholarship in regard to wisdom and courage:

1. It invites a *self-reflexive form of inquiry* that questions openly the
   political and practical consequences of the theorizing we do as
   scholars. What happens, for example, if we continue to define or
   construct wisdom in individualistic terms?

2. It invites a *scholarship of dislodgment,* a critical theoretical
   stance that is focused on the general disruption of the conventional, on challenging those aspects of the status quo that tend to
   seal off options and leave dissenting voices unheard.

3. It invites a *scholarship of transformation,* an appreciative construction of possible worlds from anticipatory theory that offers
   new visions and vocabularies of possibility.

All of these are important forms of scholarship, and each is illustrated,
at least partially, in the chapters in Part Two.

Sheila McNamee challenges us immediately in "Reinscribing Organizational Wisdom and Courage: The Relationally Engaged Organization" (Chapter Five) by resisting anything that sounds like an

essentialist account of wisdom and courage. Essentialist talk, she elaborates, is the manifestation of our long-standing tradition of explaining things like motives, intentions, intelligence, emotions, and the like—including wisdom and courage—in terms of personal attributes. In this traditional way of explaining things, persons are viewed as containers holding the essential features of their individuality. In Western culture the individual has long occupied a place of commanding importance, and the "theoretical individualism" that has gone along with that position has made our way of talking about wisdom and courage almost automatically individualistic. McNamee demonstrates that, in contrast to our robust vocabulary about individualism, we in the West have an impoverished language of relatedness. We do not ask whether *a relationship* thinks, feels, or is wise or courageous. We identify wise men, but a wise relationship? Perhaps our ways of talking do matter.

As it has been said, the limits of our language may define the limits of our world. So the questions McNamee raises are fundamental: Can relationships become the reality by which life is lived until there is a vocabulary through which they can be realized? What will happen if we reinscribe the language of wisdom and courage with a relational intelligibility and shift our attention to what transpires between people, not what is contained within them? More important, once we achieve a relational vocabulary, do notions of courage and wisdom help us achieve the sort of multivocal, globally engaged organization so necessary to today's world? Can we locate wisdom in the "knowing heart" of an organization rather than in the minds of individuals?

The reinscription of wisdom and courage begins, submits the author, the moment our focus shifts to the movement of conversations throughout an organization. It is these conversations that give the organization life. Abandoning the idea that our organizations are led by individuals who embody courage and wisdom allows us to be attentive to organizations as communities where coordination of multiple logics, multiple meaning systems, and multiple voices becomes the primary concern. As our attention shifts toward awareness of the communal processes through which certain realities and beliefs are created, we begin to "live within conversations." We enter the interactive moment with "knowledge" that we anticipate will be altered, discarded, and reinvented as we engage others. The transformative dialogue born of the different stance we take in the interactive moment, born of our attention to the movement and connection of our conversations, offers the possibility of locating wisdom and courage in the relational heart of organizing.

In Chapter Six, "The Political Organization of Wisdom and Courage," Edward E. Sampson demonstrates one of the commitments of the social constructionist perspective—a critical scholarship of dislodgment. Too often in scientific and scholarly pursuits, attention is focused "out there," with little open reflection *inside* the discipline. Hidden from view, frequently, are potentially oppressive tendencies and values or even innocent but detrimental consequences of our work. The constructionist recognizes that any social group, whether a primitive society or a scientific subculture, develops a working language (which includes concepts, theories, and specialized vocabularies) and uses it to furnish accounts of what is real, rational, and right. Without reflexive and critical deliberation—exploration into the historically and culturally situated character and consequence of these accounts (including our own), there is always the risk of settling in too quickly. Univocal expression tends to occlude critiques.

Sampson's aim is to move the discussion surrounding wisdom and courage "away from an attachment to saintly words." For example, our tendency is to hold up courage as a universally positive attribute. But not so quick, says the author. Using *wisdom* and *courage* as his specimens, Sampson argues that terms like these are too often used to legitimate horrific actions, even genocide. And therefore, the author states, "my goal . . . is not to help organizations learn how to be wise or courageous."

Sampson's writing is compelling, even gut-wrenching. It grows out of his work in the area of intergroup relations. Researchers in this field are often astounded by the extremes to which one group will go to harm another. Through years of study, Sampson has come to realize that although we would use highly negative terms to describe such acts as a terrorist attack or genocide, their perpetrators often describe them using words such as *courageous* and *wise*—terms we reserve for acts we consider praiseworthy. Sampson asks, "If one group considers a terrorist act to be cowardly but another defines it as an act of rare bravery, which is it?" Were tobacco company executives, when they appeared before a congressional committee on health hazards, showing courage and wisdom in the face of great odds against them? What about genocide? Wasn't the Holocaust, a carefully orchestrated and highly organized enterprise, made possible only because people (a substantial number of them, in fact) accepted the plan as wise? "After all," Sampson points out, "if [the Jews] were actually cancerous growths threatening the life blood of the nation, then their elimination would appear to be a very wise course of action."

Wisdom and *courage* do not, argues the constructionist, name universal truths. They are part of the discourses of organized collectivities and are used by those collectivities to justify their actions and enlist the willing service of others. The terms we use in our everyday life, Sampson argues, do not refer to things in "the real world"; rather, they construct that world, the very world to which they appear to refer. But too often we forget the arbitrary basis of the language we employ. Over time people begin to believe that their group's way is *the* way (the wise way, the good way, and so on). As a result they begin to relate to diverse others in ways that serve to confirm for them the superiority of their way. The potential culmination of this process is the goal of eliminating the other, as the Holocaust illustrates.

Thus Sampson prefers to remain, to the very end, more than arm's length from any invitation to define wisdom. The closest he gets is in suggesting what wisdom is not: wisdom, he says, is killed by relationship-canceling conversations. In the end, Sampson concludes, monologues cave in on themselves. Without others there can be no conversation, no intelligibility, no community. Thus any silencing of the other eventually undermines the intelligibility of the social world.

But isn't the silencing of voices an everyday occurrence in our bureaucracies, our hierarchies, our organizations? Perhaps, write Mary M. and Kenneth J. Gergen in Chapter Seven, "The Relational Rebirthing of Wisdom and Courage: Voices Wise and Other/Wise," but there are vital and viable alternatives. Theirs is a wonderful example of a scholarship of transformation in a constructionist key. Even though critiques and dislodgment are valuable resources for generating ferment, by themselves they might be insufficient. Social transformation, say the Gergens, requires new visions and vocabularies, new possibilities, new practices that by their very existence begin to chart new courses.

Much needed, the authors argue, is a heightened consciousness of our connections. We need a revised understanding of organizational wisdom and courage that celebrates relatedness, interdependence, and dialogue—including even a loss of our consciousness of *self* to better sense the significance of *we*. Indeed, if we are to keep any traces of "theoretical individualism" alive, then perhaps we must become more conversant with multiple intelligibilities and viewpoints, or join in "a polyphony of multiple relationships."

The metaphor is truly interesting: as those with a musical bent will appreciate, polyphony, a composition technique that emerged in the eleventh and twelfth centuries, literally means "having multiple voices." In polyphonic music, two or more independent but organically related voices sound against one another. In polyphonic partiture we find multiple melodic lines, not just melody and chorus. Every line could in theory be performed separately, but if they are all performed simultaneously, a rich and complex totality emerges. Most important, together with the independent horizontal lines (melodies), vertical lines (harmonies) emerge, which also form a totality. In this way a network of horizontal and vertical lines is created, in which every voice is meaningful but at the same time gains meaning only in relation to the other voices. Characteristic of Flemmish polyphony in particular is the equivalence of all. There is no soloist part and chorus part. The different voices are created simultaneously in and through one another in relational practice.

It is in this spirit that Gergen and Gergen attempt to envision courageous and wise action as features distributed throughout the relational fabric of entire groups and organizations. Rather than offering a handy three-step program for achieving wisdom and courage in organizations, the authors offer a series of proposals as "incitements to dialogue and action." Providing a neat segue into Part Three, they leave us with a number of compelling questions: Can organizations as a whole differ along a "continuum of wisdom"? Are there relational practices that carry forward the polyphonic vision? Can we envision organizations in full voice? Would such organizations be wiser?

THE DEVELOPMENT OF WISDOM AND COURAGE

Today's global forces are creating a remarkable new set of circumstances. Organizations inherited from the modern era may be unequal to the challenges posed by overpopulation, environmental damage, ever-faster technological change, and so on. Today's challenges are international in nature, crossing borders all over the globe, simultaneously affecting local and global realities, and reminding us that the earth, for all its historically produced divisions, is a single unit.

The authors of Part Three suggest that it is time to aim higher, time to lift people's vision and provide a larger sense of purpose for the whole field of management. Isn't it time to view organization and management studies on a much broader scale than ever before—indeed, as a matter of world affairs? When we consider the needs of our day, can we say that humanity, in and through its organizations, is acting wisely? Or, more positively, is it not true that our common future depends on the extent to which today's executives, ordinary citizens, and political leaders can develop a vision of a better world and a shared will to achieve it? Organizations capable of new levels of wisdom and courage must play an integral part in this process. But can organizations, like individuals, rise above bread-and-butter concerns and realize greatness? Ultimately, is not wisdom related to a sensitive, spiritual understanding of the awesome and fragile fabric of life? Are there practical disciplines, liberating practices, that we can use in organizations to develop the kinds of wise responses the world is calling for?

Pradip N. Khandwalla launches Part Three by calling upon management professionals to explore organizational greatness. It is a daring challenge. Chapter Eight, "Thorny Glory: Toward Organizational Greatness," combines top-notch scholarship in the area of organizational strategy with empirical research and exceptional vision. It invites all of us to aim higher.

"Organizational greatness ascends on two legs," Khandwalla writes. One leg is the familiar notion of organizational excellence (especially performance excellence) in a competitive context. The other is what Khandwalla calls exalted striving—working strategically to advance the social condition of humanity and the ecological well-being of the earth. In organizational terms, exalted striving means going beyond business as usual to promote some ethic, social concern, or spiritual state.

In many ways Khandwalla has produced an iconoclastic chapter. The conjoining of profits and social ideals is a disquieting proposition for some people. There is "business," and there is "good works," and never the two shall meet (see Bollier, 1996). But Khandwalla proposes exactly the opposite. Story after story demonstrates their constructive (but not always easily obtained) synergy. It is about "thorny glory." The pursuit of the sublime along with the mundane is no easy path; there are numerous challenges that call for increases in organizations' operating complexity and require more differentiated strategies, structures, know-how, and rules.

Khandwalla demonstrates that organizations can indeed rise above their bread-and-butter concerns. Several "paths to organizational exaltation" are discussed, including stakeholder orientation, corporate social responsibility, strategic domain development, institution building, organizational ethics, organizational justice, organizational altruism, radical humanism, and organization spirituality. Each of these are well researched. Likewise, Khandwalla provides useful and concrete illustrations, with material from organizations like Johnson & Johnson;

Ben and Jerry's; the House of Tatas; the Grameen Bank; Bharat Heavy Electricals, Ltd.; the Swadhyay Movement; and others. Each illustrates one or more of the paths to exaltation, and each helps develop the concept of greatness as something beyond performance excellence. Gandhi's concept of trusteeship is a case in point: it is not enough to create wealth; the businessperson must administer it as a trustee for society.

Let's be part of it as a field, says Khandwalla. Not only are all the necessary materials there (practice is way out in front of theory), but fusing the mundane with the sublime may well provide a vast new impetus to management innovation and new organizational forms, which in turn can sustain managerial creativity in the coming decades. Khandwalla asks, "Will organizational researchers rise to the occasion and build a paradigm of organizational greatness? Will they show wisdom and courage?"

Nancy J. Adler, in "Societal Leadership: The Wisdom of Peace" (Chapter Nine), agrees with Khandwalla—it *is* time to aim higher. "Why not have peace in the twenty-first century?" she asks. Would not wise leaders declare peace instead of continuing to resolve the world's conflicts through violence? What would it take to marry the practical idealism found in communities like Çatal Höyük (archeological records date these peaceful communities to 7,000 B.C., or ninety centuries ago) to contemporary reality?

Adler's thesis is that we need two things: first, a counterintuitive shift away from our widely accepted open-systems type of thinking to closed-system, global thinking, and second, a new and wiser leadership "radically different from that of the last seventy centuries." Where are we to find wise leaders to guide us toward beliefs that differ so markedly from those of the present? Adler's answer grows from her research into the leadership of women in high political offices around the world.

The myth, she explains, is that there are but a few women leaders and that women's assumption of power in not only rare but also sporadic. But in recent history, twenty-seven women have held the highest offices in their country. Moreover, their numbers appear to be rapidly increasing—over half of the twenty-seven have come to power since 1990. "While many people in search of models for twenty-first-century global leadership continue to review men's historical patterns of success," Adler states, "few have even begun to appreciate the historical and potential contributions of women leaders." Among other things, a woman's gaining her nation's highest office symbolizes that real change is possible. "If a woman can win high public office where no other woman has ever won before and few people think she can win," Adler contends, "then other national changes become believable. Bookies gave Mary Robinson only a one-in-one-thousand chance of winning her first presidential election in Ireland. She won, and today she enjoys more than a 90 percent approval rating from the electorate." Similar stories can be told about the Philippine's Corazon Aquino and Turkey's Tansu Çiller, among many others. Says Adler, "It is perhaps not coincidental that a disproportionate number of the women who have achieved such an office ... have led countries experiencing major change. Nine led countries struggling to establish their independence, and another nine led countries either attempting to reunite following a civil war or experiencing other forms of major societal upheaval, often including instituting new forms of government."

Other fascinating themes from Adler's study combine to begin making the idea of peace, perhaps even in our lifetime, more and more plausible. For example, in contrast to the majority of their male counterparts, women leaders are more likely to attempt to resolve conflicts in ways other than through military intervention. The immediate self-evident fact is that none of the women leaders Adler discusses had military training or any kind of military background prior to assuming office. Equally intriguing, says Adler, is the pattern of education shared by the women leaders. Today's women leaders, as a group, have a deeper and broader knowledge of the rest of the world than many of their male predecessors and therefore a more profound understanding of others' points of view. "It is noteworthy," Adler adds, "that two-thirds of the women leaders were educated outside their home country." Vigdís Finnbógadottir symbolizes their liberal and cross-cultural education: she finished high school in her native Iceland, then studied literature and theater in France, followed by theater studies in Denmark, French philosophy in Sweden, and finally English literature and education again in Iceland. Is it not more difficult to behave in relationship-canceling ways (such as declaring war) in relation to people whose culture you know and have taken time to deeply appreciate?

In the end Adler proposes that the biggest strides in wisdom, as it relates to leadership at the highest levels, appear to come when leaders replace open-systems thinking with closed-systems thinking—"not the local, community-based closed system of 7,000 B.C. but rather the global closed system of our planet." The reality of the shift to a closed system, Adler demonstrates, is unavoidable: consider the radiation from Chernobyl, polluting vegetables grown in Sweden and sold in

Asia; or Internet messages sent to Chinese, North Korean, and Albanian citizens, freeing them from the absolute control of totalitarian regimes; or chaos theory's butterfly, changing air currents two continents away. Adler asserts that today's women leaders are more likely to pioneer strategies for change that are based not only on closed-systems, global thinking but also on the goal of global unity versus international superiority. Her research is a promising beginning. "None of us can claim," Adler concludes, "that the twentieth century is exiting on an impressive note, on a note imbued with wisdom." And so the inquiry, the search for new leadership, is on.

In Chapter Ten, "Developing Courage and Wisdom in Organizing and Sciencing," William R. Torbert argues, much like Gandhi did, that we must be the change we want to see in the world. To aim higher in terms of wisdom and courage requires a kind of human development that involves educating not so much the mind but the attention. Educating the attention in the direction of ongoing inquiry, through what Torbert calls first-, second-, and third-person research and practice, is the kind of transformational learning that generates wisdom. In several important ways this chapter comes together with the ideas of Peter Vaill on the unspeakable texture of process wisdom and with Karl Weick's focus on improvisation. It also amplifies the relational stance of the chapters on social constructionism (for example, Sheila McNamee's call to attend to the movement of conversations in and around our organizations). The essential difference in Torbert's chapter is his clarity about methods for the development of wisdom and courage. His chapter is about "liberating disciplines," about the multiple levels of inquiry-in-the-midst-of-action through which we can open ourselves in increasingly vulnerable, wisdom-producing, life-transforming ways.

Torbert's conceptualization of three kinds of research and practice is about integrating courage and wisdom into real-time experiments and tests of validity. First-person research and practice includes all the forms of research and practice that one can do by oneself. It includes a variety of writing forms (journals, dream records, memoirs); meditation and prayer; and physical exercise performed in an awareness-widening fashion. In keeping a journal, for example, one seeks not to tell a predigested story or to construct something that others will like but rather to share the less coherent qualities of an evolving life.

Second-person research and practice includes all the times we engage in supportive, self-disclosing, and confronting ways with others as we share our first-person research and practice. It involves all conversations in which those present share an intent to learn about themselves, about the others present, and about their relationships that are forming, developing, or dissolving. Only rarely does this really happen, but if such conversations are taped, then the resulting tapes can be used to further the aims of all three kinds of research and practice, helping to alternate between rehearsal and performance, feedback and "feedforward." Finally, third-person research and practice moves in two very different ways. The most common, argues Torbert, does not really even qualify as inquiry, because it conceptually and operationally segregates research from practice and subordinates subjects into predetermined designs. Most behaviorist, empirical-positivist, and bureaucratic organizing methods fall into this category and do not encourage transformation of hierarchical power relationships; there is little in the way of collaborative inquiry or learning. The aim of "true" third-person research and practice is to integrate first- and second-person research and practice to accomplish organizational learning—that is, to widen organizational members' attention to questions and to see whether the organization's missions, strategies, present actions, and outcomes are congruent— while increasing mutuality among peers. Leaders who engage in this kind of inquiry require courage. Inquiry and vulnerability are vitally implicated in each other. Organizing becomes a process of continuous transformation and coconstruction—personally, interpersonally, and organizationally. The fruits are many, including the development of organizational wisdom. Wisdom involves widening one's awareness of purpose, process, action, and outcome; it integrates being, knowing, doing, and effecting in a timely fashion.

Torbert asks each of us to aim for wider, more humble awareness as part of the human vocation: "May this chapter invite you to explore this world of first-, second-, and third-person research and practice further for yourself, to seek out and participate in creating cooperative inquiries with colleagues and friends and to practice liberating disciplines . . . within your family and other long-term communities of practice. . . . And may you meet death inquiringly."

In the concluding chapter, "An Epilogue: An Invitation to Future Dialogue," Suresh Srivastva and Argun Saatçioğlu present a summarizing set of propositions crafted from the "cues and clues" provided in all the other chapters. Their chapter, marked by a spirit of hope for the future, concludes with the assertion that wisdom is the virtue most called for by all of us as we turn our attention to the agendas of the new century. Enriching the meaning of wisdom and looking for its sources should have a high priority in organizational life. One is struck by the passion in these authors' writing—in many ways the spirit of their medium is truly their message.

Immediately they ask, What is the most important resource organizations have for thriving in—and on—the complexities and uncertainties of our day and age? Their answer revolves around two fundamental human characteristics that they claim "are anything but new"—imagining and engaging in dialogue.

But what comes next is new. It is the treatment of these fundamentals within the conceptual context of knowing: "Knowledge is defined as a dialogic construct for the imaginative search for truth, and wisdom is defined as a virtue that promotes knowledge as such.... Courage is defined as an attitude that helps sustain wisdom." What organizations seem to be in need of is to assign imaginative knowing and dialogic construction a much higher priority. Wisdom is not something individuals have but relationships create. It is best realized, argue the authors, in an organization-wide dialogue that generates imaginative knowledge—a stance that views uncertainty as a gift; an orientation that favors experiments, spontaneity, serendipity, and surprise; a presumption that views change as opportunity; and an egalitarian value system that brings "whole systems" together in a dialogue as a mode of relating that breaks the bounds of authority and expertise. In our day, say the authors, wisdom is inspired by uncertainty, preempted by instability (change), and grounded in improvisation.

Perhaps our approach to wisdom is less than spectacular, Srivastva and Saatçioğlu insist. Indeed, their conclusion is interesting: "Given the commonsense conception of wisdom in many cultures as a quality that is extremely difficult to attain, it seems ironic that engaging in dialogue with one another, giving voice to our imagination, and never believing that our knowledge is ever sufficient are enough to pursue wisdom." Perhaps all we really need to do, in human terms, is to turn to one another in ways that involve open invitation, care, freedom, joyful ambiguity, and organizing in "full voice."

Welcome to the dialogue!

REFERENCES

Barnard, C. I. *The Functions of the Executive.* Cambridge, Mass.: Harvard University Press, 1938.

Bollier, D. *Aiming Higher: 25 Stories of How Companies Prosper by Combining Sound Management and Social Vision.* Chicago: American Management Association, 1996.

Cooperrider, D., and Dutton, J. *The Organizational Dimensions of Global Change: No Limits to Cooperation.* Thousand Oaks, Calif.: Sage, forthcoming.

Gergen, K. *Realities and Relationships: Soundings in Social Construction.* Cambridge, Mass.: Harvard University Press, 1994.

Smith, H. *The World's Religions: Our Great Wisdom Traditions.* San Francisco: Harper San Francisco, 1991.

Srivastva, S., and Cooperrider, D. *Appreciative Leadership and Management: The Power of Positive Thought in Organizations.* San Francisco: Jossey-Bass, 1990.

PART ONE

EVOLUTIONARY WISDOM

A Sensemaking Perspective

2

THE UNSPEAKABLE TEXTURE
OF PROCESS WISDOM

Peter B. Vaill

WHEN WE TALK ABOUT SOMEBODY "playing it by ear," what are we saying? What about the expression "flying by the seat of your pants"? What does that really say about taking action or getting things done in an organizational context? Expressions such as "feeling your way along," "mucking around," "going with the flow," and "taking things one day at a time" are full of implicit meaning. Is there possibly an epistemology and an ethics buried in the notion of "nursing something along," for example? It is the task of this chapter to explore such questions.

Commonplace expressions such as these are examples of what I call "process wisdom" (Vaill, 1984). (A much longer list of such phrases appears in Exhibit 2.1.) One of the delightful things about the notion of process wisdom is how frequently one hears examples of it in everyday metaphors about getting things done. (It should also be noted that this chapter resides, though modestly, within the field of "process philosophy," a good introduction to which is Browning, 1965.)

The term *process wisdom* is intended to capture the feeling of moving *through* situations and problems and yet somehow acting "wisely" in relation to them. As some readers will know, the failure of management education and training to successfully capture the process aspects of management has concerned me for some years (Vaill, 1984, 1989, 1992). It is my contention that we cannot educate managers effectively

Exhibit 2.1.   Examples of Process Wisdom.

The following expressions are heard as descriptions of the flow of an action process; the intent is to communicate the feel of the process as it is occurring.

Bouncing an idea off someone
Blue-skying a subject
Brainstorming an approach to something
Coming in on a wing and a prayer
Cutting and pasting
Dancing with a problem
Dancing with the one that brought you
Dodging bullets
Doing a dry run
Doing a quick run-through
Doing something quick and dirty
Engaging in give-and-take
Eyeballing something
Feeling your way along
Flying blind
Flying by the seat of your pants
Following your nose
Fooling around with something
Freewheeling
Getting down
Getting in sync
Getting untracked
Giving something a lick and a promise
Giving something a try
Going easy
Going for it
Going with the flow
Grooving on something
Hanging in there
Hanging loose
Having a go at something
Having a nice touch
Hitting your stride
Improvising
Keeping your head above water
Keeping your options open
Keeping the faith
Kicking something around
Landing on your feet
Learning as you go along
Letting go

Letting the chips fall as they may
Letting things take care of themselves
Living to fight another day
Making haste slowly
Massaging a problem
Mixing and matching
Mucking around in something
Nursing something along
Playing catch-up
Playing it as it lays
Playing it by ear
Playing something out
Playing the percentages
Practicing the art of the possible
Praying a lot
Retrofitting something
Riffing on something
Rolling with the punches
Romancing someone
Schmoozing with someone
Scrambling
Shooting from the hip
Staying alive
Taking a chance
Taking a leap into the dark
Taking a shot in the dark
Taking a stab at something
Taking it nice and easy
Taking things as they come
Taking things one day at a time
Thinking on your feet
Throwing away the script
Tinkering with something
Trying something on for size
Trusting your gut reaction
Trusting the process
Tweaking something
Walking on eggshells
Waltzing around something
Whistling in the dark
Whistling past the graveyard
Winging it
Working without a net
Working on-line
Writing the book as you go

This list is, in principle, unlimited if the thesis is sound that process wisdom manifests itself spontaneously in relation to action projects that are real for particular persons at particular times.

Moreover, since process wisdom is so frequently expressed metaphorically, it is likely that new phrases are rooted, at least initially, in some particular culture—whether a culture of a profession, a social class, an age group, a gender, a race, or an ethnic group. "Coming in on a wing and a prayer," for example, was probably originally about bombers returning from combat missions, and in fact was the title of a popular song during World War II. "Scrambling" originally arose to describe a quarterback's behavior during a broken play in football, but is now often heard in other contexts as well.

---

until we can incorporate time into our understanding of what managers should be doing and how they should be doing it. It is possible that considering the effect of time on management may force us to rethink what it is and how it is best performed.

A BRIEF REFLECTION ON MANAGERIAL TIME

My sensitivity to the process aspects of management was profoundly intensified by my experience as a dean of a business school in the late 1970s. As a management professor for the previous fifteen years, I had been confining myself to studying what a manager does and how, and how a manager's effectiveness could be improved. In this I was acting consistently, I think, with the dominant currents of thought in the field.

But as a dean (and thus a "midlevel general manager" myself), I quickly learned that the good things that we professors were saying managers should do are *all* time-dependent processes. Furthermore, their time-dependent quality was not usually part of the discussion of them as competencies, in the classroom or in the literature, except for the commonplace observation that managers are usually under intense time pressure. The temporal dimensions of managerial life were not well understood, I felt.

For example, how long should a planning process take? What role does time play in person-centered listening and in giving feedback? In his or her remarks and writings, how long and how frequently should a leader expound on his or her vision for the organization? At what pace can one expect to introduce new ideas and structures into an existing organization? When has a discussion gone on "long enough"?

There was nothing I could do, I learned sometimes painfully, that did not have its own rhythms and pacings, pauses and accelerations, beginnings and endings. And time was not a matter of merely academic interest; it was central to whether I got anything done at all.

Furthermore, there was the problem of the intrusiveness of events: things did not occur one at a time; no competency could be practiced in pristine singularity. Instead, at any moment I was flowing with the multiple, disjointed time streams of the various projects in which I was involved. Sometimes I had a little bit of influence over the pace and sequence of things in one of these streams, but as often I was "playing catch-up," "dodging someone else's bullets," "being overtaken by events," or "trying to get ahead" of a situation. The multiple time streams were, of course, not coordinated in space: they competed for my attention. Frequently there were three or four places I was supposed to be at virtually the same time. The calendar was filled with contingencies. I (and even more, my secretary) tried heroically to keep some harmony in this overscheduled life, but there was usually little margin for such "errors" as delayed planes, unexpected visitors, summons from top administrators, long-winded faculty members, or, heaven forbid, any of those ills of the flesh and the psyche that accompany the manager's harried life.

Another key characteristic of the temporally bound quality of my life as a manager was that I could not afford to be solipsistic about my projects and my time frames. No matter how prominent and important my projects and schedules were to *me,* I could not assume that these matters had the same subjective prominence and importance to anyone else—even if I thought I had their official concurrence (or that my position gave me the right to expect it). In many cases I was shocked to realize that something of great significance to me did not even *exist,* so to speak, for the person I was talking to, let alone inhabit the same time stream as for me or have any kind of significant influence on that person's thought and action.

Everything was interactive. (*Interaction* is a thoroughly temporal word: without interaction *in time,* the various things that are important to the various members of a system cannot become real to the others.) I simply had to learn to understand myself in a spatiotemporal field of relationships, flowing and shifting. It was a field composed of multiple players, each of whom had his or her own schedules, expectations of the rates at which things ought to proceed, and resistances to being sidetracked by other people's temporal perceptions and priorities.

I was discovering that a social system is a temporal field as well as a spatial field (Keen, n.d.) and that it cannot function as what Drath and Palus (1994) call a "community of practice" if there are not shared understandings of time. Hall (1977) makes these shared understandings a function of culture, but I was discovering that the matter is much more fine-grained than that. If two individuals' sense of pace and urgency is even slightly out of joint, they cannot communicate very well (what Hall calls "syncing" [1977, p. 72]), let alone engage in imaginative joint problem solving.

External Time Pressure

Pressures were created in this spatiotemporal field by collisions between the schedules of various projects and between the priorities of various players. But, in addition, far more powerful and implacable temporal pressures were introduced by constraints that no one within the system controlled, including constraints imposed by the marketplace, by the law, by the seasons, by contractual obligations, and by the persons who owned or controlled the system. No doubt every accounting firm has at one time or another wished it could control the timing of the tax season, and many a university admissions office would like more influence over national admissions cycles. But such external demands are generally nonnegotiable in the short run, and even in the long run they are usually almost impossible to influence. The priorities and schedules of stakeholders are relatively immutable, and all of the multiple, interacting, flowing and shifting time streams within the organization have to take account of them.

Escaping from Time?

From time to time the administrators at the business school where I was dean tried to escape the pressures of time, both those generated within the organization and those imposed from without. We sought to get away from the office and the telephones, as do many executive groups, in what we called "retreats" and "off-sites." (Today the portable and therefore even more persistent cell phone and the ubiquitous fax machine, voice mail, and e-mail make escape from the time frames of the normal workweek even more difficult.) We tried to plan off-site meetings with agendas that would permit more reflective interaction—and meetings that didn't have agendas at all, that didn't have to solve problems, reach objectives, or stay on schedule.

We, like the managers of countless other organizations, wanted desperately to believe that we could get outside of time, that we could think about our mission, our opportunities, and (most poignantly) our relationships with one another outside of the normal temporal framework of organizational life. But by and large we—like most managers—barely succeeded, if at all, in transcending time.

For one thing, the off-site meetings were extremely difficult to schedule. Parting the hours and days on a group of managers' calendars to make room for a meeting that transcends time is an act reminiscent of Moses' parting the Red Sea. Furthermore, mere removal from the site of time pressures could not alleviate our time-consciousness: it continued to intrude on our conversations at the supposedly time-sheltered sites. And then, of course, there were the time schedules and rhythms of the retreat facilities themselves—their coffee breaks and mealtimes, check-in and check-out times, schedules for use of facilities and support systems—for they too were spatiotemporal fields, with time constraints that were acutely sensed by their staffs. For all these reasons, the experience of living and working in a complex and demanding temporal process did not change that much for us in the mountains or by the seashore, let alone in a downtown hotel.

Before proceeding I want to be clear that I am *not* saying merely that because managerial life is complex and fast-paced we have to understand the role time plays in it. I am suggesting something a little more basic: managerial life is in and of itself profoundly temporal. It is temporal before it is anything else! Everything that we might say about managerial life, about what managers do and should do, is in relation to time. Even if we say, "managers have to learn to manage time effectively," that is a statement that is conditioned by the temporality of managerial life. You can't step outside of time to learn to manage it; if you try to, you will find that when you step back in, what you have decided outside of time now looks very different.

Time and Permanent White Water

With temporality understood as fundamental, let us speak further about the messiness and complexity of contemporary managerial life. Elsewhere I have written about what I call "permanent white water," the nonstop cascade of surprising, novel, obtrusive events that pepper (and sometimes bombard) all managers, events that often cannot be foreseen or planned away (Vaill, 1989, 1996). In terms of my comments so far about time, permanent white water is a form of temporality that frequently feels rather chaotic and crazy to those experiencing it. It is difficult enough to have to manage multiple, interacting time streams in the context of business as usual; it is orders of magnitude harder to manage time streams when the surprising, novel, obtrusive events—the permanent white water—involved have unknown causes, unknown remedies, unknown urgencies, unknown times to completion, and unknown compounding factors that will create additional complexity at later points in the process. The mere word *process* almost will not bear the weight of these amounts of complexity and contingency. No one is living these days in the midst of "business as usual." We are in a temporal maelstrom as much as a substantive one. "Process," Hamlet might as easily have said, "is out of joint."

Out of joint or not, "process," I can see now in retrospect, was everything in my managerial life. Whether we were working smoothly and effectively or sputtering and cursing one another and "spinning our wheels," how well we understood the process quality of our relationships was key to understanding why anything was happening at the moment.

I don't think there is anything in all of this that is unique to a university setting or to me as an individual. If anything, university settings are tranquil compared to today's high-tech corporate environments. Outside of academe there is if anything more deadline pressure, more clamorous stakeholders, more complex projects with more aggressive players and more multiple interacting time streams.

There is acute time-consciousness in all of these settings, I find, but it appears in the form of time *pressure*. Time is considered mainly in terms of aberrations or deviations from a schedule, not as an existential component of situations. Time is assumed to be a controllable variable, a problem to be solved: beating time, saving time, compressing time, leapfrogging time—these are the preoccupations of today's managers. (This view of time as a problem to be solved or a variable to be controlled is seen in the current fascination with "just-in-time" integration of various streams of events. The effect of just-in-time thinking on the basic temporality of situations is perhaps worth studying.)

But as noted earlier, no matter what we do to time, we cannot detemporalize managerial life. Process will always be there: action may not always be "just in time," but it will always be just "in time."

THE NATURE OF PROCESS WISDOM

Even though discussions such as the one above are not common, the time-driven and time-obsessed organizational world we live in is very familiar. Everyone has lived through these experiences. Everyone understands how fragile an orderly and effective process is in the modern organizational world and how rare it is to even hope to achieve one. So why take time to spell out the pain and frustration? First, because it is there as a reality of organizational life. Second, because definitions of effective management skills (or "competencies") put forth by academics and practitioners alike tend not to include time in the way I have talked about it here. And third, the more problematic temporal processes become, the more we need to understand effective management *in terms of* time—both each person's subjective perception of time and a more objective view of the effect time has on organizational behavior.

I opened this chapter with references to everyday idioms that are generally about taking action in complex situations. I called these phrases examples of "process wisdom." They express our consciousness, I believe, of the complexities and contingencies of the spatiotemporal field of relationships I have just been describing. These phrases represent charming, memorable, sometimes brilliant, sometimes bittersweet distillations of what it feels like to try to go forward in the face of great uncertainty, confusion, and time pressure.

These phrases are important in another way: they are testimonies, almost confessions, of the meaning of personal experience. They remove the rationalistic gloss from behavior and attitude, and as such they are bridges between people who are not sure anyone else understands what they are going through: "I know I am feeling my way along. You are too?"

These phrases, in other words, are *data of consciousness:* they confirm empirically the commonality of process complexity, contingency, and fragility that we all experience. They capture metaphorically the adaptations people make to the spatiotemporal swirl I call permanent white water. As such, these phrases are attempts to describe what behaving wisely means under these circumstances: "The best I can do under the circumstances is to feel my way along." These phrases embody the process wisdom that continually arises spontaneously. Their emergence and the flash of recognition they evoke is testimony to the commonality of the experiences they refer to.

This chapter's title refers to the unspeakability of process wisdom. I do not know whether we will ever have an operational language for talking about the spatiotemporal swirl of organizational life. It may be that lived temporal experience in today's and tomorrow's organizations perpetually transcends academic categories. Metaphor may be all we have.

Perhaps there will be no Chester Barnard (1938) for the spatiotemporal swirl of contemporary organizational behavior to supply exact names for the functions and processes we are experiencing. Indeed, perhaps Barnard was thinking too statically even in 1938! Maybe there has been an invisible process wisdom operating all along that accounts for things getting done, a process wisdom that we have never quite captured. Barnard, after all, in a brief epiphany, did say that effective executive behavior is composed of "feeling, judgment, sense, proportion, balance, appropriateness" (1938, p. 235) before returning to the impersonal categories he primarily employed. Feeling, judgment, sense, proportion, balance, appropriateness—these are not bad descriptions of what I have been calling process wisdom.

Other writers have intuited an "art" to the process of management; a few years ago I pushed that idea one step further with the notion of managing as a *performing* art (Vaill, 1989). Today I would say that if managerial leadership is a performing art, it is definitely street theater, where the script, the characters, the props, and the drama are all unfolding in real time.

My basic thesis is that in a world of rapid change "wisdom" is not so much a stock of knowledge and experience that can be drawn on or applied as it is an ability to "size up" situations and "learn as you go." Wisdom is a way of thinking and being in relation to motion and change, to the spatiotemporal swirl.

Yet this is still not quite an adequate way of talking about process wisdom. A principal meaning of *wisdom,* one might argue, is precisely that quality of human intelligence that does not change, that is above the swirl, beyond contingency and the immediate idiosyncrasies of situations. Interestingly, *Roget's Thesaurus* (Chapman, 1992) gives approximately 170 words and phrases as synonyms for *wisdom.* The overwhelming majority of these signify a fixed characteristic or possession of a person or a mind. Only *nimbleness, adroitness, dexterity, quick-wittedness, sprightly wit,* and *streetwise* seem clearly to view wisdom as something that is flexible in relation to its objects.

There is no doubt that wisdom does have a transcendent and timeless quality. But then we are left with the question of what "wisdom" is in situations where rapid change is under way and in emerging situations that have never been seen before—precisely the conditions I have called permanent white water: surprising, novel, ill-structured, obtrusive events and processes that may bear little resemblance to anything those involved have ever faced before. Executives all over the developed world are saying they are constantly facing such problems. What needs to be added to "wisdom" to truly make it "process wisdom"— the ability to act wisely in relation to confusion and mystery?

Here is a provisional answer: process wisdom, as distinct from wisdom by itself, is wisdom *about* change and fluidity. Process wisdom is insightful about the very phenomena that so many people experience as crazy, messy, and confused. Where others perceive only "the blind leading the blind," "the train leaving the tracks," "things spinning out of control," "the patients running the asylum," or "rearranging deck chairs on the Titanic" (all expressions one routinely hears in situations of high turbulence, uncertainty, and rapid change), those with process wisdom manage to continue to perceive meaning and possibility. Those with process wisdom are able to see how work can continue on the human projects being buffeted by continual change. As such, process wisdom combines the qualities of mind and character we have always meant by *wisdom* with the ability to "dance" with change and instability without losing one's sense of purpose and direction. Process wisdom continues to see pathways through complexity and confusion, how purpose can remain alive and relevant when, for those distracted by the temporal maelstrom, the sense of direction and order has become utterly splintered. Defined this way, there can hardly be a more important quality for managerial leadership than process wisdom.

BREAKING OFF FROM *IS* TO *FLOWING*

As is usually the case with subtleties of any kind, a poet has said it better than ordinary language seems to permit. Following is A. R. Ammons's "Guide" (1977, pp. 22–23) in its entirety:

GUIDE

You cannot come to unity and remain material:
in that perception is no perceiver:
     when you arrive
you have gone too far:
     at the Source you are in the mouth of Death:
you cannot
     turn around in
the Absolute: there are no entrances and exits
     no precipitation of forms
to use like tongs against the formless:
     no freedom to choose:
to be
     you have to stop not-being and break
off from *is* to *flowing* and

　　　　this is the sin you weep and praise:
origin is your original sin:
　　　　the return you long for will ease your guilt
and you will have your longing:
　　　　the wind that is my guide said this: it
should know having
　　　　given up everything to eternal being but
direction:
how I said can I be glad and sad: but a man goes
　　　　from one foot to the other:
wisdom wisdom:
　　　　to be glad and sad at once is also unity
and death:
　　　　wisdom wisdom: a peachblossom blooms on a particular
tree on a particular day:
　　　　unity cannot do anything in particular:
are these thoughts you want me to think I said but
　　　　the wind was gone and there was no more knowledge then.

Without motion (process) there is no knowledge: this poem by one of America's greatest living poets seems to be exploring the same idea as this chapter: being *is* process. Process is not random; it has direction. But it is quintessentially particular, not universal. It always "goes from one foot to the other," "blooms on a particular tree on a particular day." It is never sure what it is or has, whether this "knowledge" is real—even though the other kind of absolute knowledge cannot be knowledge at all, for "in that perception is no perceiver."

The poem argues against the quest for universal, extra-process knowledge of anything, including managerial leadership. However, too much insistence on exactly what the poem is saying would violate its own injunction: the poem is its own peach blossom. Therefore I will refrain from further exegesis and let this artist's vision of process wisdom stand by itself.

PROCESS WISDOM AND LEARNING

As I have argued elsewhere (Vaill, 1996), in the permanent white water of novelty, surprise, and messiness, the ability to engage in continual learning is crucial. Although we may not notice, the term *learning process* is redundant. Learning *is* a process. What kind of learning is process wisdom? Unfortunately, most of the folk wisdom of Exhibit

2.1 does not refer directly to learning. The remainder of this chapter is devoted to some reflections on the kind of learning that may aid in the development of process wisdom.

However, to speak of how process wisdom is learned is possibly to commit the very error that this chapter is calling attention to—the tendency to think of various qualities of managerial leadership as fixed qualities or competencies that are somehow acquired like possessions or personal characteristics and then applied to situations. In a turbulent environment, the core competency is learning; therefore management is not learned, it *is* learning. This I call the "learning premise." The learning premise follows directly from the nature of permanent white water and from the temporal nature of all acts of management. *Process wisdom, we may then say, is not learned; it* is *learning.* What then is the learning (process) of process wisdom?

Another way to put the question is to ask, If one is to practice wisdom in relation to continual change—which is what we have said process wisdom is—then what is being practiced?

The most general answer to this question, I think, is that what is being practiced is what might be called a *philosophy of temporality.* In the opening section of this chapter I described how I had gradually and painfully discovered the temporality in everything I did as a manager. Temporality conditioned everything; nothing was exempt, even the most insignificant acts.

But I was not yet practicing a philosophy of temporality; I was a prisoner of temporality, struggling against it, still thinking I could get outside of it and get control. I barely even realized the role of temporality at that time; only later, with hindsight, could I see how time conditioned everything.

The concept of permanent white water contributes to our understanding of temporality. Reflecting on the extreme turbulence and multiple interacting uncertainties of modern organizations forces us to reflect on time: We do *not* control schedules and times to completion. We do *not* unilaterally control the pace or rate of change. We do *not* control the rate at which others in a given situation can absorb change, nor can we control how they will interact with changes we initiate. Fundamentally, we do *not* control the agenda (with *we* in all of the above examples understood to mean "we who would influence, manage, and lead a system of human beings"). It is not surprising that so many of the entries in Exhibit 2.1 have to do with relinquishing control (or the absence of control in the first place). The more that our impulse to control processes causes us to ignore the natural but invisible temporality of situations, the more we can expect resistance, conflict, and misunderstanding of our efforts as a manager. Rethinking the nature and limits of control is the primary content of process wisdom.

It is worth noting in passing that the idea of process wisdom as a philosophy of temporality throws new light on the nature of leadership. As this discussion has alluded to all along, leadership is a thoroughly temporal phenomenon; I am hard put, however, to recall ever seeing it characterized that way. The primary content of leadership is a philosophy of temporality: leadership may be that set of influences in a system that helps members come more fully to experience the mutual, interacting temporality of their attitudes, abilities, and actions.

Additionally, process-wisdom-as-learning is concerned with the maintenance of certain crucial values and priorities—about human beings, about purposes, about responsibilities. These values and priorities may be any of a very large set; their content is not the point. The point is that process wisdom is not mere expediency. It does not sacrifice principle to process but finds a way to understand and express principles-in-process. Because of our culture's extreme preoccupation with the Absolute (the right answer, once and for all), for which the Ammons poem says there are no tongs to understand, saying "principles-in-process" *sounds* like expediency, *sounds* like selling out, *sounds* like saying anything goes.

Here, perhaps, is one of the most important characteristics of *process* wisdom as distinct from wisdom outside of time and change. "Principles-in-process" means (temporally) living a value system as opposed to (atemporally) holding one.

A very nice example of an ethical principle that contains its own temporality is Viktor Frankl's famous admonition to "live as if you were living already for the second time and as if you had acted the first time as wrongly as you are about to act now!" (1963, p. 173).

"Principles-in-process" means the ongoing (temporal) *discovery* of the meaning of principles, for only in process (that is, over time) do their meanings emerge. It means keeping principles rooted in one's temporal consciousness, not treating them as entities ("unity," "the Absolute") existing independent of consciousness. For process wisdom, after all, is an attitude and action of persons. Principles exist in a person's processes of relating to the world.

Moreover, the use of the plural—*principles*—is deliberate. Process wisdom finds in a moving present multiple principles in play, not just one single overriding imperative. It is the intellect standing outside of process, concreteness, and change that confidently (smugly?) declares the overriding priority of some single principle or value. Process wisdom never finds things quite that neat. Process wisdom thus interweaves principles and priorities and emerges with insights, understandings, and ideas about courses of action. These matters are often of the "unspeakable texture" mentioned in the title of this chapter, however. This is why practicing leaders have such trouble with their memoirs. Away from flow, from what Eric Trist used to call "the action station," the ingenuity of the things they did is often not apparent.

And so we return to the folk wisdom of Exhibit 2.1. Perhaps in the final analysis these metaphors, and the continuing flow of new expressions that we know will appear, are the best statements we have of what process wisdom entails. Each of these expressions is itself learning, and taken together they capture as thoroughly as we could want the extraordinary variety and subtlety of the ways of wisdom available to us in social contexts.

REFERENCES

Ammons, A. R. *The Selected Poems, Expanded Edition.* New York: Norton, 1977. Copyright © by A. R. Ammons, from *The Selected Poems, Expanded Edition* by A. R. Ammons. Reprinted by permission of W. W. Norton & Company, Inc.

Barnard, C. I. *The Functions of the Executive.* Cambridge, Mass.: Harvard University Press, 1938.

Browning, D. (ed.). *Philosophers of Process.* New York: Random House, 1965.

Chapman, Z. L. (ed.). *Roget's Thesaurus.* New York: HarperCollins, 1992.

Drath, W. H., and Palus, C. J. *Making Common Sense: Leadership as Meaning-Making in a Community of Practice.* Greensboro, N.C.: Center for Creative Leadership, 1994.

Frankl, V. E. *Man's Search for Meaning.* New York: Washington Square Press, 1963.

Hall, E. T. *Beyond Culture.* New York: Anchor Books, 1977.

Keen, E. *A Primer in Phenomenological Psychology.* Lanham, Md.: University Press of America, n.d. (Originally published 1975).

Vaill, P. B. "Process Wisdom for a New Age." In J. Adams (ed.), *Transforming Work.* Alexandria, Va.: Miles River Press, 1984.

Vaill, P. B. *Managing as a Performing Art: New Ideas for a World of Chaotic Change.* San Francisco: Jossey-Bass, 1989.

Vaill, P. B. "Notes on Running an Organization." *Journal of Management Inquiry,* 1992, *1*(2), 130–138.

Vaill, P. B. *Learning as a Way of Being: Strategies for Survival in a World of Permanent White Water.* San Francisco: Jossey-Bass, 1996.

3

THE ATTITUDE OF WISDOM: AMBIVALENCE AS THE OPTIMAL COMPROMISE

Karl E. Weick

WHEN PEOPLE CREATE MAPS of an unknowable, unpredictable world, they face strong temptations toward either overconfident knowing or overly cautious doubt. Wisdom consists of an attitude toward one's beliefs, values, knowledge, and information that resists these temptations through an ongoing balance between knowing and doubt (Meacham, 1983, 1990). In an earlier article (Weick, 1993b) I used this view of wisdom to reanalyze the Mann Gulch wildfire disaster, made famous in Norman Maclean's book (1992) *Young Men and Fire.* I suggested that the firefighters became trapped by the fire partly because of overconfidence that they would have it extinguished by 10:00 the next morning. Failure to treat this belief as fallible led the firefighters to ignore growing signs that the fire was about to explode. Although my discussion in that article of the attitude of wisdom was a mere sketch (it covered forty-one lines of text in a specialized academic journal), the idea struck sufficient resonance among wildland firefighters that it has since been incorporated into some of their training programs.

The purpose of this chapter is to explore the idea of an attitude of wisdom in greater detail. I intend to focus on issues related to action, information processing, and thought in complex social systems and to argue that adopting an attitude of wisdom is one way complex systems function reliably and heedfully even though they work with fallible knowledge. Before moving to these issues, I first sample the wisdom literature and connect some of its themes to a piece of wisdom in wildland firefighting.

THE WISDOM LITERATURE AND FIREFIGHTING

People in charge of wildland firefighting crews have begun to follow the maxim, "Never hand over a fire in the heat of the day." What this maxim means is that when a departing crew hands over a fire to an incoming crew, they should do so when it is easiest for the incoming crew to understand what is happening and step in and continue the strategy used by the departing crew. The easiest transitions normally take place at night, when the combination of low winds, high humidity, and cool temperatures will stabilize a fire and render it the most predictable. In the heat of the day, by contrast, the fire is at its most dynamic and most volatile, which makes it harder for the incoming crew to catch up with its rapidly changing character. When there is an attempted handoff in the heat of the day, the incoming crew is always behind. The crew's understanding of what is happening lags behind what is actually happening, making it difficult to properly adjust their actions to a rapidly developing situation. As a result, the level of danger increases dramatically.

The firefighters' heat-of-the-day maxim is a good example of wisdom because it reflects several ways in which wisdom has been described. For example, it is consistent with Blanshard's all-purpose description (1967) of wisdom as "sound and serene judgment regarding the conduct of life" (p. 322). The maxim represents sound judgment because it is based on an actual wildland fire tragedy, the Dude Fire in Payson, Arizona (see Johns, 1996). Six firefighters burned to death when a change of command was botched at 1:00 P.M., on a hot, windy day with temperatures in the high nineties, while the fire was making spectacular runs. The maxim represents serene judgment because it counsels against brash, impulsive action, because it is based on distance and detachment from the Dude Fire tragedy itself, and because it is conveyed to crew chiefs in training settings, where reflection is possible. Furthermore, it is a recipe for preserving control and stability without making a situation worse, and it is a calming edict intended to provide firm guidance in chaotic moments. The heat-of-the-day maxim is also relevant to two properties of wisdom that are often mentioned: reflection and judgment.

The Theme of Reflection

● Reflection, understood as "the habit of considering events and beliefs in the light of their grounds and consequences" (Blanshard, 1967, p. 323), is synonymous with wisdom when wisdom is considered a "mode of knowledge that tries to understand the ultimate conse-quences of events in a holistic, systemic way" (Csikszentmihalyi and Rathunde, 1990, p. 32). "Whether a belief is warranted must be decided by the evidence it rests on and the implications to which it leads, and one can become aware of these only by reflection" (Blanshard, 1967, p. 323). The reflection associated with wisdom con-sists of "a well-ordered and controllable series of symbolic links in a train of thought, to the exclusion of the more 'natural' meandering of the stream of consciousness" (Csikszentmihalyi and Rathunde, 1990, p. 39). Reflection also involves the articulation of the "big picture" that results from a grasp of multiple connections. The reflective component of wisdom may be thought of as the substantive side of wisdom. It is implicit in current discussions of cause maps (Huff, 1990), interactive complexity (Perrow, 1984), causal interdependence (Maruyama, 1963), and systems (Roberts, 1991).

Reflection on the tendency of the diverse, interrelated components of systems—for example, weather forecasting, the necessary conditions for fire (the "fire triangle," consisting of flammable material, a temper-ature above the point of ignition, and oxygen), shared meanings based on briefings, experience levels, and availability of air reconnaissance—to generate conflicting cues about unstable events led to the wisdom of the heat-of-the-day maxim. To be wise, in this case, is to be aware of the systemic quality of firefighting, to envision longer causal chains among the components within that system, and to appreciate what happens when these complex interdependencies are allowed to unfold in the absence of clear communication.

The Theme of Judgment

If reflection is about substantive wisdom, then judgment can be said to be about process wisdom. This second component of wisdom is found in descriptions such as these: "Wisdom is the capacity of judging rightly in matters relating to life and conduct" (Simpson and Weiner, 1989, p. 3,794), and wisdom is "informed judgment based on a com-parison of situations" (Sakaiya, 1991, p. 233). Blanshard (1967, p.

323) describes judgment as the "wisdom of ends," by which he means the appraisal and choice of values, intrinsic goods, and ends.

While many scholars are eager to equate wisdom with judgment, few of them seem willing to say what they mean by judgment. One is tempted to fill this void by adopting William James's (1963, p. 75) description: "In practical talk, a man's common sense means his good judgment, his freedom from eccentricity, his *gumption*." "Gumption" is a colloquial expression that means resourcefulness, enterprise, and a quality of mind that enables one to make intelligent choices. As a potential descriptor of wisdom, *gumption* implies sense, "but in addition it suggests a capacity to estimate shrewdly or cleverly the possibilities of success or failure, of change for the better or worse, or the like; as, an investor without *gumption* is bound to lose money; he is a dreamer and, what is worse, he hasn't the slightest bit of *gumption*; if the voters have *gumption* they will re-elect the mayor" (Webster, 1951, p. 737). Thus, when judgment is incorporated into wisdom, it contributes the relatively rare quality of "discernment of facts or conditions that are not obvious as well as knowledge of those that are ascertainable, an ability to comprehend the significance of those facts and conditions" (p. 737). To process the data of reflection with special attention directed to that which is nonobvious, significant, clever, shrewd, and a harbinger of possibilities is to engage in activities that simultaneously know and doubt.

Judgment, understood as the appraisal of ends, is evident in the heat-of-the-day maxim in that it places higher value on informed transitions than on uninformed ones. Judgment is also understood as the prudent use of knowledge, and this is evident in the presumption that knowledge of a fire should be used not just to fight it but also to decide how and when to walk away from it. Consistent with Sakaiya's description (1991) of judgment as making comparisons, the maxim suggests that compared to making the transition in cool temperatures, hot transitions are more dangerous. Even the old-fashioned, commonsense aspect of judgment connoted by the word *gumption* figures in the maxim. The advice to avoid handoffs in the heat of the day reflects a shrewd awareness that even a relatively small event in the complex mobilization of resources to suppress a large fire will have an important bearing on the success or failure of the mission. It is *not* obvious that when a tired crew leaves a fire and is replaced by a fresh crew, things will get worse. The addition of fresh resources normally would be expected to produce a redoubled effort and faster success. The maxim alerts people that precisely the opposite could occur. That fore-warning is a mark of wisdom, facilitated by good judgment that com-prehends significance in unexpected places.

The Theme of Metaphysical Commitments

While various treatments of wisdom share the themes of soundness, serenity, reflection, and judgment, one crucial theme they don't share turns on the question, "What is the 'it' that wisdom understands bet-ter?" This is shorthand for Robinson's concern (1990, p. 22) with metaphysical commitments in discussions of wisdom:

> The concept of wisdom is perforce dependent upon a prior meta-physical commitment, taking metaphysics to be composed of onto-logical and epistemological elements. To regard one as *wise,* after all, is to ascribe a deeper understanding of reality, but this assumes that a more or less settled (ontological) position has been reached on the question of what is *real.* And this very position can be reached only after taking a stand (epistemologically) on the ques-tion of *how one can know anything.* Thus, to regard one as "wise" for knowing an absolute, universal, and nonempirical ("transcen-dent") truth is at once to accept that there is such a truth and that it *can* be known through, for example, contemplation, revelation, logic, intuition, or genius. If, instead, the official ontology leaves room only for the reality of physical things, then "wisdom" can be nothing but a scientific understanding of the laws governing matter in motion. The greater the inclination toward a materialistic ontol-ogy, therefore, the greater will be the degree of synonymy among *sophia, phronesis,* and *episteme.* In the end, "wisdom" would then refer to no more than a technical knowledge of how things work, its claims exhausted by purely pragmatic modes of evaluation.

To specify the ontology and epistemology behind the view of wis-dom described here would take us too far afield, if in fact it could even be accomplished. In lieu of that, one is tempted either to invoke Robin Williams's exclamation—"Reality. What a concept!" (Davis, 1993, p. 74)—or to argue that "ontological oscillation" is a constant in everyday sensemaking (Weick, 1995, pp. 34–37) and let it go at that. Actually, both of those shortcuts are close to the presumptions that lie behind the present argument. The argument presumes, along with James (1963, p. 85), that "profusion, not economy, may after all be reality's key-note." It presumes, following lessons from chaos theory and quantum theory (McDaniel, 1996), that the world is largely unknowable and unpredictable, which means that sensemaking is all we have. And it also presumes that the maps people form to deal with unknowable territories are influenced by generic categories (such as "thing," "the same or different," "kind," and so on; James, 1963, p. 76) handed down by fallible predecessors: "Reality is an accumulation of our intellectual inventions, and the struggle for 'truth' in our progressive dealings with it is always a struggle to work in new nouns and adjectives while altering as little as possible the old" (p. 169).

The "reality" that wisdom more deeply understands consists of tenacious categories, constructed and validated consensually by both contemporaries and predecessors. Mere empirical technical knowledge plays a relatively minor part in this validation. The larger part—the part contributed by wisdom—lies in awareness of influences like legacies, predecessors, contingencies, and relationships as the object of wisdom (Follett, 1924, pp. 62–63); interpersonal relations as the vehicle for wisdom (Gergen, 1994); and questions as the output from wisdom. The reality behind wisdom is prefigured by symbolic systems that people have invented and imposed on one another because they seem to make a difference in practice (James, 1963, p. 75). People see and are bound by the constraints and categories they enact. Thus it is the task of wisdom to remain mindful of this ongoing fallible knowing and to witness both for its fallibility, through acts of doubt, and for its knowing, through acts of affirmation.

Returning to the heat-of-the-day maxim and the metaphysical commitments that drive it, the maxim's claim to wisdom is that it understands better than do formal models of fire behavior (Rothermel, 1993) the unknowable, unpredictable profusion of interdependencies associated with dynamic events such as uncontained wildland fires. The maxim, in other words, embodies an appreciation of ignorance and of the fact that actions such as crew transitions and fire suppression often occur in the midst of such ignorance. The maxim represents a consensus among the people who investigated the Dude Fire incident, including the crew chiefs involved in the incident. The maxim introduces new nouns, adjectives, and categories (for example, handoffs in the face of dynamic uncertainty) that supplement older understandings inherited from predecessors. Finally, this maxim, considered as a product of wisdom, is as much a question as it is an answer: "How knowable and predictable is this fire that I am about to inherit [or hand over]?" No matter how the crew chiefs answer this question, their answer will be flawed and incomplete. To be wise is to proceed anyway, knowing that your knowing is fallible and that whatever you do will shape what you face.

The Theme of Wisdom as an Attitude

To conclude this introduction to the literature on wisdom, I want to return to Meacham's formulation (1990). Meacham argued that "the essence of wisdom . . . lies not in what is known but rather in the manner in which that knowledge is held and in how that knowledge is put to use. To be wise is not to know particular facts but to know without excessive confidence or excessive cautiousness. . . . To both accumulate knowledge while remaining suspicious of it, and recognizing that much remains unknown, is to be wise" (pp. 185, 187). Thus "the essence of wisdom is in knowing that one does not know, in the appreciation that knowledge is fallible, in the balance between knowing and doubting" (p. 210). Wisdom is a quality of thought that is animated by a dialectic in which the more one knows, the more one realizes the extent of what one does not know. Defined algebraically, wisdom equals the ratio of knowledge one has acquired and not lost (k) to the knowledge one believes might be accumulated or acquired (K), expressed as one's confidence in what one knows ($p = k/K$) and one's doubts ($u = K-k$).

These four variables interact to form a context of knowledge that describes what one knows in relation to what is not yet known. If one presumes that there is a fixed upper boundary on knowledge to be acquired, then the closer one comes to that limit, the greater one's confidence. This gain in confidence is at the expense of wisdom, because new questions, doubts, and uncertainties are ignored. People are lured away from wisdom and toward more extreme confidence by pressures to "accumulate" knowledge, power that deters other people from challenging one's apparent knowledge, and an intellectual climate that forces premature foreclosure of possible conceptual positions (Meacham, 1990). Movements in the opposite direction, from wisdom toward overcautiousness, involve forgetting or dismissing what one knows and inflating the amount of potential knowledge that remains to be known. People are lured toward excessive caution when they get overwhelmed by rapid technological change, doubt what they have come to know, or suffer personal tragedies that dissolve the intellectual frameworks that had previously given meaning to their actions.

Wisdom, defined conceptually as a balance between knowing and doubting, or behaviorally as a balance between too much confidence and too much caution, is set at $k/K = .5$ to capture the dialectical assumption that an increment in what one knows is matched by an equal increment in one's realization of what one does not know but could know. Deviations above this value are associated with confidence, purchased at the expense of ignoring questions and uncertainties. Deviations below this value represent insufficient confidence, due to the ignoring of answers and certainties. These patterns form a "knowledge context" that shapes the meaning of incoming data. The same piece of information could add to or dissolve what one thought one already knew and enlarge or shrink the perceived size of what one does not know but could potentially know.

If we reexamine the firefighting maxim in light of Meacham's argument, we see that it is about the deployment of fallible knowledge. The maxim reminds firefighters that fires in the heat of the day are least knowable, which means that this is when the firefighters' knowledge of the fire will be most fallible. The maxim reminds firefighters that they do not (and cannot) know midday fires as well as they know midnight fires. They are perfectly free to ignore their ignorance, of course, and they may be tempted to do so if they *have* to accept a midday fire and do their best to continue the effort to suppress it. But even if the hand-off must proceed at midday, the fire can still be fought with either more or less wisdom.

Wise firefighting is indexed by how firefighters hold and use the knowledge they do have about a fire they are fighting. If they engage the fire warily, having first located escape routes, safety zones, look-outs, and communication links (Gleason, 1991), then they perceive their knowledge about the fire without either excessive confidence or excessive caution. They hedge their confidence by having a way out in case they are wrong or conditions change. But they also hedge their caution when they engage the midday fire believing that their crew chief knows what the previous crew chief knew and that their chief would not have let the other chief leave the scene until a satisfactory picture of the fire had been conveyed. There are several presumptions in those beliefs (for example, questions of trust and trustworthiness are central). Those presumptions are things that are *not* known for sure. They are the ambiguities that one is tempted to ignore in the name of boldness or magnify in the name of caution. Those are the same ambiguities that are neither ignored nor magnified but are balanced during wise moments when people act with full attention. That is Meacham's point. And that is the lesson of the Dude Fire.

REFINEMENTS IN THE ATTITUDE OF WISDOM

I chose Meacham's ideas about wisdom as the basis for this chapter because they are relevant to organizational learning and knowledge creation (for example, see Nonaka and Takeuchi, 1995). The ideas also provide a platform to fold action and knowledge together, which fits my ongoing interest in adaptation (Weick, 1969) through actions that incorporate qualities of thought, as in "heedful interrelating" (Weick and Roberts, 1993), "acting thinkingly" (Weick, 1983), and "committed interpretation" (Weick, 1993a). The idea that wisdom may be an attitude rather than a body of thought also has a certain appeal because it implies that people can improve their capability for wise action. Furthermore, once wisdom is decoupled from specific knowledge, we expect to find it expressed by more people more often, in more diverse settings. That very pluralism could strip the idea of its nuance, but not if the nature of the attitude is specified with some precision. There is also a certain attractiveness to the notion that wise people recognize the limits of their knowledge.

These attractions notwithstanding, one does encounter limits when trying to work with Meacham's ideas. As it stands, Meacham's definition is a bit too cool in its heavy dependence on cognition, a bit too solitary in its focus mainly on a single actor (although Meacham, 1990, pp. 207–208 does discuss wisdom communities), a bit too passive in its focus on deliberation rather than action, a bit too structural in its failure to describe processes that move toward wisdom, a bit too silent about doubt and caution, and a bit too preoccupied with overconfident knowing. Take, for example, the case of wildland firefighting that we started with. People who do that kind of work need to see what they don't know, because it can kill them. But they also need to remain confident if they are to muster the courage to face fire and knock it down. To doubt and to hesitate is to let events get irretrievably beyond control. People responsible for wildland firefighting need both to keep asking questions and to act like they have most of the answers. The same holds true for people in any other high-tempo setting where complex interdependencies can swiftly unfold, out of sight and out of mind, with irrevocable, possibly catastrophic consequences. Thus the question is, how do people in any of these settings simultaneously know and doubt? The answer I am pursuing is the possibility that successful simultaneity lies in how people deploy the attitude of wisdom. This possibility makes more sense, however, if we develop Meacham's ideas further. That is the task to which we now turn. We take a closer look at overconfidence, overcaution, and balance and conclude that the attitude of wisdom makes action more intelligent and adaptive because it recapitulates the wisdom inherent in all evolutionary processes.

CONFIDENCE AND ITS EXCESSES

The attitude of wisdom is relatively rare, because people find it hard to doubt what they know or to admit to themselves that the knowledge they possess is only a small portion of what could be known. At first that sounds absurd. Everyone knows that there is much they don't know. But people often judge what they don't know to be unimportant, absurd, irrelevant, of little use, or lacking in credibility. Judgments of importance tend to be negatively correlated with judgments of ignorance. If I don't know it, it's probably not important, or even likely to be true. People feel attached to old ideas and tend to modify new inputs to fit them. These tendencies have been recognized for a long time, as in this eloquent description from William James (1963):

> The individual has a stock of old opinions already, but he meets a new experience that puts them to a strain. Somebody contradicts them; or in a reflective moment he discovers that they contradict each other; or he hears of facts with which they are incompatible; or desires arise in him which they cease to satisfy. The result is an inward trouble to which his mind till then had been a stranger, and from which he seeks to escape by modifying his previous mass of opinions. He saves as much of it as he can, for in this matter of belief we are all extreme conservatives. So he tries to change first this opinion, and then that (for they resist change very variously), until at last some new idea comes up which he can graft upon the ancient stock with a minimum of disturbance of the latter, some idea that mediates between the stock and the new experience and runs them into one another most felicitously and expediently.
>
> This new idea is then adopted as the true one. It preserves the older stock of truths with a minimum of modification, stretching them just enough to make them admit the novelty, but conceiving that in ways as familiar as the case leaves possible. . . .
>
> New truth is always a go-between, a smoother-over of transitions. It marries old opinion to new fact so as ever to show a minimum of jolt, a maximum of continuity" [pp. 29–30].

The combination of tenacious older "truths" and the tendency to assimilate the novel into one's existing stock of knowledge often results in the belief that what one knows is what is true. And if it is true, why doubt it? Remember, we are talking about an attitude toward knowledge, not the substance of knowledge itself. Tendencies toward "extreme conservatism," exemplified by the assimilation of new information into old understandings, systematically remove grounds for doubt. Therefore, to increase wisdom we need to sharpen our ability to distinguish the bases on which we judge events to be the same or different. It is this distinction that is blurred during assimilation. We also need to be more stingy in our use of *same* and more generous in our use of *different*.

If this is plausible, then it raises interesting questions about the role of metaphor in making wise judgments. While the use of metaphor may promote one form of wisdom—holistic, systemic awareness (for example, the Gaia hypothesis)—it may undermine the attitude of wisdom. Metaphors obscure difference in favor of sameness, which should encourage assimilation, more confidence in one's stock of knowledge, and a heightened reluctance to doubt oneself. Even though metaphors hold the potential to increase doubt when they uncover neglected dimensions and differences, assimilation masks those differences, and the metaphor appears to confirm this masking. Instead of new questions, there is strengthened conservatism.

If doubt is made difficult because people seldom add new facts raw but instead embed them in their thoughts "cooked, as one might say, or stewed down in the sauce of the old" (James, 1963, p. 75), then doubt is made doubly difficult by tendencies toward selective perception in the service of justification. When people take actions that are visible (the act clearly occurred), irrevocable (the act cannot be undone), and volitional (the act is the responsibility of the person who did it), they often feel pressure to justify those actions, especially if their self-esteem is shaky. The felt need to justify committed action is the antithesis of doubt. Justification is about mobilizing good reasons that show, beyond a doubt, that one knows what one is doing. Thus commitment, like metaphor, can be an enemy of wisdom. Both of them minimize doubt and doubting.

If it is the case that once people begin to act they become attached to their choices and defend them, then adjustments toward wisdom should occur when people become more aware of their attachments and of reasons that favor other attachments. (A prominent theme in wisdom literatures, such as Buddhist texts, is the avoidance of attachments.) With respect to attachment per se, one might expect to find an attitude of wisdom expressed in receptiveness to beliefs that minimize the visibility of action (for example, "people are so wrapped up in their own world that they fail to notice anything that anyone else does"), in beliefs that downplay the irrevocability of action ("the world has changed, so the act no longer means what it once did"), and in beliefs that discount the responsibility for action ("at the time it seemed like the right thing to do, I had no choice"). Oddly enough, an attitude of wisdom may be expressed in the form of worldviews that emphasize narcissism, relativity, and fatalism, not because these views are "true" but because they weaken commitments, arrest the tendency to justify, and sustain doubt in contexts that might otherwise trigger commitment and overconfidence. Again, reluctance to engage in committed action may be too big a price to pay for wisdom, which could explain why wisdom is hard to find.

The commitment scenario can be taken one step further. One could choose to become committed, knowing full well that commitment encourages things like blind spots, overconfidence, and inattention to questions and alternatives. This is equivalent to *doubting* the merits of committed action itself, which introduces the attitude of wisdom at a meta-level. One doubts the commitment to commitment. If one doubts a commitment to commitment, then this should at least weaken the property of irrevocability. If the commitment to commitment is potentially revocable because it is doubted, then the strength of the commitment itself should be weakened. That, in turn, should produce more openness to information suggesting the merits of alternative actions.

Both assimilation and justification can weaken doubt and put wisdom out of reach. These two mechanisms reduce the occasions for surprise, which means people have more confidence in what they know and are less willing to doubt it. The problem, of course, is that people badly underestimate how much they overlook to keep surprise at arm's length.

Overconfidence may be an impediment to wisdom, but it persists because structures and cultures support it. In an unknowable, unpredictable world, bold actions can shape events and enact realities that favor capabilities people already possess. For example, hubris (insolent presumption) shapes markets, which can make it a virtue in many organizations. The liabilities (for the individual) normally associated with hubris get attenuated in organizations because the executives who act with hubris are located higher in the hierarchy, where their informational inputs are filtered more heavily to support their perspectives. People in high places are able to ignore their ignorance because organizational designs make this possible. Central placement of executives in networks encourages the fallacy of centrality (if this existed I surely would have known about it, but since I don't know about it it doesn't exist: Westrum, 1982; Weick, 1995). Furthermore, their success at shaping events, their continual receipt of supportive information, and their search for confirming instances under the pressure of speed (Fiske, 1992) reinforce the notion that they know most of what there is to know. Thus there's no reason for them to doubt their knowledge. If we add to these organizational dynamics that of anticipatory socialization (by which people lower in a hierarchy imitate those higher up), culture that mirrors the values of top management, and constant pressure for results rather than reflection, it is not surprising that overconfidence in the form of hubris is common in organizations and that the attitude of wisdom is rare. Not only is wisdom rare, but there is no incentive to introduce it.

Thus the achievement of ignorance is harder than it looks because there are strong incentives for bold action that can blur into overconfidence. Furthermore, organizational designs can shape information in ways that minimize doubt. Organizations are action generators (Starbuck, 1983), and anything that gets in the way of action, including wisdom, is discouraged. Thus it becomes important to look more closely at ways in which an attitude of wisdom and action can coexist. I explore two options here and additional ones later. The first option is to accept ignorance as an inevitable accompaniment of acting, but to act anyway. The second option is to use action to shift the domain and size of ignorance.

To be aware that one is ignorant but to act anyway is made possible when people trust that a combination of attentiveness, resilience (Wildavsky, 1988), and improvisation can substitute for omniscience. The social version of this option is to spread ignorance around but ensure that different people are ignorant in different ways and that they are trustworthy reporters of what they know and trust those who know what they do not. Schulmann (1993) describes this strategy as the creation of "conceptual slack," which he equates with requisite variety. Conceptual slack represents the attitude of wisdom embodied in an organizational design. The resulting design may look a lot like distributed information processing. What's significant about this design, from the standpoint of wisdom, however, is not that it increases the amount that people know but that it reminds individuals of what they don't know. Distributed information processing, by this line of reasoning, is effective not because it makes knowing less fallible but because it makes it more so. The fact that knowing is distributed makes people more aware of what they don't know, which heightens their attentiveness to the limits of what they do know. As a result, all of them act with more wisdom and update their knowledge more often with greater attention to larger systemic consequences.

A second way to act without ignoring one's ignorance is to use action to shift the timing, domain, and size of that ignorance. Here the focus is less on accepting the inevitability of one's ignorance and more on shifting it from one set of concerns to another. An example of this form of wise action is found in the way some physicians modify the traditional sequence symptom-diagnosis-treatment to symptom-treatment-diagnosis. In the modified approach they treat the symptoms in order to be able to make the diagnosis. This is not as irrational as it might sound. Since any diagnosis will ignore some presenting symptoms, to refrain from making a diagnosis is to remain attentive to more symptoms. To do this, physicians start with a plausible treatment and observe its effects on the presenting symptoms. Obviously the tricky phrase here is "plausible treatment," since "arriving at a plausible treatment" could simply be another way of saying "making a diagnosis." The nuance I want to accentuate is not that a bundle of symptoms is either explained (that is, a diagnosis is made) or not. Instead I want to preserve the quality of understanding that is associated with an attitude of wisdom. When physicians make a formal diagnosis under time pressure, their rush to label the disease, begin treatment, and achieve closure leads them to overlook and then forget the symptoms that don't fit the diagnosis. This forgetting encourages more confidence in their diagnosis than may be warranted. Doubt, correction, and revision of the diagnosis do not occur, because they are deemed unnecessary. One way around this is to postpone making a diagnosis. If doctors substitute modest hunches for full-blown diagnoses, modest treatments for "cures," and frequent monitoring for occasional monitoring, then they are likely to ignore fewer symptoms. A hunch held lightly (that is, without commitment) is a direction to be followed, not a decision to be defended. It is easier to change directions than to reverse a decision, simply because less is at stake. Similar flexibility has been demonstrated on battlefields where commanders "fight empirically" in order to discover what kind of enemy they are up against (Isenberg, 1985).

Whether one accepts one's ignorance and acts anyway while trusting to one's resilience, improvisation, and attentiveness, or one accepts one's ignorance and acts in order to shift it to another domain, the result represents an application of the attitude of wisdom. Fallible knowing replaces overconfidence. The important point is that, in both cases, action does not grind to a halt. Instead the action becomes infused with learning, and adaptation improves. The one problem associated with both of these scenarios is that they may occur mostly near the bottom of the organization, where information is filtered less fully. As we move higher up, more filtering leads to more overconfident knowing. With overconfidence comes blind spots, crises, and face-saving downsizing that diverts attention from the effects of hubris in high places. When organizations ignore their ignorance, they mistake arrogance for good management. If this happens, wisdom could become the ultimate source of competitive advantage, since it is so hard to duplicate.

CAUTION AND ITS EXCESSES

There is an imbalance in the wisdom literature that is reflected in Meacham's discussions—namely, excess confidence is treated as more of a threat to wisdom than is excess caution. As a result we know less about what it means to apply an attitude of wisdom to doubts than about what it means to apply it to certainties. Consider, for example, this account from Plato, quoted by Meacham (1983, p. 127): "Socrates questioned a man with a reputation for being knowledgeable and seeming to be wise both to others and to himself. *Plato* reports *Socrates'* conclusion: 'I went away thinking to myself that I was wiser than this man; the fact is that neither of us knows anything beautiful and good, but he thinks he does know when he doesn't, and I don't know and don't think I do: so I am wiser than he is by only this trifle, that what I do not know I don't think I do.'" And consider this bit of doggerel from R. D. Laing, quoted by Mangham and Pye (1991, p. 31): "The range of what we think and do is limited by what we fail to notice. And because we fail to notice *that* we fail to notice there is little we can do to change until we notice how failing to notice shapes our thoughts and deeds."

If I admit what I don't know, or if I notice that I fail to notice, then my knowledge declines, my doubt increases, and I move toward wisdom, *if* I had too much confidence to begin with. But I move even farther away from wisdom if I make these same changes from a prior position of caution. In the case of excess caution, I need to ignore what I don't know rather than admit it, if I want to increase wisdom. When I adopt the attitude of wisdom under conditions of excess caution, I need to doubt my doubts and learn more of what there is to know. I need to repunctuate my state, from *fallible* knowledge to fallible *knowledge*. If I can make this shift, then I should move toward a more balanced state of knowing and doubting. Shifts from more caution to less caution can occur in many ways. In terms of the variables specified by Meacham, I can increase confidence if I eliminate a potential area of knowledge (reduce K), acquire information at a faster rate than the rate at which new questions develop, or lose information that I have acquired at a slower rate than the rate at which potential questions disappear.

The nature of these moves can be illustrated using the example of wildland firefighters facing a fire that defies categorization. Suppose they believe initially that the fire could be anything from a minor fire that will be out by 10:00 the next morning to a fire that is just about to explode (K is high, k is low, p is low, u is high). The firefighters face a knowledge context characterized by excess caution. The amount of information they have acquired relative to the amount that could be known is small, possibly too small. There may be pieces of information that they have already acquired even though they do not yet realize it, or there may be pieces they could easily acquire.

Suppose the firefighters observe that small pieces of burning wood (firebrands) are being thrown out ahead of the flames. This information suggests that the fire is at least volatile enough to throw spots. If the fire is capable of doing that, then it is less likely to be a minor fire at 10:00 the next morning. They now have a reason to decrease their doubts about what kind of fire they face. Furthermore, their reason for decreasing their doubts is a good reason, backed by their prior experience in firefighting. When this piece of information is interpreted in a knowledge context of caution, it raises doubts about their doubts and increases their confidence. Expressed in Meacham's notation, caution gives way to more confidence when there is an increase in k (knowledge already acquired) and a decrease in both K (knowledge potentially acquirable) and u (size of one's doubts).

All of this may sound like much ado about traditional information processing. It is more than that. It is about the deployment of an attitude that creates a knowledge context that then affects how information is interpreted. The meaning of any informational input is determined by whether it flows into a condition of excess confidence or one of excess caution. The very same input could either (1) invalidate other acquired information without necessarily suggesting what is correct, (2) raise new questions and possibilities, (3) be a newly acquired piece of knowledge, or (4) eliminate a potential area of knowledge. Any one of these results is possible. Which meaning actually sticks will depend on the importance of an attitude of wisdom, the value placed on a balance between knowing and doubting, and the state of the knowledge system prior to the input.

So far we have remained within Meacham's system in our efforts to develop a fuller picture of excess caution as a knowledge context. To adopt an attitude of wisdom toward deep doubt and to reduce some of that doubt, one can either learn something new while holding new uncertainties constant, or eliminate potential domains of questions and uncertainties.

There are other options, however. Some of these simply reverse prescriptions discussed earlier in discussions of overconfidence. For example, excess caution may be reduced if people are encouraged to assimilate new inputs into old understandings. When assimilation is encouraged, acquired knowledge should climb faster than new questions, which means that both confidence and tendencies toward wisdom increase. The same conversion of caution into wisdom should occur when new inputs are interpreted to justify old behavioral commitments.

Other options, not yet discussed, introduce some unexpected themes. Postmodernism, normally thought to epitomize relativity and doubt, actually can also be viewed as a source of confidence, belief, and certainty when it is incorporated into an attitude of wisdom. Postmodern doubt can apply just as readily to one's doubts as to what one knows. If the world is unknowable—a possibility implicit in quantum theory, chaos theory, and postmodern thought—then the amount of potential knowledge that could be known (the denominator K in the attitude of wisdom) *shrinks* relative to what is known, which means confidence and wisdom should increase. If, in addition, multiple readings of any "text" are equally plausible, then the knowledge that comes from any one reading is a credible acquisition. If one makes a credible acquisition in a domain where there is *less* to be acquired, then this is equivalent to a simultaneous increase in k and decrease in K. Caution should change into wisdom.

Tendencies to discard complexities, to increase knowing through an increase in requisite variety, or to make meaningful connections can all be viewed as efforts to deploy an attitude of wisdom toward doubts and to weaken doubts by eliminating potential areas of knowledge (K). The strategy of small wins could have a powerful impact on doubt. When people create controllable opportunities of modest size that produce visible and tangible outcomes (Peters, 1977; Weick 1984), they increase what is known, thus raising k. Since this learning derives from a modest intervention that produces a tangible, incremental result, the learning tends *not* to raise new questions. Instead, since the small win is basically a self-contained episode, learning reaffirms rather than reopens issues previously settled. Furthermore, since the intervention is also controllable, it remains completely knowable and within the intellectual grasp of the person performing it. This means that once the knowledge attendant to it is acquired, there is little residual uncertainty to raise new questions and doubts. Encoded into Meacham's notation, a small win adds learning (k) but does not enlarge the size of the domain to be known (K). Previous doubts about the malleable world are successfully doubted and replaced by something known, with more certainty than before. Because the win is so small, it raises few questions while supplying a clearer understanding of what the world may be like.

BALANCE AND IMPROVISATION

To portray wisdom as an attitude is to suggest that it is a dynamic process in which people make sense of information differently depending on which side of the knowing-doubting scale they find themselves. If they are above the scale, the input is used to raise questions and move downward, toward wisdom. If they are below the scale, the input is treated more like new learning or as information that reduces what there is to know. The choice of interpretation is affected not just by its relationship to a balance point, however, but also by the implications for action. And therein lies the rub. Action benefits from *higher* levels of confidence. Thus demands for wisdom and demands for confidence to strengthen action can work at odds, especially when confidence is already high. The ways in which people balance interpretations, confidence, knowing, and doubting to sustain action have not been given much attention. Instead, "balance" is usually invoked in discussions of wisdom as a kind of mantra and left at that.

I want to argue that one way out of this dilemma is to conceptualize balance as confidence in one's skills of improvisation. Improvisation can be defined as "reworking precomposed material and designs in relation to unanticipated ideas conceived, shaped, and transformed under the special conditions of performance, thereby adding unique features to every creation" (Berliner, 1994, p. 241). Since improvisation involves the flexible treatment of preplanned material, it is an ideal means to stretch existing knowledge in the interest of confident action and still preserve an attitude of wisdom.

Improvisation is not "making something out of nothing." Instead, it is making something out of previous experience, practice, and knowledge during those moments when one surfaces and tests intuitive understandings of experienced phenomena—while the ongoing action can still make a difference (Schön, 1990). Jazz musician Stan Getz described the preplanning of improvisation using the metaphor of language: Jazz is "like a language. You learn the alphabet, which are the scales. You learn sentences, which are the chords. And then you talk extemporaneously with the horn. It's a wonderful thing to *speak* extemporaneously, which is something I've never gotten the hang of. But musically I love to talk just off the top of my head. And that's what jazz music is all about" (Maggin, 1996, p. 21).

Gilbert Ryle (1979) discussed improvisation as one means to convert knowledge and doubt into adaptive action. He argued that virtually all behavior has an ad hoc adroitness akin to improvisation, because it mixes together a partly fresh contingency with general lessons previously learned. Ryle (1979) describes this mixture as paying heed. Improvisation enters in the following way: "To be thinking what he is here and now up against, he must both be trying to adjust himself to just this present once-only situation *and* in doing this to be applying lessons already learned. There must be in his response a union of some Ad Hockery with some know-how. If he is not at once *improvising* and improvising *warily,* he is not engaging his somewhat trained wits in a partly fresh situation. It is the pitting of an acquired competence or skill against unprogrammed opportunity, obstacle or hazard. It is a bit like putting some *new* wine into *old* bottles" (p. 129).

These ideas about improvisation can be spliced into the emerging picture of an attitude of wisdom in the following way. So far we have seen that to adopt the attitude of wisdom is to treat one's "beliefs, values, knowledge, information, abilities, and skills as fallible" (p. 187). This fallible knowledge may represent a wise blend of knowledge and uncertainties, but this blend holds down confidence ($k/K = .5$). However, higher levels of confidence necessary for bold action can be achieved if the wise person also believes that what is already known can be combined in novel ways to deal with previously unmapped uncertainties. Faith in one's ability to recombine items already in one's repertoire in effect raises the amount of information already acquired and lowers the amount that is potentially knowable. Faith in improvisation, in other words, creates a shadow equation that has a much higher level of confidence than does the equation that represents a wise balance between knowing and doubting.

Both equations are plausible. The wisdom equation is a plausible representation of the ratio of what one knows to what one does not know. What the wisdom equation does not capture are the potential ways in which novel combinations of what is already known can create new knowledge that reduces old domains of uncertainty. Faith in this possibility creates a higher level of confidence than does the simple ratio of acquired to potential knowledge.

Once we define balance as a capability for improvisation, then we can keep the idea that to deploy an attitude of wisdom is to doubt that what is known and done is necessarily true, valid, or an exhaustive set of those things that could be known (Ryle, 1979). Knowing and doubt remain balanced, and confidence remains modest. What we add with the idea of improvisation is the possibility that what people know is sufficient to move ahead. Modest as their knowledge may be relative to what they could know, it is nevertheless sufficient because of the possibility of recombination. Belief in the power of improvisation animates an attitude of wisdom. The inability to juxtapose wisdom and improvisation may lie behind arrogant boldness that backfires (for example, the "dynamic entry" of first the Bureau of Alcohol, Tobacco, and Firearms and then the FBI at Waco failed to generate a peaceful resolution of the Branch Davidian standoff). If people are unable to decouple wisdom from confidence and pursue both, then they tend to act with dogmatic overconfidence and suppress their doubts. However, if they balance knowing and doubt around the belief that their fallible knowledge can be recombined to deal with the unexpected, and if they remain attentive, wary, and willing to explore, then they tend to remain wise and retain sufficient confidence to act. Improvisation enables people to wade into situations with fallible knowledge, secure in the belief that they can recombine that knowledge by shifting their fallibilities around. Faith in their ability to "make do" infuses confidence into their balance of knowledge and doubt.

CONCLUSION

An attitude of wisdom may be one way people in complex systems deal with the fallibility of their knowledge and remain adaptive. To maintain an attitude of wisdom, people can introduce doubt into a state of overconfidence by emphasizing differences and contrasts among events, minimizing connections between new facts and old facts, reducing their tendency to overjustify their actions, uncovering unexpected surprises, raising new questions, removing filters on informational inputs, recognizing the fallacy of centrality, increasing conceptual slack to show that there is more than one way to interpret data, and distributing different portions of what is known among several people. People can introduce confidence into a state of doubt by focusing on what they do know, shrinking their estimates of the size of what is not known but could be known, raising doubts about their doubts, generating experiences that answer larger sets of basic questions, enlarging the relevance of what is already known to new areas of potential information, assimilating new inputs to old understandings, and originating small wins. The balance point toward which these operations move can itself encourage these adjustments, even when there is continuing pressure for bold action. These conflicting pressures can be accommodated if the balance point consists of an attitude of improvisation that supplements an attitude of wisdom. Improvisation does not deny that knowing is fallible. Instead, it overlays that fallibility with the confidence-restoring prospect of adaptive recombination. Adaptive recombination of fallible knowledge produces wise action.

I want to conclude by suggesting that wisdom, conceived as an attitude that balances knowing and doubt, mirrors an even more basic principle of adaptation—namely, that ambivalence is the optimal compromise. The idea is Donald Campbell's (1965); the inspiration for it comes from William James (1890). First, the inspiration:

> The whole story of our dealings with the lower wild animals is the history of our taking advantage of the way in which they judge of everything by its mere label, as it were, so as to ensnare or kill them. Nature, in them, has left matters in this rough way, and made them act *always* in the manner which would be *oftenest* right. There are more worms unattached to hooks than impaled upon them; therefore, on the whole, says Nature to her fishy children, bite at *every* worm and take your chances. But as her children get higher, and their lives more precious, she reduces the risks. Since what seems to be the same object may be now a genuine food and now a bait; since in gregarious species each individual may prove to be either the friend or the rival, according to the circumstances, of another; since any entirely unknown object may be fraught with weal or woe, *Nature implants contrary impulses to act on many classes of things,* and leaves it to slight alterations in the conditions of the individual case to decide which impulse shall carry the day. Thus, greediness and suspicion, curiosity and timidity, coyness and desire, bashfulness and vanity, sociability and pugnacity, seem to shoot over into each other as quickly, and to remain in as unstable equilibrium, in the higher birds and mammals as in man. . . . We may confidently say that however uncertain man's reactions upon his environment may sometimes seem in comparison with those of lower creatures, the uncertainty is probably not due to their possession of any principles of action which he lacks. *On the contrary, man possesses all the impulses that they have, and a great many more besides.* In other

words, there is no material antagonism between instinct and reason. Reason, *per se,* can inhibit no impulses; the only thing that can neutralize an impulse is an impulse the other way. Reason may, however, make an *inference which will excite the imagination so as to set loose* the impulse the other way; and thus, though the animal richest in reason might be also the animal richest in instinctive impulses too, he would never seem the fatal automaton which a *merely* instinctive animal would be. . . .

Curiosity and fear form a couple of antagonistic emotions liable to be awakened by the same outward thing, and manifestly both useful to their possessor. The spectacle of their alternation is often amusing enough, as in the timid approaches and scared wheelings which sheep or cattle will make in the presence of some new object they are investigating. I have seen alligators in the water act in precisely the same way towards a man seated on the beach in front of them—gradually drawing near as long as he kept still, frantically careering back as soon as he made a movement. Inasmuch as new objects *may* always be advantageous, it is better that an animal should not *absolutely* fear them. But, inasmuch as they may also possibly be harmful, it is better that he should not be quite indifferent to them either, but on the whole remaining on the *qui vive,* ascertain as much about them, and what they may be likely to bring forth, as he can, before settling down to rest in their presence. Some such susceptibility for being excited and irritated by the mere novelty, as such, of any movable feature of the environment must form the instinctive basis of all human curiosity; though, of course, the superstructure absorbs contributions from so many other factors of the emotional life that the original root may be hard to find [James, 1890, vol. 2, pp. 392–393, 429].

Here, now, is Campbell's distillation (1965, p. 305) of the key point he draws from James: "The presence in moral codes, proverb sets, and motivational systems of opposing values is often interpreted as discrediting the value system by showing its logical inconsistency. This is a misapplication of logic, and in multiple-contingency environments, the joint presence of opposing tendencies has a functional survival value. Where each of two opposing tendencies has survival relevance, the biological solution seems to be an ambivalent alternation of expressions of each rather than the consistent expression of an intermediate motivational state. Ambivalence, rather than averaging, seems the optimal compromise."

If we return once more to the world of wildland firefighting, ambivalence in assessing the dynamic Mann Gulch fire might have taken the form, "We believe this is a fire we'll extinguish by 10:00 tomorrow morning, but we can't say for sure. We will fight it as if we're right, but we will remain attentive as if we were wrong." As Carl Wilson's later analysis (1977) showed, attentiveness was warranted because the small Mann Gulch fire had all four of the signs that suggest that a minor fire is just about to explode.

We can illustrate ambivalence as the optimal compromise in a different aspect of wildland firefighting, designs for organizing fire crews. There is growing use of Paul Gleason's LCES system (1991), which prescribes that a crew should not attack a fire until the crew's lookouts, communication links, escape routes (at least two), and safety zones are in place and known to everyone. What's interesting about an LCES design is that it is a blend of knowledge and doubt. The lookouts and communication capabilities imply that the crew knows what is going on and how the local conditions are related to the big picture. The attention to escape routes and safety zones, however, implies that what the crew knows may be incomplete and that this potential ignorance needs to be recognized and hedged. The crew is simultaneously confident and cautious. This is made possible because they trust that their ability to pool and recombine what they know, should the unexpected occur, will enable them to keep acting. The escape routes and safety zones preclude hubris on the part of the crew, and the lookouts and communication links preclude timidity. The combination of these four LCES components encourage an attitude of wisdom in the face of danger, without paralyzing action. Knowledge and ignorance balance on the pivot of improvisation. This configuration exhibits the ambivalence of wisdom and celebrates the wisdom of ambivalence.

REFERENCES

Berliner, P. F. *Thinking in Jazz: The Infinite Art of Improvisation.* Chicago: University of Chicago Press, 1994.

Blanshard, B. "Wisdom." In P. Edwards (ed.), *The Encyclopedia of Philosophy.* New York: Free Press, 1967.

Campbell, O. T. "Ethnocentric and Other Altruistic Motives." In D. Levine (ed.), *Nebraska Symposium on Motivation.* Lincoln: University of Nebraska Press, 1965.

Csikszentmihalyi, M., and Rathunde, K. "The Psychology of Interpretation: On Evolutionary Interpretation." In R. J. Sternberg (ed.), *Wisdom.* New York: Cambridge University Press, 1990.

Davis, M. S. *What's So Funny?* Chicago: University of Chicago Press, 1993.

Fiske, S. T. "Thinking Is for Doing: Portraits of Social Cognition from Daguerreotype to Laserphoto." *Journal of Personality and Social Psychology,* 1992, *63,* 877–889.

Follett, M. P. *Creative Experience.* New York: Longmans, Green, 1924.

Gergen, K. J. *Realities and Relationships.* Cambridge, Mass.: Harvard University Press, 1994.

Gleason, P. "LCES—A Key to Safety in the Wildland Fire Environment." *Fire Management Notes,* 1991, *52*(4), 9.

Huff, A. (ed.). *Mapping Strategic Thought.* New York: Wiley, 1990.

Isenberg, D. J. "Some Hows and Whats of Managerial Thinking: Implications for Future Army Leaders." In J. G. Hunt and J. D. Blair (eds.), *Leadership on the Future Battlefield.* New York: Pergamon Press, 1985.

James, W. *The Principles of Psychology.* New York: Dover, 1890.

James, W. *Pragmatism and Other Essays.* New York: Washington Square Press, 1963.

Johns, M. "Dude Fire Still Smokin'." *Wildfire,* 1996, *5*(2), 39–42.

Maclean, N. *Young Men and Fire.* Chicago: University of Chicago Press, 1992.

Maggin, D. C. *Stan Getz: A Life in Jazz.* New York: Marrow, 1996.

Mangham, I., and Pye, A. *The Doing of Managing.* Oxford, England: Blackwell, 1991.

Maruyama, M. "The Second Cybernetics: Deviation Amplifying Mutual Causal Processes." *American Scientist,* 1963, *51,* 164–179.

McDaniel, R. R., Jr. "Strategic Leadership: A View from Quantum and Chaos Theories." In W. J. Duncan, P. Ginter, and L. Swayne (eds.), *Handbook of Health Care Management.* Cambridge, Mass.: Blackwell, 1996.

Meacham, J. A. "Wisdom and the Context of Knowledge: Knowing That One Doesn't Know." In D. Kuhn and J. A. Meacham (eds.), *On the Development of Developmental Psychology.* Basel, Switzerland: Karger, 1983.

Meacham, J. A. "The Loss of Wisdom." In R. J. Sternberg (ed.), *Wisdom.* New York: Cambridge University Press, 1990.

Nonaka, I., and Takeuchi, H. *The Knowledge-Creating Company.* New York: Oxford University Press, 1995.

Perrow, C. *Normal Accidents.* New York: Basic Books, 1984.

Peters, T. J. "Patterns of Winning and Losing: Effects on Approach and Avoidance by Friends and Enemies." Unpublished doctoral dissertation, Stanford University, 1977.

Roberts, K. H. "Structuring to Facilitate Migrating Decisions in Reliability-Enhancing Organizations." In L. Gomez-Meija and M. W. Lawless (eds.), *Top Managerial and Effective Leadership in High Technology Firms.* Greenwich, Conn.: JAI Press, 1991.

Robinson, D. N. "Wisdom Through the Ages." In R. J. Sternberg (ed.), *Wisdom.* New York: Cambridge University Press, 1990.

Rothermel, R. C. *Mann Gulch Fire: A Race That Couldn't Be Won.* [General Technical Report INT-299.] Ogden, Utah: Intermountain Research Station, U.S. Forest Service, 1993.

Ryle, G. "Improvisation." In G. Ryle (ed.), *On Thinking.* Cambridge, Mass.: Blackwell, 1979.

• Sakaiya, T. *The Knowledge-Value Revolution.* Tokyo: Kodansha International, 1991.

Schön, D. A. *Educating the Reflective Practitioner: Toward a New Design for Teaching and Learning in the Professions.* San Francisco: Jossey-Bass, 1990.

Schulmann, P. R. "The Negotiated Order of Organizational Reliability." *Administration and Society,* 1993, *25,* 353–372.

Simpson, J. A., and Weiner, E.S.C. (eds.). *The Compact Edition of the Oxford English Dictionary.* (2nd ed.) New York: Oxford University Press, 1989.

Starbuck, W. H. "Organizations as Action Generators." *American Sociological Review,* 1983, *48,* 91–102.

Webster, N. (ed.). *Webster's Dictionary of Synonyms.* (1st ed.) Springfield, Mass.: Merriam-Webster, 1951.

Weick, K. E. *The Social Psychology of Organizing.* Reading, Mass.: Addison-Wesley, 1969.

Weick, K. E. "Managerial Thought in the Context of Action." In S. Srivastva (ed.), *The Executive Mind: New Insights on Managerial Thought and Action.* San Francisco: Jossey-Bass, 1983.

Weick, K. E. "Small Wins: Redefining the Scale of Social Problems." *American Psychologist,* 1984, *39,* 40–49.

Weick, K. E. "Sensemaking in Organizations: Small Structures with Large Consequences." In J. K. Murnighan (ed.), *Social Psychology in Organizations: Advances in Theory and Research.* Englewood Cliffs, N.J.: Prentice Hall, 1993a.

Weick, K. E. "The Collapse of Sensemaking in Organizations: The Mann Gulch Disaster." *Administrative Science Quarterly,* 1993b, *38,* 628–652.

• Weick, K. E. *Sensemaking in Organizations.* Thousand Oaks, Calif.: Sage, 1995.

Weick, K. E., and Roberts, K. H. "Collective Mind in Organizations: Heedful Interrelating on Flight Decks." *Administrative Science Quarterly,* 1993, *38,* 357–381.

Westrum, R. "Social Intelligence About Hidden Events." *Knowledge,* 1982, *3*(3), 381–400.

Wildavsky, A. *Searching for Safety.* New Brunswick, N.J.: Transaction, 1988.

Wilson, C. C. "Fatal and Near-Fatal Forest Fires: The Common Denominator." *The International Fire Chief,* 1977, *43*(9), 9–15.

4

FACING THE FUTURE:
BACKING COURAGE WITH WISDOM

Janice M. Beyer and David Niño

SOMETIMES IT TAKES COURAGE for employees to honor their convictions. No doubt there are some instances in which managers are wise enough to listen to employees who report wrongdoing (Beyer, 1989), but in other cases managers ignore or deny allegations of wrongdoing until employees feel they must go public to achieve redress. Consider the words of one whistle-blower who uncovered serious wrongdoing in his organization: "I said to myself: 'Look, you are at a crossroads and you have to decide which way to go. You can either roll over and play dead or stand up and say what you think.' I [had] hit the wall, the red line. I could not go beyond that line. I was being asked to become a party to an act of fraud on the public where health and safety are concerned" (Glazer and Glazer, 1989, p. 78). But to go public requires overcoming legitimate fears. And some of those fears involve considerations other than what one might expect, as another whistle-blower explains: "It's not exactly a fear of what could happen to me, although

Many of our friends and colleagues contributed to the development of our ideas and referred us to likely sources. We especially want to thank Donde Ashmos, Tom Denton, Mimi Drumwright, Frances Hauge, John B. Henneman, III, George Huber, Esther Wyss, Bill Zelazny, and any others we may have forgotten for sharing their insights and knowledge with us. What we have written is, of course, solely our own responsibility.

that certainly crossed my mind. What it is is a fear of being found out not to stand up to standards that I have claimed as my own. . . . I mean, why is it in life today that we have to deny any morality at all? . . . What is right in the corporation is not what is right in a man's home or in his church. What is right in the corporation is what the guy above you wants from you. That's what morality is in the corporation" (Jackall, 1988, p. 109).

Both of these individuals faced isolation and possible reprisals for their actions, but they took them anyway. In this chapter we argue that their actions evinced both courage and wisdom. Sometimes they received support from coworkers, but never from management. Indeed, had management been wise enough to listen to the evidence of wrong-doing these employees described and act on it, there would have been no need for whistle-blowing.

These whistle-blowers' fears were well-founded; their organizations retaliated in horrendous ways against them.[1] Their managers also lost, because they ended up being exposed anyway and often had to pay damages. How can we understand the courage and wisdom of these employees' actions and the lack of both reflected in what their managers did and failed to do? One approach may be to inquire into how organizational cultures support or undermine courageous and wise actions.

TABOO OR OVERSIGHT?

A few years ago a group of leading management researchers set about measuring the fit between organizational culture and individual values. They searched both the scholarly and popular management literature for central values important both to individuals' self-concept and identity and to organizational value systems (O'Reilly, Chatman, and Caldwell, 1991). The 54 items they culled from an initial list of 110 included neither courage nor wisdom.[2]

We decided to do our own search, starting with the subject indexes of more than a dozen leading texts surveying the field of organizational behavior. We failed to turn up any entries for either courage or wisdom. Searches of the leading books on organizational culture and the leading scholarly management journals produced similar results. We found only two books (both on leadership) that substantively addressed the issue of courage (Kouzes and Posner, 1987; Chaleff, 1995) and two articles on wisdom (Bigelow, 1992; Weick, 1993). In other sources these terms were used only in passing.

The neglect of these concepts in the management literature indicates a significant gap in the knowledge base from which we teach future managers. Other fields of study have treated these subjects at length. For example, when we searched the literature on philosophy, psychology, and sociology, we found in-depth analyses of both courage and wisdom (some of which we will use in this chapter).

Why have these subjects been neglected in writings on management yet examined in some detail in other social science fields? One excuse might be that both *courage* and *wisdom* describe something that is exceptional—not expected to occur very often—and therefore peripheral to management concerns. But genuine vision and charisma are likewise exceptional, yet they are frequently discussed in the management literature. A second possibility is that these terms seem too idealistic to be relevant to the customary, pragmatic concerns of managers and their organizations. A third possibility is that they describe qualities to which managers do not aspire. Maybe there is something in the current practice of management that is antithetical to or at least at odds with the concepts of courage and wisdom. Perhaps it is taboo to connect the ideals behind courage and wisdom to those that underlie management. In order to weigh the last possibility, we must sort out what the two terms mean and what implications they have for the practice and culture of management.

DEFINITIONS OF COURAGE AND WISDOM

Dictionary definitions of courage describe it as facing and dealing with danger, difficulty, or pain (Guralnik, 1979). Psychological definitions add the element of emotion: courage is persistence in the face of emotional and physical sensations of fear (Rachman, 1990). We prefer a more complete definition, developed by a philosopher (Walton, 1986). He argues that courage should meet all of the following conditions:

1. The actor intends to realize some moral end.
2. The actions taken are practical, skilled, and deliberate. They go beyond the call of duty and involve overcoming fear.
3. The actor expects the actions taken to make a difference in furthering his or her moral end in a specific situation.

Courage, in this view, is not a personal trait; rather, it is defined in terms of practical actions taken to realize moral objectives in dangerous or threatening situations. Moral objectives are those involving inner convictions about what is right and wrong; they are based on conscience and ethical judgments. According to this definition, whistle-blowing is courageous when those who do it are driven by moral considerations, realize that they face serious risks of reprisals and other dangers, but act anyway in a practical and effective way. It is not courageous if the whistle-blower feels no fear, makes accusations that are ill-founded, or is motivated by revenge or a desire to divert attention away from his or her own incompetence.

We also prefer a comprehensive, philosophical definition of wisdom. According to Blanshard (1967, p. 322), wisdom involves an intellectual grasp of and insight into the means and ends of practical life. Like courage, wisdom is grounded in what is practical and possible. Other qualities that constitute wisdom are reflectiveness, judgment, and recognition of limitations and possibilities. *Reflectiveness* means considering events and beliefs in light of their likely consequences; it thus focuses on means. *Judgment* involves weighing ends in terms of values and experience (Blanshard, 1967). Wise persons evaluate objectives according to their ideals and in terms of the cumulative learning derived from the trials and errors of life. Wisdom presumes self-direction. *Recognition of limitations and possibilities* begins with the self and extends to other people (Kekes, 1983) and to situations. Like judgment, it grows from experience and can be transferred to others through socialization and culture. The quotations at the beginning of the chapter reveal considerable reflection and judgment on the part of the two whistle-blowers, as well as recognition of the limitations and possibilities in their situations. These two men reflected before they acted, based their actions on strong personal values, and took action with awareness of the possible repercussions. Whistle-blowing is not wise unless it involves sound judgment based on "evidence that would persuade a reasonable person" that the situation the whistle-blower seeks to correct is indeed wrong or dangerous (Bowie, 1982, p. 143).

If, as Trice and Beyer (1993) argue, cultures are repositories of the beliefs and practices people use to cope with life's uncertainties, then it makes sense that culture would shape the enactment of courage and wisdom. Both emerge in uncertain situations and characterize the actions taken to deal with uncertainty. Culture influences courage by dictating which ends are moral, by providing routines and other means to effect practical action and overcome fear, and by offering ideologies that enable people to have faith that their actions will result in desired outcomes. Culture also embodies accumulated knowledge (Sackmann,

1991) derived from collective experience, and as such it informs wisdom. It does so by providing ideologies, values, and norms that provide substance for reflection and inform judgments; an array of cultural forms and practices communicate and affirm this substance and help people define who they are.

As we see it, courage and wisdom are complementary but not inseparable. Wisdom does not require courage, but courage inevitably involves some measure of wisdom since it requires actions that are practical, skilled, and deliberate. Therefore, by analyzing courageous actions in organizations we may learn something about both wisdom and courage.

COURAGE IN ACTION

In our readings on courage in organizations we encountered two quite different types of courage, what we call exceptional courage and everyday courage. One occurs only occasionally and is thus, in that sense, exceptional. The other occurs on a day-to-day basis. Examples of exceptional courage that we discuss in this chapter include whistleblowing, exemplary social activism, and courageous following. Examples of everyday courage that we discuss here come from the taken-for-granted cultural practices of highly dangerous occupations.

Exceptional Courage

Occasionally members of an organization are compelled to take extraordinary measures to remedy a perceived wrong or otherwise change the direction of their organization. We identified three types of individuals that display exceptional courage in organizations: whistle-blowers, moral exemplars, and courageous followers.

WHISTLE-BLOWERS. In their study of whistle-blowers, Glazer and Glazer (1989) document how the strong professional and religious values held by these individuals propelled them to protest what they saw as immoral or unethical practices: "Once the resisters had defined the conflict in moral terms, no organizational demands and priorities could persuade them to abandon their strong commitment to actions they . . . deemed appropriate for an ethical, religious person" (p. 98). These whistle-blowers derived their strong values from the culture of their religion or profession, both of which instilled in them a sense of right and wrong. Most initially expected their organizations to uphold the same values, but they soon learned otherwise. Because they believed that overcoming wrongdoing was the right thing to do, it became a personal mission, usually involving actions that they saw as their duty but that their employers and coworkers usually saw as disloyal—that is, as contrary to their duty to their organizations and coworkers.

When those to whom they reported the wrongdoing denied it or failed to act to correct it, the whistle-blowers came to see the correction of the wrongdoing as their personal responsibility. A woman physician in a Veterans Administration hospital put it this way: "First of all, there wasn't anyone else willing to do it. There was no one else around. Secondly, some of the things they did were so unfair that my conscience simply bothered me and I couldn't allow these things to go unnoticed. . . . I know it may sound like a hackneyed phrase today, but I believe it: 'The only thing necessary for evil to prevail is for good men to do nothing.'. . . I felt if I didn't do anything, who will?" (p. 86). This particular resister received support from another female physician at the hospital; however, most whistle-blowers end up acting alone, with no support from coworkers.

All of these whistle-blowers had to overcome fear to persist in their dissent. Their superiors and coworkers repeatedly warned them that they would pay dearly for their actions. As they suffered retaliation, the whistle-blowers kept expecting some support for their ethical position from the institutions and individuals around them. As one put it, "I kept thinking that they would not get away with it." (p. 157). They were right, but they received support only after remarkable persistence on their part. All eventually won enough support from agencies outside their employing organizations that the wrongdoing was acknowledged and to some degree corrected. Sadly, however, they failed to win support from the very religious or professional organizations from which they drew their convictions. Instead they were helped by the press, politicians, and organizations specifically founded to help whistle-blowers.

The price for making a difference was often high. In one well-publicized case that Glazer and Glazer felt helped to encourage later cases of dissent, Frank Serpico, a police officer who exposed corruption in the New York City Police Department, was ostracized by his fellow officers and eventually shot and killed during a drug raid. Many suspected his fellow officers had set him up or, at a minimum, failed to back him up during the raid. (In dangerous occupations like police work, the support of coworkers can mean the difference between life and death—an issue we will discuss more fully later.) One of the whistle-blowers studied by Glazer and Glazer lost custody of her children for a substantial period of time because the superior whose wrongdoing she exposed told scurrilous lies about her personal behavior to her former husband, the children's father.

MORAL EXEMPLARS. A similarly high degree of moral certainty characterizes another type of documented exceptional courage—that exhibited by moral exemplars. Colby and Damon (1992) studied twenty-three extraordinarily altruistic social activists. These individuals felt they had no choice but to act on their principles, often in ways that involved heavy personal sacrifice. They displayed "an unhesitating will to act, a disavowal of fear and doubt, and a simplicity of moral response. Risks were ignored and [personal] consequences went unweighed" (p. 69). Their moral convictions developed and deepened over the years as they made contact with and learned from others in their own and other activist and political organizations. One such moral exemplar spent most of her adult life caring for people living in a trash dump in Juarez, Mexico. Although she was a high school dropout herself and a single mother of four, she was able to raise funds to clothe, feed, and educate these desperately poor people. She secured their trust and love to a degree that protected her from the crime around her. She felt fear at first, but she went to the dump and helped them anyway because she believed the Holy Spirit was leading her. She said her actions were based in faith, not courage.

Another was a southern woman who spent over thirty years leading the struggle against the poll tax, working to desegregate restaurants and hotels and other public facilities, and helping her lawyer husband serve black clients who were fighting discrimination, segregation, and exploitation. During that time she came into contact with most of the leading civil rights leaders, those opposing McCarthyism, and many others with strong social concerns. These contacts contributed to her moral development, which was "co-constructed by the continual interplay between her and her chosen community" (p. 120). She and her husband suffered ill health and considerable financial hardship; sometimes they had so little money that they could not afford to maintain their own household. Much of the time they lived in communities that were hostile toward their activities and views. But her many connections to other morally concerned individuals and organizations helped this activist sustain her courage and efforts.

Most of these activists said that the notion of courage did not capture anything they had felt or done; rather, they had acted out of a sense of moral necessity. One even commented, "It would take more courage for me not to do it because . . . how could I live with myself afterwards? . . . It wasn't a courageous act. . . . It was a *normal* act" (p. 75). Nevertheless, all shared an awareness of the risks they faced. But they put considerations of risk aside, sometimes making a conscious effort to do so. One who admitted to feeling scared said he faked courage and acted anyway. After a while he realized that faking courage worked and that it had helped him move ahead. Strong moral convictions are apparently enough to lead some people to believe that they have no choice but to take actions entailing personal risk.

It is clear from their accounts that Glazer and Glazer (1989) and Colby and Damon (1992) considered the whistle-blowers and social activists they studied to be unusual people. A quite different conclusion, drawn in some of the literature on whistle-blowing, is the idea that ordinary people caught in unusual circumstances may feel impelled to take courageous action. A recent review states that "Empirical research to date has not shown that whistle-blowers are inherently different from those organization members who observe wrongdoing but choose not to report it" (Near and Miceli, 1996, p. 515). These observations underline our earlier contention that courage is not a personal characteristic of specific individuals but rather a distinguishing feature of specific actions taken in specific situations. It may be that wrongdoing has to reach some degree of perceived severity and that observers have to believe they can make a difference before they will report it (p. 515). Courage has a practical aspect, even when persons are driven to act courageously primarily by their strong moral convictions.

COURAGEOUS FOLLOWERS. Chaleff (1995) provides a provocative recent addition to the literature on courage, in which he addresses the issue of good followership. His central argument is that leaders need courageous followers who will protect them from their own weaknesses and help them to evaluate ideas by standing up to them when necessary: "Devoted leaders and followers enter a kind of sacred contract to pursue their common purpose. They are both guardians of that purpose. Part of the followers' role is to help the leader honor that contract. If we do not challenge the leader about dysfunctional behavior, the contract is slowly shredded before our eyes. The longer we wait, the less is left of the contract" (p. 81). Chaleff goes on to point out that it takes more courage to challenge a leader's behavior than it takes to challenge policy. He also says that followers sometimes have a duty to disobey their leaders; the list of circumstances he lists in which disobedience is appropriate (risks to life or health, sacrifice of the rule of law, and so on) make it clear that such disobedience must be in the service of a moral purpose. Opposition involves other risks, he points out, including the risk of being proved wrong later. But he argues that "We should never berate ourselves for having had the courage to act on our convictions" (p. 164). Although Chaleff's treatment is more theoretical than empirical, and it seems impossible to determine the prevalence of courageous followers, organizations probably do indeed produce some of these individuals.

Everyday Courage

The nature of some occupations requires those in them to overcome fear and face dangers and risks on a daily basis. Police officers, soldiers, pilots, firefighters, high steel ironworkers, demolition workers, underground miners, and even butchers face very real dangers in carrying out their work. Although members of these occupations tend to lay claim to exceptional character traits, in reality the ideologies and cultural forms they cultivate help them vent their emotions and deal with their fears (Trice and Beyer, 1993). It is their cultures that make their everyday courage possible.

OCCUPATIONAL IDEOLOGIES. Ideologies are important to dangerous occupations because their members must perceive some rationale for taking the risks inherent in their work, and they must have some mechanism for overcoming their fear so that they can carry out their duties. To the police, the ability to confront danger is considered a core skill, and dangerous acts are seen as characteristic of the profession (Manning, 1977). To help themselves justify taking such risks, the police cultivate an ideology of absolute morality. They regard what they do as agents of the state as, by definition, good and proper, because they are protecting the state and the public from criminals. This ideology suffuses police work with "a moral integrity" and, in so doing, conceals as well as reveals its realities (p. 5).

The police also claim the mantle of professionalism, which serves their self-esteem and gilds "the entire enterprise with the symbols, perquisites, tradition, power, and authority associated with the most respected occupations" (p. 129). A prevalent myth that also serves to elevate police work is that the police control crime. Of course they cannot completely do so, but many police believe firmly in the myth because it makes the risks they take seem worthwhile. Furthermore, they are often called on to enforce standards with which segments of the population disagree. They deal with these cultural conflicts and ambiguities by assuming a frame of reference that stresses that the police protect their communities, enforce the law, and prevent law-breaking. All of these are moral objectives worthy of courageous acts.

Another occupation with an ideology that gives it a moral purpose is military service. The military has the dual duty of fighting wars and generally protecting a country's interests from enemies. Both aims are, in the eyes of those prosecuting them, morally justified. While the military employs a host of cultural forms to buttress its purposes and identity (Trice and Beyer, 1993), a particularly relevant cultural form to the issue of everyday courage is the taboo. Soldiers, especially officers, are not supposed to exhibit fear, even in the face of mortal danger. One theory explaining this taboo says that soldiers overcome their fears—they find courage—largely through social pressures (Keegan, 1976). Fighting men are commonly loath to exhibit fear lest their comrades think they are cowards. The one thing a soldier fears losing more than his life, says this theory, is his reputation among other men.

This prohibition against showing fear was especially strong for officers in the British infantry during the battle of Waterloo. They "were most concerned about the figure they cut in their brother officers' eyes. Honour was paramount, and it was by establishing one's honourable-ness . . . that leadership was exercised over the common soldiers" (p. 189). When one officer followed an order that he knew would lead him and his men into certain death, his death was considered the ultimate mark of honor. British officers of the day followed an abstract ideal that specified proper comportment in the face of risk, acceptance of death if it should come, and private satisfaction should it not. One analysis (Keegan, 1976) suggested that the code for such courageous behavior grew out of the coolness, endurance, and pursuit of excellence and intangible objectives learned on the football fields of Eton. Following this code induced the British officers to stand their ground in the face of repeated attacks, and because their subordinates followed suit, the British won the battle of Waterloo.

Rachman (1990) conducted psychological studies of combat pilots and bomb-disposal crews, two groups that perform courageous acts in the face of mortal danger. The pilots were less afraid when they felt they had more control. The bomb-disposal specialists were more confident, calmer, and more psychologically stable and performed more courageous acts when they had more training and belonged to cohesive groups. It follows that, to the degree that occupational cultures enhance feelings of mastery and control and reinforce group cohesion and trust, they make acts of courage more likely.

CULTURAL FORMS. There are a wide variety of other dangerous occupations for which a moral purpose is less clear-cut. Members of these occupations see a clear moral purpose in their work to the degree that they believe it is essential to society and that society would suffer if they did not do it. They view their work as more than morally neutral because it provides something good for someone else or for society.

Smoke jumpers are an instructive example. By parachuting into forests to put out fires, they may protect lives as well as forests and property. Since saving lives is a moral purpose, it is clear that they sometimes display courage, by our definition. (Community firefighters more readily fit our demanding definition of courage, because in communities lives are always at risk. However, it is interesting to note that smoke jumpers probably have the more dangerous occupation.) In any case, smoke jumpers face very dangerous conditions and employ a rich mix of cultural forms to help their members overcome their fears, reflect carefully, and use good judgment (McCarl, 1976). Their cultural forms express ideas and lessons learned from experience that help their members behave courageously and wisely.

One cultural form they use is the story. One night around a campfire, an experienced smoke jumper gave an extensive account to a group of rookies about how he and a companion, who was an awkward rookie, got out of trouble even though everything went wrong (McCarl, 1976). Their saga began with both men hanging from their parachutes, caught in a tree. After cutting themselves down, they could not reach their food, which was caught in another tree. They were lost, and the rookie was injured. They stayed calm, persevered, and managed to walk twenty-five miles, weak from hunger and exhaustion, before reaching help three days later. Such stories remind listeners of both limitations and possibilities learned through experience and convey practical knowledge that can be used in dangerous circumstances. They also stimulate reflection and courage in those listening.

A rather strange rite of passage undergone by neophyte smoke jumpers before their first jump can be seen as a ceremonial act intended to reduce fear and thus bolster courage. The neophyte is subjected to an elaborate series of ordeals—being bound with tape, lathered with soap, doused with water, and kept awake with repeated hazing all through the night before. The rationale behind this ritual is that the neophyte will be too tired to think much about what he or she is doing when the time for the jump arrives and will therefore behave automatically as trained and not hesitate.

Even meat cutters, who have a dirty, dangerous, and (to many people) rather disgusting job manage to instill social value into their work. At least until recently they assumed value for their occupation from the value placed on meat as an expensive, healthful, and highly valued product (Meara, 1974). They were thus able to display confidence, honor, and pride in their work. Because the work is dangerous, involving exceedingly sharp knives, saws, and cutting machines, they develop stories and rituals to dissipate and deal with their fears. Meat cutters who have been disfigured by accidents make a point of showing their injuries to newcomers and telling them the story of how they got them. Such stories serve to reinforce warnings and promote safe practices; they also display pride and courage. To cope with the morbid conditions of their work, butchers use ritual humor. While cutting up meat, for example, they make jokes about animal parts that are analogous to those of humans. They also heighten their sense of masculine "honor" and identity through irreverent talk about women, whom their culture assumes to be incapable of doing such physically demanding and dangerous work (Meara, 1974).

Other dangerous occupations with an important social value that does not quite equate with a moral purpose are miner and high steel ironworker. In both of these occupations, workers realize that their safety may depend on the performance and skills of others. Such recognized interdependence builds extremely strong subcultures that help members deal with their fears.

Fitzpatrick (1980) describes how miners socialize newcomers into their occupation with a variety of cultural rites. Through these rites newcomers learn the practical and technical skills miners need to help them gain a sense of control over the dangers they will face: explosions, cave-ins, fires, rock falls, and cave floodings. Neophyte miners must pass through a rite of passage in which they learn that everyone does their fair share of the work, adheres to a code of mutual assistance, works moderately (because trying to do too much can jeopardize everyone's safety), and controls their emotions, even under stress. New miners also learn that they should never work alone. Miners know that because of the many hazards they face they must watch out for and keep tabs on one another. They also have a norm that says they should never attempt to perform work beyond their capabilities. Miners must be able to trust their coworkers to know their own limitations and not accept an assignment if it will jeopardize anyone's safety.

"They are therefore especially accommodating to one another's fears, wishes, and personal idiosyncrasies" (p. 147). If a miner expresses any desire to avoid a certain task, he is never considered a coward. Miners also continuously remind one another to "play it cool" and not get excited, even if trapped by a cave-in. They evince a stoic acceptance of the risks they face. Newcomers are advised not to worry about danger, because there is nothing they can do about it anyway.

Three of the cultural forms used by high steel ironworkers to deal with their fears are a testing ritual, stories, and taboos. "Binging" is a ritual used to test other workers' trustworthiness, competence, and self-control under pressure. Workers provoke one another with verbal abuse and even sparring matches to see what the other guy is "made of" (Haas, 1977). Information is gained and relationships defined through this ritual. Newcomers usually receive the most binging. Stories are also told to warn workers of dangerous conditions. But perhaps the strongest cultural form among the high steel ironworkers is a taboo about talking about danger. As in the military, fear must be kept private; it cannot be publicly displayed, lest it spread to others.

The subcultures of these occupations foster courage by providing belief systems and practices that help their members accept and deal realistically and practically with their dangerous working conditions. Their ideologies elevate the social significance of the work they do and thus give it a moral purpose. In some occupations, the social significance is not a stretch—in others, it requires some myth building. Their taboos, rituals, rites, stories, and other practices provide culturally accepted ways for them to acknowledge the dangers they face and control the fears they feel, thus enabling them to carry out their work despite these emotions. The strong social bonds they forge with other members working near them help them sustain their courage by giving them a sense of shared control and responsibility.

A less admirable side to these macho occupational subcultures is that they tend to exclude women. Some of the rituals used by smoke jumpers and miners, for example, are not suitable for mixed-sex groups because they involve nudity and intimate physical contact (Trice and Beyer, 1993). Since more women are entering traditionally male occupations, some of these rituals must be changing, but we found no scholarly accounts of such changes. The existence of these traditional rituals, to the degree that they are valued and still practiced, forms a symbolic barrier to the entry of women into these occupations.

It also seems clear that some traditionally female occupations require courage. Nursing, for example, not only requires the ability to cope with stress and life-and-death situations but also may involve real physical danger from violent patients, especially in the case of psychiatric and geriatric nursing. Also, caring for some patients (especially AIDS patients) involves some risk of contracting a fatal or highly damaging disease. Interestingly, however, the nursing subculture does not seem to include any particular stories or rituals related to these dangers. Rather, it has traditionally stressed patient welfare as the nurse's top priority, even when it puts the nurse at risk. One story told among nursing students questions hospital policies that advise nurses to protect themselves. In the story, nurses are instructed not to hold the hand of a patient in labor, lest the patient inadvertently crush their nurse's hand. The nursing students questioned this advice because they felt it was dehumanizing for both patients and staff (Dingwall, 1977).

THE WISDOM UNDERLYING COURAGE

In the examples of exceptional courage given in this chapter, wisdom is apparent primarily in the strong influence that personal values and ideals had on the actions of those involved. The whistle-blowers and morally exemplary social activists described previously followed their moral convictions in attempting to correct social wrongs and to help other people. They made judgments that said that what was going on was a violation of their inner beliefs, and they acted to mitigate that violation. Data from interviews with them gives evidence that they did not act precipitously but reflected on and weighed their possibilities before acting. Any potential personal harm they perceived was outweighed by the harm they saw being done to others and to society. (Courageous followers, if such persons do indeed exist, would follow a similar path, weighing the possibilities and limitations of their leaders and their situations and using their personal values to guide their judgment.)

Our examples of exceptional courage and whistle-blowing are also consistent with Kekes's notion (1983) of the self-directed nature of wise acts. According to Kekes, wisdom involves judging actions against one's own hierarchy of ideals and commitments, which determines the ends toward which one's actions are directed. Self-direction is derived from a form of self-knowledge about what is good and important in life. Wisdom guides action when people act according to this self-knowledge with great commitment and constancy. This is especially true in what Kekes calls hard cases, in which one's commitment to one's hierarchy of ideals is put to a tough and sometimes painful test. We saw vivid examples of these wise acts in the self-directed behavior of both the whistle-blowers and the moral exemplars.

The cultures of dangerous occupations exhibit wisdom both in their ideologies and in the cultural forms they employ. Since these cultural forms are the chief observable manifestations of their ideologies, they express and reflect the accumulated wisdom of the culture in which they appear. However, occupational cultures may also encourage automatic behavior that may be unwise in unanticipated circumstances. Weick's analyses (1996) of the Mann Gulch and South Canyon disasters, in which groups of smoke jumpers lost their lives, suggests that if the smoke jumpers had dropped their tools while fleeing the fires they could have moved faster and would have had a good chance of escaping. He suggests that among the reasons they did not drop their tools was that they were given no clear reason to change, and their tools symbolized the essence of what it means to be a firefighter. To be a firefighter without tools was inconceivable to the smoke jumpers. As he argued earlier in connection with the Mann Gulch disaster, "In a fluid world, wise people know that they don't fully understand what is happening right now, because they have never seen precisely this event before" (p. 641). Thus wisdom can also be defined as a balance between knowing and doubting, between too much confidence and too much caution (see Chapter Three).

In contrast, the taboo against fear that is prevalent among soldiers and high steel ironworkers is wise in several respects. Fear is contagious (Rachman, 1990), and people overcome by fear tend to perform poorly. Soldiers may run away and start a panicked retreat. This is highly dangerous to the whole group, because retreating soldiers are more easily killed than those who stand their ground (Keegan, 1976). Workers overcome by fear on the high steel may freeze in position, unable to help their coworkers or themselves. They then create additional danger, because someone else must come and rescue them (Haas, 1977). Thus the taboo against fear in these occupations seems to illustrate sound judgment and collective knowledge based on accumulated practical experience. It recognizes the probability of fear and regulates its expression by setting limits on acceptable behavior.

Stories foster wisdom because they encourage reflectiveness and the rethinking of past events. They contribute to the listener's judgment by informing him or her of the experiences of others and suggesting right and wrong courses of action. They also alert listeners to what could happen and warn them of possible limitations in themselves, their coworkers, and various situations. They often impart cautionary lessons about what can happen that cannot be anticipated. In this sense they create the wisdom that comes from realizing that one cannot possibly know everything one might need to know (Weick, 1993).

Rituals and rites create wisdom because they test newcomers and dramatize the hazards present in their situations. They also define the boundaries of appropriate and safe behavior. After undergoing the rite or ritual, the newcomer is better informed and emotionally hardened to face the dangers of the occupation.

MANAGEMENT IDEOLOGIES

The occupational cultures described previously provide an instructive contrast with that of the management community. Managerial work is commonly considered an occupation or profession, although the boundaries and precise duties of managers are not so clear-cut as in the occupations already discussed.[3] As with other occupations, people are attracted to management by their beliefs and preferences. Some have argued that people with an orientation toward control are attracted to management (Jackall, 1988). In the terms of scholarly definitions, however, managers do not qualify as professionals, because their occupation lacks a formal code of ethics and formal qualifications for licensure (Wilensky, 1964; Trice and Beyer, 1993). (Although there are some managers who do come from within recognized professions, such as accounting and engineering.) Given the lack of a code of ethics to set forth a moral purpose for management, it is far from clear whether the management culture in the United States contributes to organizational courage. It is also not clear whether the predominant culture in U.S. management circles contributes to organizational wisdom.

Moral Mazes

Not only does the management occupation lack codified moral or ethical standards, but as one observer of managers in several organizations concluded, the bureaucratic organizations in which most managers work tend to encourage a kind of moral relativism: "In the welter of practical affairs in the corporate world, morality does not emerge from some set of internally held convictions or principles, but rather from ongoing albeit changing relationships with some person, some coterie, some social network, some clique that matters to a person" (Jackall, 1988, p. 101).

In U.S. corporations, with their bureaucratic hierarchies and their reverence for individual achievement and heroes, managers soon learn that their success depends on a patrimonial system—on fitting in and pleasing the boss—as much as on their expertise and personal achievements.

They must develop an ethic that allows them to use their personality as a commodity to please and impress others; to get ahead in the organization (and often just to survive), they must become socially skilled actors (Jackall, 1988). All of these pressures favor allowing oneself to be directed by others (Whyte, 1956) and militate against self-direction.

Extensive observations and interviews have shown that managers learn to adapt their personal beliefs, values, and behavior to the socially defined culture around them and to appear comfortable in doing so. Truth is thus socially defined within the organization. Its norms rest on an institutional logic that is unquestioned, and the principle managerial virtue is pragmatism. Maintaining the appearance of consistency is important. What matters is not whether managers stand by their personal principles, but their agility in avoiding blame; not their acuity in perceiving falsity or errors, but their adeptness at protecting others; not their talents, abilities, or hard work, but how these are harnessed to serve the particular exigencies faced by their organization; not what they believe or say, but how well they have mastered the ideology and rhetoric that serve their organization; not what they stand for, but whom they stand with (Jackall, 1988). The best way for managers to maintain their personal integrity is to avoid knowing about what might be wrong: "Without clear authoritative sanctions, moral viewpoints threaten others within an organization by making claims on them that might impede their ability to read the drift of social situations" (p. 105).

Given this logic, it is not surprising that managers fear and despise whistle-blowers. The latter exhibit a courage based in self-direction and moral convictions that is contrary to the prevailing relativity of management rationales and thus threatens to overthrow or undermine them. Also, people who become managers like to control what happens, both to reassure themselves and to assert their own will (Jackall, 1988). Whistle-blowers challenge managers' control and threaten to expose their weaknesses and ineptitude.

The Myth of Rationality

Another factor discouraging courage in organizations is the emphasis the U.S. management culture puts on an ideology of rationality (Trice and Beyer, 1993). Much of the language employed by managers and in the training of managers connotes an image of rational calculation: terms such as *information, efficiency, optimization, implementation,* and *design* occur frequently (Scott, 1987). Many analysts have agreed that rationality is expected, encouraged, and celebrated in organizations (Pfeffer,

1981; Moore, 1962), even if it is not always practiced (Staw, 1980; Feldman and March, 1981; Meyer and Rowan, 1977).

The ideology of rationality refers to more than a belief in the use of reason. It also implies a lack of emotionality, including the kind of caring that undergirds strong moral convictions. Rationality's preeminent place in the management ethos is buttressed by a belief in the superiority of a scientific, often quantitative, approach to problems. Economics, finance, management science, and accounting are the disciplines that adhere most tightly to this belief. The ideology of rationality also includes a belief in efficiency, predictability, calculability, and substitution of technology for human involvement—all of which are supposed to contribute to managers' control over uncertainty (Ritzer, 1983). Uncertainty is, of course, the enemy of managerial control.

Rationality in its purest form requires a unified and consistent set of purposes, knowledge of all relevant alternatives, and goals that reliably guide behavior (Thompson, 1967). To practice such rationality would require managers to possess perfect know-how and to consistently achieve logical judgments and actions. As Simon (1957) and others have pointed out, perfect rationality is seldom possible.

Thus the idea that some kind of super-rationality underlies managerial action and expertise is a myth. And like the myths surrounding police work, the myth of managerial rationality hides as much or more than it reveals. The myth helps managers to persuade themselves and others that they have techniques at their disposal that will enable them to control their organizations. It thus helps to justify their high salaries, status, and other perquisites. The myth also helps to deflect criticisms and inconvenient questions.

When managers put aside their personal moral convictions in pursuit of supposed rationality or some perceived social pressure, they can act with neither courage nor wisdom. Their relative, situational morality is not anchored in sustained moral convictions and thus precludes their acting with true courage as we have defined it. Their shifting allegiances and opportunism devalue their self-direction, accumulated experience, and knowledge. They thus lack a basis for wisdom as we have defined it. Various current events and trends in organizations dramatically reveal managers' lack of conventional wisdom.

CONSEQUENCES OF A LACK OF WISDOM

Perhaps the most telling recent example of an organization's lack of wisdom was the Barings Bank fiasco. Lacking experience in the kind of financial trading done in the United States, British bankers deluded themselves into thinking that to make huge profits in financial markets did not require formal preparation so much as a kind of knack or intuition (Lewis, 1996). Thus some British firms hired relatively uneducated, working-class young men and put them in front of trading screens in the belief that some of them were bound to make big money. Nick Leeson was a young, working-class man who, although he had no college degree, had worked for Morgan Stanley in Britain. That was enough, apparently, to make him seem a good bet for Barings. Since top management really didn't know what Leeson should be doing, they gave him an incredibly free hand. And even though he was operating in faraway Singapore, they failed to set up any meaningful supervision of his trades and allowed him to handle his own financial reporting back to the firm. As it turned out, Leeson lacked even an elementary understanding of the markets and made disastrous, speculative trades at the Singapore Exchange that eventually cost the bank $1,400,000,000, forcing it into receivership. Clearly neither Barings nor Leeson himself understood his limitations. Barings management also failed to reflect carefully on what it took to be a successful trader; they apparently never knew that U.S. traders handling comparable volumes of trade tend to have Ph.D.'s in mathematics and physics.

Another example of the disastrous results of a lack of wisdom is the fateful decision to launch the *Challenger* space shuttle on January 29, 1986 (Maier, 1992). Despite warnings from engineers worried about damage done to the shuttle's O-rings in previous launches and the unusually cold temperatures at launch time, managers at the highest levels of NASA decided to go ahead with the launch. With many schoolchildren watching on-site and much of the world watching on television, the shuttle blew up seventy-three seconds after launch. To add to the trauma of the event, the seven-member crew included, for the first time, a school teacher, who was supposed to translate her experience in space into an educational lesson for American children. As it turned out, the launch was a very sad lesson and a collective trauma that required psychological counseling for many children. In addition to the tragic deaths of seven brave people, the *Challenger* disaster had serious repercussions for NASA, whose proud reputation has never been completely restored and whose budget has been under fire ever since.

Testimony from NASA engineers and subsequent analyses of this decision revealed that NASA administrators had failed to take account of the possible risks of the low-temperature launch and the safety implications of possibly damaged O-rings (Maier, 1992). The agency managers responsible for making the decision to launch did not reflect as carefully as they should have on the disastrous possibilities warned of in the reports of their engineers and on the limits on their own technical knowledge. At one point the chief engineer, who was hesitant to approve the launch, was asked to "take off his engineering hat and put on his managerial hat." He then went along with the decision to launch. Putting this kind of pressure on an expert who was supposed to use his expertise to inform the decision was poor judgment when so much was at stake.

Dumbsizing

A collective lack of wisdom seems to be reflected in the rash of downsizings that have occurred in U.S. corporations over the last two decades. Despite numerous studies showing that downsizing has many costs and negative effects and seldom produces gains (except in short-term stock prices), U.S. firms continue to downsize. One set of analysts has deplored this trend, calling downsizing the "equivalent of corporate anorexia" (Hamel and Prahalad, 1994, p. 10). The *Wall Street Journal* (Markels and Murray, 1996) recently referred to the practice as "dumbsizing." From 1979 to 1995, forty-three million employees were laid off by U.S. corporations (Uchitelle and Kleinfield, 1996). Well-known, established firms like IBM, AT&T, General Motors, Xerox, ITT, Sears, Kodak, K-Mart, and others periodically announce layoffs of tens of thousands of employees. How wise are these decisions?

Not very wise, according to anecdotal accounts in the press and scholarly assessments (Cameron, Freeman, and Mishra, 1993). The *Wall Street Journal* article on dumbsizing gave many examples of the costs of downsizing. Some firms laid off employees and then had to hire them back as consultants at up to four times their original rate. Others that offered early retirement plans found that many valued old-timers left—sometimes to go to work for competitors—or found they had to hire back some retired employees and managers and pay them both retirement pay and a salary. The worst case was a gas company that laid off its meter readers and contracted out the work. When one of the contracted employees allegedly raped a customer, the gas company found itself with an expensive lawsuit and a public relations nightmare on its hands.

Furthermore, research on downsizing has shown that those employees that remain often feel demoralized, guilty, and anxious (Brockner, 1988), and those who are laid off become less trusting of future employers. There is some evidence that the deleterious consequences of downsizing are beginning to be recognized. Management attitudes, according to one human resources manager, have gone from seeing employees as disposable to recognizing them as a critical renewable asset. Some firms are thus trying to rebuild loyalty in their workforce by extending new assurances about security and commitment to their employees (White and Lublin, 1996). Since employees are the main repository of accumulated knowledge and experience in an organization, treating them as disposable ignores the value of their collective wisdom.

Various explanations can be offered for why organizations downsize without a clear need for it or clear benefits from it. As Selznick (1996, p. 273) points out, "organizational adaptation is often more compulsive than problem-solving." Organizations may downsize because they think society expects them to, because others are doing it, or because once other companies do it it seems legitimate, even obligatory, to do so as well. A primary rationale underlying downsizing is the still-dominant view of the corporation as an instrument for maximizing return on capital and profits for shareholders. Since this rationale has gained increasing legitimacy, corporations have engaged in repeated rounds of mergers and downsizing—and each round helps in turn to further strengthen that rationale (Goodrick, Meindl, and Flood, 1997) and undermine broader, less shortsighted views of corporate responsibility that include the likely impacts of these actions on employees and society.

Research also shows that the majority of managers contemplating downsizing prefer a quick-hit approach to both planning and implementing it (Cameron, Freeman, and Mishra, 1993). One justification for speeding up the process is that doing so minimizes employees' pain, fear, and anxiety, which would otherwise drag on for months. But whose pain and anxiety are managers really concerned with minimizing—their employees' or their own? If they were wise and a bit courageous, managers might go slower and make sure that they attend to the welfare of those being laid off. Rather, they rush through the process, often taking two months or less to plan and implement a substantial downsizing (McCune, Beatty, and Montagno, 1988). This hardly leaves time for careful reflection on what downsizing can and cannot accomplish, on the best way to carry it out, or on its possible consequences.

Research indicates that those organizations whose performance benefited the most from downsizing were those that implemented a gradual, incremental approach (Cameron, Freeman, and Mishra, 1993). In these organizations managers took time to reflect on their circumstances and the possible consequences of alternatives, and they ended up surgically eliminating unnecessary and redundant functions rather than cutting across the board. Some organizations were able to downsize without laying off any employees. Managers in these organizations showed more wisdom than those who acted hastily and with less careful reflection.

A second rationale for rapid downsizing is a current, very popular ideology that favors sudden, radical change in organizations. It has been described and sold with various labels: punctuated equilibrium (Tushman and Romanelli, 1985; Gersick, 1991), reengineering (Hammer and Champy, 1993), revolutionary change (Tushman and O'Reilly, 1996), and discontinuous change (Nadler, Shaw, Walton, and Associates, 1995). Despite the aura of difficulty associated with doing what this ideology prescribes, it is questionable whether pursuing radical change usually reflects either wisdom or courage.

Devaluing the Past

All of the current approaches that advocate radical change devalue past learning and experience. The basic argument against following the past is that it hinders an organization's ability to adapt to major environmental changes. The punctuated equilibrium model of organizational evolution, for example, assumes that adaptation sometimes requires fundamentally new practices, structures, strategies, and values. Old organizational systems that resulted in great organizational success are especially likely to require change, because such success increases inertia and resistance to change (Tushman and Romanelli, 1985). This perspective has been retained in current discussions about the need for revolutionary change, or the "inevitable revolutions required by discontinuous environmental change" (Tushman and O'Reilly, 1996, p. 11). (Revolutionary change theorists do recognize, however, that both revolutionary and evolutionary change are desirable; their emphasis is on how to combine or alternate between the two types of change.)

This dim view of organizational experience underlies the prescriptions set forth in the widely read management book *Reengineering the Corporation* (Hammer and Champy, 1993). The basic argument behind reengineering is that dramatic improvements are gained when managers forget about past practices and take a radically new, "clean-slate" approach to thinking about and designing organizational processes. The objective is to implement revolutionary changes that represent a complete break with the past. With worldwide sales approaching two million copies, the book and its prescriptions have grown into a $30 billion global consulting empire. Many firms have tried or are trying reengineering, but the question is whether they are making change for the sake of change alone (Bruce, 1994).

Whereas reengineering practitioners target organizational processes, promoters of discontinuous change also advocate getting rid of people who might be envoys of the unwanted past. Their rationale is that because of their past experiences with the organization, senior managers will either resist or not be able to recognize the changes needed to adapt to new environmental conditions. Even if they did accept the need for change, these analysts contend, senior managers may not be up to the task: "Frequently those who have been part of the organization, part of its history and traditions and part of the web of relationships, are not capable of administering the needed shock. That is why most of the cases of successful re-creation start with the replacement of the CEO and much of the senior team" (Nadler, Shaw, Walton, and Associates, 1995, p. 13).

The problem with these ideas is that they assume that the existing organizational culture is dysfunctional and a barrier to desired change, and that since past practices and top management are agents of that culture, they must be removed and replaced. They further assume that the practices and people associated with the past have little to offer and may actually interfere with what is needed for the future. This is not necessarily true, as Wilkins (1989) and Hamel and Prahalad (1994) have pointed out.

If acting with courage requires an underpinning of wisdom, the lack of wisdom evident in recent managerial fads and actions is disquieting. How can we expect managers to act courageously if their culture lacks wisdom that can be translated into moral and practical actions that make a difference?

BACKING COURAGE WITH WISDOM

Perhaps the picture is not as black as a review of the business press might suggest. Some organizational scholars have questioned the assertions cited previously. Their analyses, if heeded, may help show the way to courageous and wise managerial action.

In his discussions of cultural change, Wilkins (1989) suggests that managers should honor the past. Before embarking on wholesale

change, they should reflect on what has become distinctive and endur-
ing in their organizations and then act to preserve and build on those
distinctive competencies. They should also seek to understand and
appreciate how these distinctive skills and attributes came into being,
so that these generative processes can perhaps be replicated to create
new distinctive competencies in the future. He counsels managers to
ask themselves, "How can we take advantage of our past learning, values, and traditions to develop answers to future problems?" (p. 51).

In a similar vein, Hamel and Prahalad (1994) argue that it takes
many years for organizations to develop core competencies. If kept
vital, such competencies can enable organizations to seize future
opportunities. They argue that "consistency of effort is key.
Consistency depends first of all on a deep consensus about which competencies to build and support, and second, on the stability of the management teams charged with competence development" (p. 231). They
see stability of senior management as critical because it helps ensure
consistent strategic agendas and cumulative learning.

Their view is supported by longitudinal data from a Stanford
Business School study (Collins and Porras, 1994) that found many benefits in executive continuity. It found that those organizations that had
consistently outperformed their industry rivals were "six times more
likely" to promote and develop their top managers from within (p.
173). Examples of firms that had promoted no outsiders to CEO at the
time of the study included the following industry leaders: 3M,
American Express, Boeing, Citicorp, Ford, General Electric, Hewlett
Packard, Johnson & Johnson, Mariott, Merck, Motorola, Nordstrom,
Procter & Gamble, Sony, and Wal-Mart. Because the insider, "home-
grown" CEOs at these companies had shared their firms' historical
experiences and been thoroughly socialized into their cultures, they
provided important consistency and cultural continuity even as they
upgraded and adapted their firms to new circumstances. The changes
they introduced were not always gradual or small; often they were able
to bring about drastic changes in their organizations, contrary to what
Nadler and his coauthors (1995) predicted.

Because of the tendency of the business press to consider change and
anything unusual as more newsworthy than continuity and solid
accomplishment, it is hard to assess how many more managers and
organizations are following prescriptions for radical change than paying attention to analysts who advocate building on the past. What
seems clear, however, from the popularity of the reengineering
approach, is that there may be a bias in the management culture and in

organizational reward systems toward the pursuit of radical change. First, as noted previously, managers want to exercise control. They want to make a difference. What better way to make a difference than to change something from what it was? Pursuing dramatic change is especially tempting when it may make you appear heroic and daring and get you lots of attention in the business press. Second, managers are ambitious, and many want to advance their careers and make more money as fast as they can. Radical change promises dramatic short-term results, which may enable managers to quickly move on to bigger and richer positions and cash in on their stock options. Third, institutional pressures from the stock market favor signs of change over signs of continuity. The markets always want still-better performance, and perhaps change will deliver it, especially change that follows currently popular prescriptions (Powell and DiMaggio, 1991). Fourth, managers want to be "in the know" and "in the swim of things." If their competitors are reengineering or downsizing, they may feel they have to imitate them just to keep up and not be left behind. All of these tendencies reflect the propensity of managers to constantly look outside themselves and their organizations for affirmation and approval. The current emphasis on satisfying the customer is yet another example of this propensity, elevated to an almost sacred commandment.

It is possible, however, to find some traces in the business press of managerial courage and wisdom—examples of managers who do not follow the crowd. Whether these are rare exceptions or not is impossible to tell without more research along the lines of the Stanford study (Collins and Porras, 1994).

A prominent example of resisting popular management thought is provided by Lou Gerstner's decision not to break up IBM (Meyer, 1996). Institutional investors would like to see parts of the company sold off to realize what they consider to be its full market value. One expert argues that the sum of IBM's parts is greater than the whole. He calculates that if each of the company's major operating units were valued as separate companies relative to their competitors in those industries, IBM would be worth $115 billion—$50 billion more than its current market value. Resisting the logic behind such analyses, Gerstner, IBM's current CEO, considers all such talk "dumb." "'IBM's size and breadth,' he says, 'gives the company a leg up in the fastest-growing segment of its business—helping customers integrate technologies and manage large information systems.'. . . A spokesman for Gerstner says, 'Those who advocate breaking up IBM don't understand either the company or the technology industry'" (Meyer, 1996, p. 50).

Gerstner seems to be facing the future with both courage and wisdom. He cannot know whether his courage and wisdom will translate into organizational success. But after reflecting on the limitations and possibilities within his company and the market, he has decided to take the risk of following his own convictions. If his strategy is unsuccessful, he will undoubtedly lose his job. He may anyway, if his board of directors grows impatient before his strategy pays off. So Gerstner faces the danger of failing even if he is right. Clearly his decision makes a difference to the future of the company. Keeping the company intact is a moral end if it brings better returns to stockholders and a better future to employees in the long run. (As of this writing, IBM stock is doing much better than Gerstner's critics had predicted.) For this CEO and others, it takes courage and unconventional wisdom to resist the conventional wisdom.

But managerial wisdom requires more than resisting external pressures. It also requires exercising sound judgment that not only relies on the current strengths of the company but also is highly self-critical and searches for ways to do things better (Collins and Porras, 1994). Managers of successful organizations "know who they are" and use that knowledge as the basis for self-improvement. They are, in that sense, self-directed. In Weick's terms (see Chapter Three), they display both self-confidence and self-doubt.

A seventy-year-old woman who is an amateur sculptor and former medical technician provides another unlikely example of apparent courage coupled with wisdom. After sixteen years of toiling and tinkering, Patricia Billings finally succeeded in developing a fireproof, nontoxic building material that seems to be the best alternative to asbestos yet discovered. Tests of the material show that it doesn't burn even at temperatures surpassing two thousand degrees Fahrenheit; it doesn't even produce smoke. Ms. Billings has started her own company, called GeoBond International, to manufacture the fireproof material. Large companies are interested in buying the company for more than $20 million, but Ms. Billings won't sell. She fears that these big companies would simply bury her invention because they have too much invested in the status quo—and she wants people to know that she saved lives (Naj, 1996).

Clearly this entrepreneur-inventor has moral ends as well as profits in mind. To make sure her product reaches the market, she is willing to forego large financial rewards. Realizing the enormous benefits that her product could have for humanity, she is making judgments based on her ideals rather than on selfish material advantage. She is demonstrating wisdom, but is she also demonstrating courage? Much depends on how we interpret the risks of continuing to operate a small start-up company in competition with giant firms. What might she fear? Perhaps bankruptcy. Perhaps failure to ever successfully market the product in which she believes. The latter is probably the biggest fear for this entrepreneur—the fear of not making the difference she hopes to make.

Another interesting example of courage and wisdom in organizations is that of the policy entrepreneur—a manager who advocates socially responsible buying practices in his or her firm (Drumwright, 1994). A study of policy entrepreneurs showed that most are well-respected middle managers with considerable persuasive skill and high energy for their cause. They act based on personal commitment to a cause and after deliberate consideration of their personal beliefs. As one of these managers explained, "I did it purely from wanting to do the right thing" (p. 4). It seems clear that policy entrepreneurs act courageously in the sense that they pursue moral ends in which they have strong convictions, they have relevant practical knowledge and skills, they go beyond the call of duty, and if successful they make a difference.

The final criterion for courage—overcoming fear—was apparent in at least some of the cases considered in the study. Some of the policy entrepreneurs felt secure enough that they saw no personal threat in advocating socially responsible actions. Others, however, clearly saw substantial risks. One manager was worried about misjudging the cause he was championing and thus losing credibility. Another said the policy entrepreneur has to be willing to accept rejection and be prepared to fail. Although policy entrepreneurs do not face physical danger, they do face possible damage to their career and reputation and even the possible loss of their job. It seems clear that they fear such possible outcomes, and so by our definition the actions they take are courageous. They also appear to be wise, because they have clearly reflected on the possibilities open to them and have used skills and knowledge gained from their experience to realize their aims.

CONCLUSION

Although distinct, the qualities represented by the terms *courage* and *wisdom* are complementary. Both are based in culture and evidenced in individual actions. Courage, according to a thoughtful philosophical definition, is not a personal characteristic of individuals but a distinguishing feature of practical, skilled, and deliberate actions that go beyond the call of duty, involve overcoming fears, are intended to realize moral aims, and make a difference. Individuals who exhibit courage may draw their moral aims and their practical knowledge and skill from their religious or occupational culture. Wisdom concerns the means and ends of practical life; it involves reflection, sound judgment, and the recognition of limitations and possibilities. Wisdom depends on culture as a repository of lessons learned from accumulated experience. There is nothing in either of these definitions to preclude the emergence of courage and wisdom in organizations. Yet the topics of courage and wisdom have been neglected in the literature on management and organizational culture. It seems worthwhile to inquire why.

We suspect that what these terms connote is at odds with conventional management thought and practice. Although there are well-documented examples of courage and wisdom in organizations, these qualities have seldom been noted in managers. Rather, they have been seen in employees who have publicly exposed wrongdoing and in members of dangerous occupations. One analysis theorizes that followers may also sometimes be courageous.

Juxtaposing examples of exceptional individual courage and of everyday courage within specific occupations with an analysis of the ideology and culture of management has proved instructive. The whistle-blowers and moral exemplars described in this chapter drew on their religious and professional cultures for moral guidance and scripts. They had unwavering convictions that they followed at great personal risk and cost. In contrast, because it lacks a code of ethics or any established moral principles, the management profession offers no cultural basis for the practice of courage. Indeed, studies of managers reveal that they practice moral relativism, marked by shifting allegiances and response to social pressures. Such pragmatism is not consistent with courage. Without a fixed base of beliefs and values, the occupational culture of managers provides no anchor for acts of courage. Any courage that individual managers practice must therefore be derived from their religion or their personal value system.

Comparing the manager's experience with that of members of dangerous occupations has also been instructive. Examining the benefits provided by the occupational cultures of miners, smoke jumpers, butchers, and so on makes it even more clear what the management culture lacks. People in dangerous occupations band together to provide one another with practical knowledge and social support that buttresses the courage it takes to face danger on a daily basis. The cohesiveness of these groups is an important bulwark against fear and foolhardy or cowardly behavior. Experienced members of these occupations provide role models and teach lessons to newcomers through expressive cultural forms. They also pass on the accumulated wisdom of the occupation. Studies of managers and writings about management do not reveal similar practices or tendencies (although they may exist and have simply not been studied). Newcomers to management may acquire mentors or sponsors, but they do not encounter any rich set of historically based cultural practices that tell them how to face the risks of the occupation. Rather, prevailing management ideologies exhort new managers to be completely rational, to avoid emotion and make decisions scientifically. But not only is complete rationality impossible, it is also at odds with the compassion required for the type of moral convictions that drive courageous behavior.

If the management culture can be said to have one central concern, it is probably control. Managers want control, believe in control, and value control. They want to be able to determine what happens; they want to make a difference. Thus managers tend to avoid even the appearance of a loss of control. Although total managerial control is a myth, the strong urge to maintain it can lead managers into some unwise decisions and actions. In particular, they may be loath to admit a lack of relevant knowledge, or they may fail to take the superior knowledge of others fully into account. The managers at Barings did not seek enough information before embarking on trading activities with which they were unfamiliar. The tragic decision to launch the *Challenger* space shuttle illustrates how a group of managers proud of their "can-do" attitude can discount the critical advice of experts, leading to disaster. The popularity of one management fad after another suggests that managers feel they must actively pursue some course of action to make things different from how they have been—change evinces the manager's control. Those who are taken up by the latest fad, like downsizing, ignore its historical record and the data on its effects and adopt it anyway. They devalue the past and any collective wisdom that they might draw on, in favor of making a major change that demonstrates their power and control.

Fortunately the management culture is not sufficiently powerful to influence all managers in this direction. There appear to be some wiser managers around who resist the latest fad and the institutional pressures of the stock market and the business community and instead follow their own convictions about what is best for their organizations or for society. In resisting the conventional wisdom, such managers perform acts of courage. They have much to fear, including the loss of their reputation, career, and financial rewards, but probably, like the moral exemplars we have discussed, what they fear most is failing to realize their aims.

Managers and others in organizations may engage in acts of courage and wisdom more often than we know. Policy entrepreneurs are one example, and it seems likely that others dedicated to socially responsible corporate behavior can be found if we look for them. The prevalent approaches to management research seem to have made us myopic and blinded us to courageous and wise behavior in organizations. The terms *wisdom* and *courage* do not even appear in lists of established management concepts. It is time to look for more that is admirable in management practice; looking for courage and wisdom is a good place to start.

NOTES

1. The Glazer and Glazer study (1989, p. 4) adopted a demanding definition of whistle-blowing, derived from Bowie (1982). The whistle-blower's actions had to have been morally motivated, and he or she had to have exhausted all available internal procedures for rectifying the wrongdoing. Furthermore, the whistle-blower had to have possessed evidence that would persuade a reasonable person, perceived serious potential danger from the violation, and acted out of felt responsibilities for exposing moral violations. Finally, the whistle-blower's actions had to have had some reasonable chance of success. The whistle-blowers they studied suffered many forms of retaliation, including ostracism, humiliation, stalled careers, firings, and smearing of their reputations. Another study of less damaging and public revelations—complaints of sexual discrimination (Near and Jensen, 1983)—found that 59 percent reported no retaliation.

2. Those that came closest to courage were related to innovation—experimenting and risk taking (which both loaded positively), and care and security (which loaded negatively). Another related value—social responsibility—loaded negatively on the aggressiveness factor. The value closest to common definitions of wisdom—being reflective—failed to load on any of the factors used and was therefore excluded from further study.

3. In a general sense, an occupation consists of any line of work or set of tasks. However, over time occupations tend to develop other characteristics that give them a distinct identity and influence: they become full-time work with special training, occupational associations, exclusive rights to perform certain sets of tasks (sometimes through licensure), and codes of ethics (Trice and Beyer, 1993).

REFERENCES

Beyer, J. M. "Ethical Dissent in a New Mode." *Science*, 1989, *244*, 835–836.

Bigelow, J. "Developing Managerial Wisdom." *Journal of Management Inquiry*, 1992, *1*, 143–153.

Blanshard, B. "Wisdom." In P. Edwards (ed.), *The Encyclopedia of Philosophy*. New York: Free Press, 1967.

Bowie, N. *Business Ethics*. Englewood Cliffs, N.J.: Prentice Hall, 1982.

Brockner, J. "The Effects of Work Layoff on Survivors: Research, Theory, and Practice." *Research in Organizational Behavior*, 1988, *10*, 213–255.

Bruce, R. "Reengineering: The Fun and the Hype." *Accountancy*, Mar. 1994, p. 54.

Cameron, K. S., Freeman, S. J., and Mishra, A. K. "Downsizing and Redesigning Organizations." In G. P. Huber and W. H. Glick (eds.), *Organizational Change and Redesign: Ideas and Insights for Improving Performance*. New York: Oxford University Press, 1993.

Chaleff, I. *The Courageous Follower: Standing Up To and For Our Leaders*. San Francisco: Berrett-Koehler, 1995.

Colby, A., and Damon, W. *Some Do Care: Contemporary Lives of Moral Commitment*. New York: Free Press, 1992.

Collins, J. C., and Porras, J. I. *Built to Last: Successful Habits of Visionary Companies*. New York: Ballinger, 1994.

Dingwall, R. "Atrocity Stories and Professional Relationships." *Sociology of Work and Occupations*, 1977, *4*, 371–396.

Drumwright, M. E. "Socially Responsible Organizational Buying: Environmental Concern as a Noneconomic Buying Criterion." *Journal of Marketing*, 1994, *58*, 1–19.

Feldman, M. S., and March, J. G. "Information in Organizations as Signal and Symbol." *Administrative Science Quarterly*, 1981, *26*, 171–184.

Fitzpatrick, J. S. "Adapting to Danger: A Participant Observation Study of an Underground Mine." *Sociology of Work and Occupations*, 1980, *7*, 131–158.

Gersick, C.J.G. "Revolutionary Change Theories: A Multilevel Exploration of the Punctuated Equilibrium Paradigm." *Academy of Management Review*, 1991, *16*, 10–36.

Glazer, M. P., and Glazer, P. M. *The Whistleblowers: Exposing Corruption in Government and Industry*. New York: Basic Books, 1989.

Goodrick, E., Meindl, J. R., and Flood, A. B. "Business as Usual: The Adoption of Managerial Ideology by U.S. Hospitals." In J. J. Kronenfeld (ed.), *Sociology of Health Care*. Greenwich, Conn.: JAI Press, 1997.

Guralnik, D. B. (ed.). *Webster's New World Dictionary of the American Language*. Springfield, Mass.: Merriam-Webster, 1979.

Haas, J. "Learning Real Feelings: A Study of High Steel Ironworkers' Reactions to Fear and Danger." *Sociology of Work and Occupations*, 1977, *4*, 147–170.

Hamel, G., and Prahalad, C. K. *Competing for the Future.* Boston: Harvard Business School Press, 1994.

Hammer, M., and Champy, J. *Reengineering the Corporation.* New York: Ballinger, 1993.

Jackall, R. *Moral Mazes: The World of Corporate Managers.* New York: Oxford University Press, 1988. From *Moral Mazes* by Robert Jackall. Copyright ©1989 by Oxford University Press. Used by permission of Oxford University Press, Inc.

Keegan, J. *The Face of Battle.* New York: Viking Penguin, 1976.

Kekes, J. "Wisdom." *American Philosophical Quarterly,* 1983, *20,* 277–286.

Kouzes, J. M., and Posner, B. Z. *The Leadership Challenge: How to Get Extraordinary Things Done in Organizations.* San Francisco: Jossey-Bass, 1987.

Lewis, M. "Snobs and Yobs: How British Banking Produced Nick Leeson." *The New Yorker,* 1996.

Maier, M. *"Red Flags," "Smart People," "Flawed Decisions": Morton Thiokol and the NASA Space Shuttle* Challenger *Disaster.* Binghamton: State University of New York, 1992.

Manning, P. K. *Police Work: The Social Organization of Policing.* Cambridge, Mass.: MIT Press, 1977.

Markels, A., and Murray, M. "Slashed and Burned: Call It Dumbsizing: Why Some Companies Regret Cost-Cutting." *Wall Street Journal,* May 14, 1996, sec. A1.

McCarl, R. S. "Smokejumper Initiation: Ritualized Communication in a Modern Occupation." *Journal of American Folklore,* 1976, *81,* 49–67.

McCune, J. T., Beatty, R. W., and Montagno, R. V. "Downsizing: Practices in Manufacturing Firms." *Human Resource Management Journal,* 1988, *27,* 145–161.

Meara, H. "Honor in Dirty Work: The Case of American Meat Cutters and Turkish Butchers." *Sociology of Work and Occupations,* 1974, *1,* 259–283.

Meyer, J. W., and Rowan, B. "Institutionalized Organizations: Formal Structure, Myth, and Ceremony." *American Journal of Sociology,* 1977, *83,* 340–361.

Meyer, M. "Defending Big Blue: Why IBM Doesn't Think It's Smart to Break Up." *Newsweek,* Sept. 30, 1996, p. 50.

Moore, W. E. *The Conduct of the Corporation.* New York: Random House, 1962.

Nadler, D. A., Shaw, R. B., Walton, A. E., and Associates. *Discontinuous Change: Leading Organizational Transformations.* San Francisco: Jossey-Bass, 1995.

Naj, A. K. "Burning Passion for Her Art Leads to Hot Invention." *Wall Street Journal,* Sept. 26, 1996, sec. A1.

Near, J. P., and Jensen, T. C. "The Whistleblowing Process: Retaliation and Perceived Effectiveness." *Work and Occupations,* 1983, *10,* 3–28.

Near, J. P., and Miceli, M. P. "Whistle-Blowing: Myth and Reality." *Journal of Management,* 1996, *22,* 507–526.

O'Reilly, C. A., Chatman, J., and Caldwell, D. F. "People and Organizational Culture: A Profile Comparison Approach to Assessing Person-Organization Fit." *Academy of Management Journal,* 1991, *34,* 487–516.

Pfeffer, J. *Power in Organizations.* Marshfield, Mass: Pitman, 1981.

Powell, W. W., and DiMaggio, P. J. (eds.), *The New Institutionalism in Organizational Analysis.* Chicago: University of Chicago Press, 1991.

Rachman, S. J. *Fear and Courage.* (2nd ed.) New York: Freeman, 1990.

Ritzer, G. *Contemporary Sociological Theory.* New York: Knopf, 1983.

Sackmann, S. A. *Cultural Knowledge in Organizations: Exploring the Collective Mind.* Thousand Oaks, Calif.: Sage, 1991.

Scott, W. R. *Organizations: Rational, Natural, and Open Systems.* (2nd ed.) Englewood Cliffs, N.J.: Prentice Hall, 1987.

Selznick, P. "Institutionalism 'Old' and 'New.'" *Administrative Science Quarterly,* 1996, *41,* 270–277.

Simon, H. A. *Administrative Behavior.* (2nd ed.) Old Tappan, N.J.: Macmillan, 1957.

Staw, B. M. "Rationality and Justification in Organizational Life." *Research in Organizational Behavior,* 1980, *2,* 45–79.

Thompson, J. D. *Organizations in Action.* New York: McGraw-Hill, 1967.

Trice, H. M., and Beyer, J. M. *The Cultures of Work Organizations.* Englewood Cliffs, N.J.: Prentice-Hall, 1993.

Tushman, M. L., and O'Reilly, C. A., III. "The Ambidextrous Organization: Managing Evolutionary and Revolutionary Change." *California Management Review,* 1996, *38,* 8–30.

Tushman, M. L., and Romanelli, E. "Organizational Evolution: A Metamorphosis Model of Convergence and Reorientation." *Research in Organizational Behavior,* 1985, *7,* 171–222.

Uchitelle, L., and Kleinfield, N. R. "The Downsizing of America: On the Battlefields of Business, Millions of Casualties." *New York Times,* Mar. 3, 1996.

Walton, D. N. *Courage: A Philosophical Investigation.* Berkeley: University of California Press, 1986.

Weick, K. E. "The Collapse of Sensemaking in Organizations: The Mann Gulch Disaster." *Administrative Science Quarterly,* 1993, *38,* 628–652.

Weick, K. E. "Drop Your Tools: An Allegory for Organizational Studies." *Administrative Science Quarterly,* 1996, *41,* 301–313.

White, J. B., and Lublin, J. S. "Some Companies Try to Rebuild Loyalty." *Wall Street Journal,* Sept. 27, 1996, p. 97.

Whyte, W. H., Jr. *The Organization Man.* New York: Simon & Schuster, 1956.

Wilensky, H. L. "The Professionalization of Everyone." *American Journal of Sociology,* 1964, *120,* 137–158.

Wilkins, A. L. *Developing Corporate Character: How to Successfully Change an Organization Without Destroying It.* San Francisco: Jossey-Bass, 1989.

PART TWO

INTO THE RELATIONAL HEART OF ORGANIZATION

The Social Construction of Wisdom and Courage

5

REINSCRIBING ORGANIZATIONAL WISDOM AND COURAGE: THE RELATIONALLY ENGAGED ORGANIZATION

Sheila McNamee

THE TERMS *courage* and *wisdom,* as they might be applied to our understanding of organizational life, present some interesting challenges. They are terms that we more readily associate with individuals. We might, for example, talk about a wise leader, a courageous leader, or a series of courageous acts performed by some one person. These terms are deeply inscribed in essentialist talk—that is, talk about a person's innermost, basic qualities. Essentialism refers to our long-standing tradition of locating attributes, motives, intentions, desires, emotions, and virtually all psychological qualities, traits, or characteristics within the individual. In the essentialist frame, persons are viewed as containers (Sampson, 1993); these containers hold people's "essence" and thus define their individuality. To use the terms *courage* and *wisdom,* then, connects us to a long tradition of attempting to delineate individual qualities that make a wise person wise or a courageous person courageous. Others in this volume have provided illustrations of the limiting and even damaging effects of this tradition (see especially Chapters Six and Seven).

These critiques and other challenges to this tradition are rapidly growing. Technological innovation has expanded our concerns beyond self-contained individuals, because it has provided us with ready access to competing "rationalities," ways of living, belief systems, rituals, and opinions (Gergen, 1991). Our daily activities, by and large, now require that we acknowledge and coordinate with diverse views. From the mundane activities in which we engage every day to the broad-reaching implications of far-reaching organizational change, it is difficult to ignore news from other communities, both disparate and similar. With satellite television, the Internet, fax machines, teleconferencing, and easy global transportation, our exposure to diversity is growing exponentially. With this growth our own beliefs and rituals appear parochial in their local focus and thus become more and more difficult to sustain as universally applicable.

Our attention shifts toward our increasing interdependence with different communities, organizations, and cultures. One important implication of this for organizational life is the growing difficulty of holding on to the view that individuals should be the primary source of decisions and action in organizations. With access to diverse forms of understanding, questions emerge concerning what can be considered a competent, moral, ethical, or rational choice. Our task in organizations is to coordinate our local realities with other local realities, communities, organizations, and cultures.

For example, what good is accomplished by providing leadership consulting if the community and corporate contexts remain unchanged? What is the benefit of expanding productivity if doing so exploits workers or leaves other communities impoverished? Each local decision or action has broader consequences, and it is difficult to ignore these. How do we engage in organizational development that is not insignificant? Considering organizational wisdom and courage provides an opportunity to contemplate what is at stake in moving from an individualist focus to one that emphasizes the relational construction of meaning. Further, it allows us to explore how an understanding of meaning as a relational by-product might recast *courage* and *wisdom* as orienting and enlivening terms for organizational life.

A relational understanding of organizational life is revitalizing. It focuses on microsocial processes—the interchange among persons in relationships—and the broader networks of relationships they inhabit. When considered in relational terms, a person's problems are not his or hers alone. Similarly, world crises are not divorced from the ways in which we raise our children, participate in our communities, and conduct our work. With a relational intelligibility in place we can shift our attention to, as Sampson (1993) says, what transpires between people, not what is contained within them. This shift revitalizes our sense of community, lends broad social and cultural significance to our local actions, and provides discursive options that centralize our relational engagement. The question at stake here concerns what different kinds of social worlds are possible if we move from an individualist tradition to a relational intelligibility?

How might a relational sensibility reconfigure *courage* and *wisdom*? More important, once they are situated within a relational reality, do notions of courage and wisdom help us achieve the sort of multivocal, globally engaged organization so necessary to today's world?

The dictionary identifies *wisdom* as coming from the Old English word meaning "to know" and *courage* as being derived from the French word for "heart." Perhaps we should think about organizational wisdom and courage as a "knowing heart" (Srivastva, 1996). Can this image, this theme, move us beyond our focus on individuals in organizations?

THE PROBLEM WITH INDIVIDUAL NOTIONS OF WISDOM AND COURAGE

To locate wisdom and courage within persons is to expect individuals to know, to decide, and to solve problems based on their ability to think rationally. Rationality, in this tradition, places emphasis on a knowing mind. Persons are expected to illustrate their reasoning abilities so that others might objectively determine how well matched reason is to reality. Such expectations—whether placed on ourselves or others—can be quite burdensome. Which is the right answer, the correct technique or method, the proper analysis? And what are we to say when what we think is right, correct, proper, or best does not fit with what others believe? Who will determine the truth, and by what criteria? Who will win and who will lose? With the presumption of individual rationality, the responsibility one carries within each social interchange is potentially enormous. And when one part of an organization is dissatisfied with what is happening, the first move is toward evaluating, reprimanding, and "repairing" the person responsible. Ultimately, when something fails in an organization we are encouraged, in this individualist tradition, to identify individuals as lacking in wisdom, courage, or both.

But what if we locate knowledge in the heart of the organization rather than in the minds of individuals? Can a "knowing heart" generate an alternative to this individualist discourse? Can it move us toward a relational sensibility in our understanding and living in organizations? A knowing heart, as opposed to a knowing mind, raises all sorts of questions. What *is* the heart of an organization? Who is to define it? Can we expect that our notion of our organization's heart will vary depending on who we are in that organization—which in turn depends on who we talk with and in what ways? And "knowing" from the heart—what would such "knowledge" look like? How can we distinguish a knowing heart from a passionate heart or a cold heart—or is there not a difference?

There are more questions raised here than ready-made answers. I am hesitant to simply do as the title of this chapter suggests: "reinscribe organizational wisdom and courage" in relational terms. Indeed, I am curious whether we need wisdom and courage in organizations at all. Are these terms that we really want to reinscribe, or would we be better served to move in a direction that requires no reinscriptions and offers, instead, new relational realities, new potentials for action, new venues for global connection—that is, new ways of talking about organizational life?

Let me attempt to sketch briefly where I think each of these directions (that is, the reinscription of wisdom and courage as well as the crafting of new ways of talking about organizational life) might take us. They need not be seen as separate paths, however, as the latter can also serve as a reinscription of wisdom and courage. Let us, if you will, travel two paths in our exploration that eventually may converge into one.

DECONSTRUCTING WISDOM AND COURAGE

Having already identified the meaning of *wisdom* and *courage* within the individualist tradition, the first move toward reinscription is to deconstruct these terms, in an attempt to illuminate their relational origins.

Drawing on a long heritage of critiques of traditional, modernist understandings of the social world, Derrida (1978) points out that terms used to describe the world (that is, to "tell it like it is") are not simply reflections of an individual's "sound" observations of the world; rather, language is a system unto itself. To Derrida, words derive their meaning from how they relate to other terms or words within a system. So, for example, courage is not determined by careful observation of persons who might be deemed courageous. Rather, the term *courage* gains its meaning from contrasting it with other relevant terms in use within the community. One community might assign value to courage in contrast to timidity or cowardice. Within other language communities, however, timidity might well be championed over courage (for example, it might be considered more admirable to appear timid when asking for a favor from a superior). The deconstructive mode of analysis reminds us that our ways of talking about the world cannot stand unquestioned as objective, stable, or universally rational statements. They are, instead, descriptions that are coherent within local discourses—that is, the discourses of situated activities of persons in relation. The following is an attempt to explore some of the "less certain" locations of wisdom and courage.

Wisdom

Wisdom, we know, refers to the quality of having or showing good judgment. Someone who is wise makes sound decisions based on knowledge. But who is to say that one's decisions or judgments are wise? Are they wise regardless of what others claim? Can I profess my words on this page to be wise without other voices declaring them so? And beyond the affirmation of my words' or actions' wisdom, we must ask from where those words and actions come. I pose this question not with the goal of locating the precise origins or causes of particular ways of talking or acting. Rather, I am interested in exploring within which communities, which networks of relationships, a person's behaviors gain their significance. Here the emphasis is placed on discourse, our way of connecting with others. Discourse is always situated in some tradition, some set of relationships, some historical frame. Thus to locate wisdom is not to somehow articulate unique qualities but instead to draw on the conversational resources made available by virtue of our relationships with others.

For example, does a manager, in establishing close working relationships with others, draw on her conversations with her mentor and manager from her early career and on conversations with her spouse, her children, and individuals in her community? How are these conversations brought into the present one? Do not these communities provide conversational resources (that is, ways of talking, acting, and interpreting) that, perhaps, the present situation invites but does not necessarily make obvious? What would it take to bring these resources into the current conversation?

We can now describe wisdom, which has been viewed popularly as a trait of individuals, as a relational accomplishment. A person cannot be or act wise if others do not grant wisdom to that person or his or her actions. Additionally, what we take to be behavior born out of an individual's capabilities we can more generatively see as a thread from one or more communities. To introduce this thread into a conversation is to weave together networks of relationships and thus communities of meaning. This reconfigured, relational definition of wisdom challenges our view of knowledge by locating knowledge within communities and within ways of talking and acting rather than within individuals.

This position raises all sorts of questions concerning our lives in organizations. Who are we selecting when we choose someone to lead a project, solve a problem, or work on some venture within an organization? Are we selecting people for their knowledge (that is, for what *they* know), or are we choosing them for the communities they bring to and create within the organization? In our search for organizational life that is marked by wisdom, how do we acknowledge the relational origins of wisdom? How do we create environments that encourage wisdom relationally? What would such encouragement look like? These are questions that I will take up later in my discussion of relational engagement.

Courage

Courage, derived from the French *coeur* ("heart"), suggests a central, essential, or core characteristic from which life flows. Thus "organizational courage" suggests a core organizational essence from which organizational life flows. Like blood circulated by the body's heart, courage must course through an organization by alternating processes of dilation and contraction. Openings to conversations and thus to realities where multiple possibilities may be entertained are met by constraints that help shape the particular form of those conversations and realities. What others do or say, the situational and environmental demands they encounter, and the practical demands such as time, distance, and cultural compatibility that they face—all narrow the scope of what any one person can or should do. Thus as we approach conversations with multiple possibilities, the need to coordinate our actions with others in *situated* practice necessarily limits our range of options and consequently establishes our lived realities.

In this deconstruction, as in the deconstruction of wisdom, we see the relational aspects of courage. No individual, no single idea or action, takes hold within an organization without the participation of others. The opening of multiple ideas and actions is constrained only in the way in which they converge with other ideas and actions. This metaphor of continual openings and closings that make an organization a living entity provokes an intriguing notion of courage.

Rather than seeing courage as a quality that allows a person to be fearless or brave (a more standard understanding of the concept), our focus on the derivation of the term itself provides a more fluid, relational understanding. Our focus shifts to the movement of conversations throughout an organization that give it life. Yet we must be cautious not to locate this movement as emanating from a core (as we do when we think of a heart). As I suggested earlier, how would we locate the heart of an organization? If it is interchange among its members that makes an organization live, then its heart must be omnipresent.

THE RELATIONAL REINSCRIPTION OF WISDOM AND COURAGE

If wisdom and courage can be understood as emerging from relationships, then how might these concepts enliven organizational life? There are several ways. Abandoning the idea that our organizations are led by individuals who embody courage and wisdom allows us to see our organizations as communities in which coordinations of multiple logics, diverse traditions and beliefs, and a multiplicity of goals are accomplished. There are many voices that each organizational member brings to the conversation. Our task is to find ways for these discursive communities—both within and around our organizations—to be heard.

Additionally, we can appreciate the fluidity with which organizations operate. We can restrain our desire to categorize and evaluate participants and their skills. We can move away from organizational practices that (perhaps unintentionally) generate anxiety, inadequacy, alienation, deficiencies, distance, frustration, and myopia with respect to our own or others' contributions. Instead we can center our concerns on how organizational participants create the realities they live in their coordinated activities together. This is best managed by attending to what we do together. This generates a sense of relational responsibility (McNamee and Gergen, forthcoming) in that our attention shifts toward an exploration of the communal processes through which certain realities and beliefs are created.

The relational reinscription of wisdom and courage displaces our reliance on "correct" methods or approaches to life in organizations. It also displaces our reliance on having one person or organization take the lead, solve the dilemma, chart the course for the future, and so on.

It disorients us by displacing our tendency to plan, to prepare, to know in advance. Instead it requires that we act, as Shotter (1993, p. 29) says, "into the conversation." That is, we come to the interactive moment with plans, preparations, and relational understandings ("knowledge") that we anticipate will be altered, discarded, and reinvented with those with whom we engage. We appreciate the uncertainty of our worlds as we seek avenues toward certainty. We appreciate our vulnerability and learn how that vulnerability positions us within the process of creating, with our partners, the realities that we live.

This reinscription suggests some different ways of talking about and experiencing organizational life. Wisdom and courage are no longer viewed as qualities of individuals or of organizations. I would like to suggest that it is our processes of relating in organizations that might be identified as emblems of wisdom and courage. Yet I would also like to question whether these terms *courage* and *wisdom,* as imbued as they are with individualist connotations, provide any generative means for operating in the relationally engaged, global organization. Might we gain further clarification about the realities we create and the possibilities for global connection and cooperation by offering new ways of talking about organizational life?

RELATIONALLY ENGAGED ORGANIZATIONAL LIFE

What would happen if we accepted the notion that any action must have a location within which it makes sense? Rather than confront situations attempting to find the best solution or path, we might then turn our attention to the various ways in which participants enter into the conversation and how these various ways open multiple possibilities for action.

The notion of relational engagement places emphasis on precisely this process. Attention is directed to the particular modes of interpretation and action by which people create their worlds (in this case, their organizations). When we centralize the discursive ways in which we engage with others, we must begin to appreciate the idea of multiple rationalities, relationally achieved realities, and indeterminacy. What is valued, what is ethical, what is made pathological emerges out of communal interchanges. Thus, to position organizational life—and its success or failure—as relational engagement invites us to foster a sensitivity to and respect for the varying constructions that emerge within different relational communities about right and wrong, good and bad, effective and ineffective, successful and unsuccessful, and so on.

Each member of an organization carries a vast network of other relationships and communities and thus brings other ways of talking, acting, and making sense to the organization. The relationally engaged organization approaches issues, topics, projects, and so forth as challenges of construction rather than as objects or problems to be solved, managed, or planned. From a relational orientation we would ask, "How is it that what we are doing together here provides the opportunity for success to emerge and gain viability, credibility, and sustainability?

This orientation carries several implications. First, if all actions are situated actions (that is, born out of relational engagement with others and thus located within communities and traditions of meaning), there is no longer a notion of an ethical or professional competency that is distinct from those communities and traditions and from the interactive moment itself. What we do with others gives life to our entire ways of being. These processes cannot be abstracted from the multiple discursive communities we inhabit.

There are no specific techniques or strategies that will ensure organizational wisdom or courage. To set out methods, techniques, or strategies would be to privilege one discursive community over others. Yet I do not want to say that there are no means by which we can evaluate, make choices, or declare one way of talking as situationally better than another. These decisions can only be made relationally. Organizational life, like all other forms of interaction, is situated practice. Its ethics, relevance, value, and appropriateness will be judged differently depending on how one situates the activity.

When we centralize relational engagement, we orient our understanding of organizational life differently. We begin to examine ways of talking and acting. We become curious about how these ways gain viability and how they are sustained within particular communities—how, in fact, they can be deemed wise or courageous. Our interest in judging ways of talking and acting wanes, however, because any judgment, by definition, is recognized as emerging within a particular discursive community. That is, any judgment is located within a relational reality that might be vastly different in its coherence and rationality from that of any other judgment.

Yet judgments, evaluations, decisions, and so forth may (and eventually must) be made. Nevertheless, when we shift our attention to the ways in which participants are relationally engaged, we suspend passing judgment or making "final" decisions until we have made inquiries into or initiated conversation about the communities that grant each action its coherence. This approach (or technique, as some might call it, although I prefer the term *stance*) has two possible outcomes. First, conversations around judgement, evaluation, decision making, and so forth look different, sound different, and are experienced differently over time because the participants' actions have been granted coherence in *some* relational network and thus have been "understood" as logical and rational within some sphere. Or, second, such conversations disappear. Judgment, evaluation, and decision making take on new meaning as members work together to make them relational actions. There is, in other words, a transformative dialogue born out of the different stance we take in the interactive moment. This is what Bateson (1972, p. 101) calls "the difference that makes a difference."

A short case study can help illustrate what this process might look like in practice. Recently I was invited to work with the management staff of a large, privately funded mental health organization. This organization had a number of locations throughout the state. Some were quite isolated. Each site dealt with a different population, depending on its location. Some sites were solely residential facilities; others offered outpatient services. As a result of these differences, the sites had varied missions and employed a variety of management styles.

In addition to managing these varied sites, the entire corporation was going through a reorganization. There was a new CEO; after an extensive study of the organization that included focus group and individual interviews, he proposed "flattening" the organization's hierarchical structure. He was attempting to create a more participatory organization in which people would be valued for their unique contributions rather than expected to perform to some preset standard. While this proposal pleased many of the staff, it also infuriated a handful of powerful managers who until this point had been quite successful in "making their unit work." I was invited to work with the entire group of managers to prepare them to implement the new plan for reorganization.

As is generally the case in any reorganization, each manager saw the reorganization plan in terms of an evaluation or judgment of his or her performance. To many it was a positive evaluation, because they saw themselves as "participatory" managers. Yet to a handful the judgment was negative, critical of their mode of operation and of the very principles they had worked so hard to uphold. There was a great deal of jealousy, vindictiveness, and hostility between these two groups.

Rather than focusing on how this group should implement its reorganization plan, I saw my job as facilitating a different kind of conversation among these managers. I was interested in providing a conversational arena in which these managers could all tell their stories about work at their site in such a way that each would come to appreciate the coherence of the others' style and philosophy. This dialogic forum was established by imposing specific rules, to which all participants agreed. I have borrowed these rules from the Public Conversations Project devised by members of the Family Institute of Cambridge (Chasin and others, 1991). All agreed to give each manager, in turn, time to speak, to tell his or her story from his or her own perspective, without interruption. All agreed that they would refrain from casting any negative remarks about others or about the operation of any other site. Once these rules were agreed on, each manager was given as much time as he or she needed to tell the story of how work proceeded at his or her site. Each was asked to describe how he or she understood or made sense of this mode of operation. Once this was accomplished, each manager was asked what was central to his or her site. In other words, what defined the site to such an extent that, without it, the site would not be that particular site? After all had answered that question they were asked to identify a central concern for them in the current reorganization plan and, in addition, their specific concerns about how things were operating at their own location. I have found that this last question never generates a productive conversation unless asked as a follow-up to the preceding two questions. When participants have been given a chance to outline the coherence of their discursive communities—their relational networks—they are much more comfortable discussing, in a public and potentially hostile forum, their doubts and concerns about them.

What happened in this consultation, as usually happens, is that once the participants were given the chance to tell their stories in their own words and articulate the issues that were of greatest concern to them, those issues begin to make sense to the others. While those others might not have agreed with their colleagues, they had access to the ways in which their colleagues approach their work.

No final results or conclusions were drawn from this conversation vis-à-vis the organization's reorganization plan. Yet, what can be said is that new conversations emerged. Conversations that had never taken place in that organization began in the process of orchestrating a different dialogic arena. Once members felt that the logic of their work sites had been voiced to their colleagues, the ensuing conversations (which may have been called judgment, evaluation, or decision making) exhibited a very different nature. Colleagues were realizing, some for the first time, the ways in which they complemented each other's work, filled it in, supplemented it in novel and useful ways. They began to *help* each other in talking through methods for more collaboration and cooperation. A transformative dialogue emerged through the simple process of giving voice to the multiple communities present in the room.

FORMS OF RELATIONAL PRACTICE

Engaging in organizational life in this manner can provide the resources for bridging or negotiating between different ways of talking. These resources bring us closer to a relational understanding of courage and wisdom. At the pragmatic level this case offers a suggestion for practices that move organizations toward relational engagement. These practices are general rather than specific. They illuminate wisdom as a communal activity that is engendered in the movement of conversations throughout and around an organization.

Expanding the Domain of Participation

To expand the domain of participation in our organization, we might invite "interested others" into our conversations. Those others might include funding sources, policymakers, legal officials, societal communities or neighborhoods, school officials, and professional groups. Typically members of all these groups have some involvement or vested interest in an organization's vitality. The very act of including their voices simultaneously expands the domain of participation as well as the domain of community and global commitment. Who are those typically silent others who might have something to say about an organization's effect and its success? By expanding the domain of participation, we can create powerful forums for promoting community and global reform. By bringing these voices together, the community of involved participants might coconstruct an understanding of the situation that does not combat the important concerns and tasks of others involved. However, this can be achieved only if conversations are created within a context that respects the coherence of these multiple communities and facilitates dialogue rather than debate.

How might we open the conversation to those who have a vested interest in our projects but might not otherwise be consulted? As we extend the network of voices involved, we expand the potential for coconstruction among broader communities. We can pose different questions such as these: "What might our organization do for this community, for this particular world problem, for this particular effort? For whom is this a problem? What would count as a success, and to whom? In what ways, if any, have we transformed others beyond the client(s)? Who among this extended group thinks our project was effective, transformative, successful? Who else might have benefited from this conversation? What new resources (financial, emotional, practical) might be generated as a result of this conversation?" The questions we ask and the conclusions we draw are coordinated within a complex network of relationships. From this process of coordination, both constraining and potentiating descriptions will emerge.

Expanding Our Conversational Resources

Another way to invite relational engagement is to encourage ourselves to draw on our own multiplicity. Can we ask questions, conduct observations, analyze data, and interpret "results" from our various identities: manager, organizational member, researcher, curious person, detective, gossip, caregiver, scholar, and so forth? Can we invite a multiplicity of voices by inviting others to assist us in our organizational tasks or by inviting those with whom we work to think of themselves as multivocal? Could we, in other words, invite our colleagues or others we draw into our conversations to bring their "internal others" (the voices of their other, less obviously relevant, relationships) into the dialogue?

Honoring Relational Responsibility

Because of our individualist orientation to organizational life, we are quick to hold individuals responsible for decisions, actions, and outcomes that actually can be seen as relationally accomplished. What if we instead embraced the notion of relational responsibility (McNamee and Gergen, forthcoming)? Instead of identifying one person who will be ultimately responsible for what takes place in and to our organizations, what would happen if we were to accept what occurs as a joint production? What would we be doing differently? We might, for one, be asking different questions. Rather than inquiring into why a project was completed in a particular manner, we might initiate inquiry into the many narratives that could be told about how that project emerged and was carried out. What stories do all participants (as well as onlookers) have to tell about this process? What is central to each story and to each storyteller? Where is the confusion for each of these stories, for each of these tellers? These questions, asked from a stance of curiosity rather than from a desire to "get to the bottom of things," generate relationally rich understanding.

This kind of conversation and inquiry dissolves the need to know with certainty and instead replenishes a sense of wonder and coherence amid diversity. Conversations like this help participants see that there is, in fact, coherence and rationality in the actions of others. Once those actions are embedded within stories—stories that embody and construct relationships, communities, and traditions—participants are free to disagree. But the disagreement that emerges from this conversational arena is vastly different from the disagreement that emerges when we enter into conversation with certainty about what is right or wrong, good or bad, successful or unsuccessful. All organizational members have their stories about each of these, but who is to determine which among all the competing stories is *truly* right, wrong, good, bad, successful, or unsuccessful?

This is a significant shift from the typical, modernist form of disagreement, based on positions believed to be objectively determined. When the coherence of participants' stories has been invited into the conversation, a willingness to engage in processes of negotiation, compromise, and transformation emerges. Any attempt to bring together in our deliberations and daily interchange the groups that we represent and the relationships of which we are a part draws our attention to the ways in which we are relationally responsible for organizational life.

Engaging in Reflexive Critiques

As mentioned previously, these practices can be encouraged by approaching organizational life from a stance of curiosity or interested inquiry. While we have a professional responsibility to act in ways that are focused, meaningful, and ethical, we must realize that too much certainty or understanding negates the argument for a relationally engaged organization. When we are too certain about our approach, our answers, our analysis, we close out the voices of others as well as our own multiplicity. In addition, we must respect that what constitutes a generative dialogue in one community might not secure the same position in another. The rhetorical force of a particular discursive argument can vary dramatically from community to community. In other words, we must constantly ask ourselves which discursive tradition warrants these particular questions, observations, and conclusions: Why this discourse and not another? Which community is being represented here, and by virtue of that community's representation, which other communities are being erased? This sort of reflexive critique is what relational engagement is about. Here we recognize the possibility of other discursive communities and traditions, and through such recognition we might grant them voice.

DIALOGUE AS METAPHOR

Finally, the relationally engaged organization I am advocating embraces the term *dialogue* both practically and metaphorically. It is worth pointing out that to engage in dialogue does not necessarily mean being an active part of the conversation, as we generally understand it. Here I am referring to the erroneous belief many have that to engage in dialogue is to have everyone talking. Quite often the "voice" one chooses to contribute is the voice of nonparticipation. These voices should be respected just as those that are "at the table" should be. Everyone does not have to participate in the same way. Participants should engage with one another in whatever way they feel appropriate, not just via "physical" participation. Nonparticipation can be seen as engagement—there is a marked difference between being invited to join and deciding not to, as opposed to not being invited at all.

Dialogue, as opposed to *debate,* is also a metaphor for the relationally engaged organization. A debate does not attempt to provide participants with a forum for articulating the coherence of their realities. In a debate, one tries only to convince the opponent that one's position is correct, true, and just. A dialogue, in contrast, attempts to engender a conversational arena in which the participants will become curious about the coherence and rationale of alternative views and garner a genuine respect for those views. This is not to imply that participants will agree with or accept another's way of talking about a situation. Rather, the curiosity and respect of the participants make possible significantly different conversations. I would suggest that these different conversations are potentially transformative in that they provide the possibility for coordinating among disparate communities. In using dialogue as a metaphor we move away from the goal of winning that is so readily invited by the debate metaphor. In place of winners and losers, dialogue offers us participants.

SOME CLOSING THOUGHTS

What does this relational view of organizational life allow us to do? What happens when there is no individual freighted with the responsibility for knowing or acting? Instead, joint action is taken as the source of knowledge. A person's actions are responsive to what is going on, to what is being offered in the interactive moment. And simultaneously, those same actions serve as invitations to certain realities, coordinations, and dances with others. With this emphasis we become curious about the conversations that create the problems, successes, and realities lived in our organization.

We now face the challenge of fostering organizational environments that invite us to focus on our reinscribed notion of courage. That is, we must consider how to attend to the movement of conversations in and around our organizations. This is what gives life to an organization. The pulsing of realities in the making is the heart of organizational life. Similarly, we are challenged to explore wisdom, now displaced from the interior of individuals and reinscribed within modes of practice, as a relational achievement. The terms *wisdom* and *courage,* reinscribed relationally, can now sensitize us to the possibilities for joint action. Without a relational understanding of organizational life in particular and human interchange more generally, we are burdened with the impossible task of knowing and acting "correctly." Yet, as we have discovered, knowing or acting correctly is problematic when there are so many different and even incommensurate communities participating. The problem is amplified when we consider the significance of the global organization in creating possibilities for today and the future. Thus, in our attempts to create effective global organizations, we must focus on giving voice to the multiple discourses present.

REFERENCES

Bateson, G. *Steps to an Ecology of Mind.* New York: Bantam Books, 1972.

Chasin, L., and others. "The Citizen Clinician: The Family Therapist in the Public Forum." *AFTA Newsletter,* 1991, *46,* 36–42.

Derrida, J. *Writing and Difference.* (A. Bass, trans.). Chicago: University of Chicago Press, 1978.

Gergen, K. J. *The Saturated Self.* New York: Basic Books, 1991.

McNamee, S., and Gergen, K. J. *Relational Responsibility*. Thousand Oaks, Calif.: Sage, forthcoming.

Sampson, E. E. *Celebrating the Other*. Boulder, Colo.: Westview Press, 1993.

Shotter, J. *Conversational Realities*. Thousand Oaks, Calif.: Sage, 1993.

Srivastva, S. *Organizational Wisdom and Courage*. [Overview of an international symposium at the Weatherhead School of Management.] Cleveland, Ohio: Department of Organizational Behavior, Weatherhead School of Management, Case Western Reserve University, 1996.

6

THE POLITICAL ORGANIZATION OF WISDOM AND COURAGE

Edward E. Sampson

AS PART OF MY TEACHING AND WRITING in the area of intergroup relations, I have become very interested in the extremes to which one group will go in harming another group, including, for example, acts of terrorism and genocide. I have come to believe that these actions, which most of us would consider evil, are usually carried out by people who would never view themselves as such. In fact, I suspect that although we would use highly negative terms to describe the perpetrators of such acts, they would use the same terms to describe themselves that we reserve for individuals we consider highly praiseworthy.

For example, in several recent bombing incidents, including in Manchester, England; Dhahran, Saudi Arabia; and Atlanta, Georgia, many people, including President Clinton, used the word *cowardly* to refer to the perpetrators. What is the likelihood that the perpetrators of these attacks considered their actions to be cowardly? Is it not more likely that the very acts we consider cowardly, they would define as highly courageous? I do not believe that their usage involves a different dictionary definition of these terms. They perceive the same meaning for *courageous* that we do. We simply refuse to apply this term of social approval to their acts—not because their acts lack courage as we define it, but because we disapprove of their acts.

The case of genocide is equally striking. In many cases genocide involves a highly organized, carefully orchestrated set of actions requiring the participation of a diverse collection of people. The Holocaust is illustrative. Many different professionals were involved in Germany's genocide, including accountants, lawyers, engineers, and architects as well as physicians and scientists. In addition, the German program of mass extermination covered an extensive geographic area, imposing major staffing, supply, and transportation demands (see Hilberg, 1992; U.S. Holocaust Memorial Museum, 1996). This was not some fly-by-night, ad hoc operation but a very well orchestrated effort requiring the cooperation of tens of thousands of people.

As evil as *we* consider the Holocaust to have been, it seems highly improbable that such a wide variety of people would have consented to participate had they believed themselves engaged in an evil, cowardly, or foolish action. In short, it seems to me that people usually consider their actions to be motivated by positive ideals rather than negative intent. Furthermore, people usually act in ways that will garner praise from the significant others in their lives. This is what occurred during the Holocaust. The guard returning home for a brief respite from his job at a concentration camp would talk openly with his family and friends about his work, fully expecting to receive a supportive response, not disapproval (see Goldhagen, 1996).

This poses a problem for those who wish to present courage and wisdom as ideals toward which we should all aspire. After all, if deeds *we* consider cowardly, brutal, or evil are seen by their perpetrators to be courageous and wise, then perhaps we need to reconsider encouraging these as ideals. Those who insist that courage and wisdom have a permanently fixed meaning, not subject to any particular point of view, will disagree with me. For them, terrorist acts *are* cowardly, no matter what their perpetrators may claim. In their view I have simply got things all wrong.

But I maintain that the perpetrators of such actions would not participate without the belief that their deeds take great courage, sharing our very understanding of that concept, and that their actions are part of a reasonable social policy that warrants high praise, not condemnation. In fact, while other terms of praise are undoubtedly also employed by terrorists and systematic mass murderers to describe themselves, I believe that the two concepts that are central to this book—courage and wisdom—are also central to the self-understanding of those individuals, whom we deem evil.

I realize that it is unsettling to link courage and wisdom with such actions as genocide and terrorism. As most of the other contributors to this volume demonstrate, these are hardly the acts that first come to mind when someone asks us to give an example of courage or wisdom. I trust that it is clear that I am intentionally using terrorism and genocide to dramatize the point I wish to make about the relational and subjective nature of meaning and because I believe that these two ideas are also central to those actions we strongly disapprove of. Because we would be highly unlikely on our own to associate either terrorism or genocide with courage or wisdom, making this association may force us to adopt a more critical view of these terms.

TYPICAL ERRORS

There are several errors we commonly make when we employ terms such as *wisdom* and *courage*. First, we usually assume that these are qualities that individuals either possess or do not possess. We say that a person *is* courageous or a person *is* wise, describing what we presume to be properties of the individual that shape his or her will, motivation, character, or personality. But like some of the other contributors to this volume, I contend that courage and wisdom are better understood as properties of social discourse, or conversations. Rather than *being* courageous or wise, people engage in discourses that *render* their actions wise or courageous, in order to achieve certain social purposes (for example, to enlist people's participation in terrorist actions by making such actions intelligible, reasonable, and approved). How could a young boy strap a bomb to his body, board a bus, and blow himself and the other passengers up unless he believed that his act would be evaluated positively by someone?

Second, therefore, we must cast a very critical eye on any claims that certain acts are inherently either wise or courageous (or foolish or cowardly). Courage and wisdom are by-products of social discourse undertaken to render actions intelligible, reasonable, and praiseworthy; they do not describe properties that are independent of such discourses. In other words, courage and wisdom are social constructions. As we have seen, an act *we* consider cowardly may very well be considered courageous by those who carry it out or endorse it.

The preceding gives rise to a troublesome issue. If one group considers a terrorist act to be cowardly but another defines it as an act of rare bravery, which is it? If cowardly prevails, are we not then simply claiming that our framework should predominate in judging others? If courageous prevails, are we not then simply claiming that their judgments should prevail over ours? Furthermore, if the same act is both cowardly and courageous, then of what use are ideals such as courage or wisdom in guiding our own actions?

Referring to an act as either courageous or wise is our way of saying "we approve," to motivate people to engage in such acts or to help people feel that what they have done is worthwhile. But what we approve of may differ from what others approve of. These ideals therefore do not stand in some objective position in the world by which we can evaluate the worth of specific acts. In short, encouraging people or organizations to behave with courage and wisdom brings no guarantees that the results will meet our general approval. Consider another example: when tobacco company executives appeared before the congressional committee investigating claims about the health hazards of cigarettes, they must have felt themselves to be showing uncommon courage in the face of great odds against them and perhaps even acting wisely in not revealing everything that they knew.

Third, because of the preceding I suggest that the only recourse available to us is to examine the forms of life and social relationships that the actions in question affirm or undermine. I will argue shortly that actions directed toward others that eliminate those others physically or psychologically undermine the very conditions necessary for intelligible action to occur, even if the perpetrators of such acts consider them to be courageous or wise.

My position then is that rather than trying to help individuals or organizations act with courage or wisdom, we should encourage ways of seeing the consequences of actions for social relationships. Our question should not be whether a given action is courageous or wise; it should be which types of human relationships are facilitated and which are thwarted by particular choices. Although there are no extrinsic foundations for evaluating our judgments even here, once the level of discussion moves away from an attachment to saintly words to examine the nature of human relations that acts sustain, I believe we will have made some significant progress.

BY WAY OF SUMMARY

For the most part we all grew up with the belief that courage and wisdom are among a short list of ideals toward which we should strive. Who would wish to socialize a child, for example, to be cowardly or foolish? Well, in fact, there are some Pacific Island groups in which timidity is highly esteemed (for example, see Howell and Willis, 1989). While following this alternate cultural direction might lead us to the same conclusion about these two cherished ideals, by linking courage and wisdom with genocide I hope to force us to question the implicit framework within which these ideals are embedded in our culture. Using *wisdom* and *courage* as examples, I argue that terms that have an ideal, positive quality to them are systematically employed by collectivities to legitimate the actions they take, including actions as horrific to us as genocide. I further maintain that acts cannot be measured against some objective standard known as wisdom or courage. Courage and wisdom do not refer to a world apart from the very human worlds that call on such ideals to justify nearly every human practice, including genocide. The measuring rod, then, cannot be these values in the abstract but must rather involve the contextual surround from which various actions emerge and the social relationships that such actions cement.

My goal, then, is not to help organizations learn how to be wise or courageous; for as I hope to show, these terms are routinely employed to justify genocide and terrorism, hardly things I believe we would wish to applaud. Rather, our task is to focus on the kind of organizational actions that sustain human relationships.

GENOCIDE

Whatever form it takes, genocide is an organized effort on the part of a dominant group to systematically eliminate others who in their eyes belong to a different collectivity or "outside" group (see Chalk and Jonassohn, 1990). Genocide tends to be a highly organized enterprise, not the random act of individuals; it is carefully orchestrated by a state or other governmental entity. To work effectively, genocide must engage the services of many people. And insofar as these people must believe that what they are doing, however horrible we may consider it, is both intelligible and praiseworthy, their actions must be placed in a context that calls on culturally esteemed values and ideals such as wisdom and courage for social sanction.

In short, for people to carry out acts of genocide, these people must come to believe that their actions are rational, even wise. They must act under the assumption that their deeds are praiseworthy. In many cases they must believe that they are engaged in acts of uncommon courage, doing what others lacking their fortitude might not be able to stomach. In short, genocide seems to offer us entry into the topic of wisdom and courage within organizations, but in a manner that will open to doubt the meaning and role of these terms. Let me illustrate what I mean.

A VIEW OF THE NAZI GENOCIDE

Of the many genocides that have been documented throughout human history—there are almost too many to list with ease, and more are being added daily—the case that continues to remain most vivid for my own and subsequent generations is the systematic destruction by the Germans of various groups during the Second World War. Acknowledging that there are a variety of accounts of these genocidal actions and continuing academic controversy about their source, meaning, purpose, and so forth, in this discussion I will follow elements of the account recently offered by Daniel Goldhagen (1996).

What I find so valuable about Goldhagen's version is its indictment of the German people as a whole and not simply the country's leadership. According to Goldhagen, in order for this genocidal organization to be effective, Germany's leaders could not have functioned alone or outside the normative framework of German society. For the Nazis to enlist such widespread cooperation, the surrounding culture had to embed genocide within a larger pattern of cultural beliefs that had widespread acceptance among the populace.

Although Goldhagen does not use these precise terms, I have little reason to suspect that he would fault my view that the genocidal actions undertaken by everyday German citizens, which Goldhagen amply documents, were experienced as acts of great courage, carried out in the service of an essential wisdom about the problems facing Germany and the solutions needed to address those problems. In other words, wisdom and courage marked these genocidal actions in the eyes of the perpetrators, for whom this understanding of their behaviors permitted those behaviors to take place.

Let me repeat: wisdom and courage are not names of universal truths; they are politically legitimating justifications that organized collectivities employ in order to enlist the willing services of others.

What I have said to this point is that the mass destruction in Germany of various peoples, especially though not exclusively the Jews, could not have occurred without the willing participation of tens of thousands of everyday German citizens, for whom such actions were subjectively experienced as involving both great courage on their part (after all, it is not easy to kill people, no matter how deceptive one is about it, without being courageous) and being part of a state program that had all the earmarks of wisdom (after all, if these people were actually cancerous growths threatening the lifeblood of the nation, then their elimination would appear to be a very wise course of action).

Goldhagen describes many incidents in which rather ordinary people—family men, in fact—carried out destructive deeds that surely must have involved their believing in the value of their actions and, indeed, believing that they were performing a courageous service that others who were less courageous simply could not stomach. The solider who walked hand in hand into the woods with a twelve-year-old girl and then put a gun to her head and shot her, splattering himself with her brains, did not undertake this deed lightly or unthoughtfully. It was ugly and unpleasant, but necessary, and he must have taken comfort in the belief that at least he had the courage to do this.

Although he claimed to have created a laboratory analogy to crimes of obedience, Milgram's research (1965) on obedience has given us an incorrect picture of what likely occurred in Germany. There was little if any blind obedience of the sort that Milgram claimed to be studying. If anything, Milgram's experimental subjects felt some empathy for their victim, a kind of empathy clearly absent in the Holocaust. The German people acted on the basis of rather strongly held beliefs about the targets of their killing and of the rightness of eliminating those people. Under these conditions they probably felt it took courage to do what was felt to be necessary but which those more cowardly were fearful of undertaking.

My readings about the German understanding of Jews and Germany's perceived mission to save the world have led me to believe that their actions were rather thoroughly guided by a system of beliefs that would fall clearly under the rubric of *wise* and *courageous* (for example, see Burleigh and Wippermann, 1991; Rose, 1990).

Do not misunderstand me here. I am not claiming that any of these horrible deeds were either courageous or cowardly, wise or foolish. As I have repeatedly commented, these are terms employed in approving or disapproving discourses, not states of being in the world as such. *We* would not describe those actions as courageous, even though they surely must have seemed so to their perpetrators. This leaves us, therefore, with the need to go beyond these terms if we hope to develop a critical understanding about situations and develop some meaningful guides for action. Genocide and terrorism are not wrong because they are cowardly. They are not wrong because they are lacking in wisdom.

Their immorality resides elsewhere. It is to this elsewhere that we must now turn our attention, not so that we will better understand genocide but so that we will be less glib about urging people to be wise and courageous, when that is not the real issue.

SOCIAL CONSTRUCTIONISM

In order to move forward with this analysis, we must turn to a conceptual framework that has increasingly guided my own work: social constructionism (see Gergen, 1994). I do not intend to outline all the details of the constructionist framework. Rather, I will use its critical stance vis-à-vis many of our commonsense notions of the world (such as courage and wisdom) as the basis for my own analysis. According to constructionism, the terms of our everyday life do not refer to things in the world; rather, these terms construct the very world to which they appear to refer.

For example, psychology and our everyday common sense assume that when we talk about individual qualities of character and personality, employing such terms as *willpower, courage, bravery, knowledge, wisdom, intelligence, motivation,* and so forth, we are referring to things in the real world (in this case, things that are usually in the mind of an individual). For constructionism, however, although these terms have real meaning insofar as they play a significant role in the way most of us carry on our own everyday affairs (indeed, we could not carry on those affairs without such concepts), they are simultaneously arbitrary in that they have been constructed for that very way of living and do not have meaning apart from it. In other words, these terms do not describe essential elements of *the* world but rather create essential elements of *our* world. This does not make them any less real; they are quite real *for us*. But because of this "for us" quality about the words and concepts we use every day, constructionism invites us to adopt a more critical stance toward them, considering that there may be and indeed are alternative ways of structuring the world.

In time most of us come to believe that these commonsense ideas are not simply *our* way of being in the world but rather are *the* way of being in the world. But as cross-cultural and historical studies have revealed, there are persons who lead perfectly satisfactory lives in cultures that are organized very differently from our own—cultures, indeed, in which even psychology as we know it could never have grown, let alone flourished (see White and Kirkpatrick, 1985, for several cogent examples).

I hope that at this point it is clear that *our* way is not *the* way; nor is *their* way *the* way, in spite of the recurring tendency to assume this to be the case. Because each way has evolved to serve the interests of a particular form of life, there is no easy way to transport our way to another's, or vice versa. None of this, however, makes either our way or theirs the preferred way in the sense of fitting some universal ground plan for living. This is the key lesson that constructionism helps us better appreciate.

RELATIVISM

At this point it should be apparent that we are wandering around in a highly relativistic world, something that many have found most distasteful, to the point of nausea, about the entire constructionist project (for example, see Smith, 1994). It seems, say the critics, that if there are only different ways of being in the world and not one proper or correct way, then not only does anything go, but in addition we have no way of discerning good ways from bad ways. How can we find proper guides to our action if all we have are different ways of being?

We have already encountered this idea in my intentional use of *courage* and *wisdom* to describe the worldview of the participants in both genocide and terrorism. For us these are anything but courageous or wise acts. But as I have maintained, I believe that this is precisely how they are experienced by the participants. In choosing the examples of terrorism and genocide, have I not therefore made the relativism of constructionism seem all the worse?

Is there any way out of what has often been referred to as a relativistic morass? Is there any way to identify which is better and which is worse? In particular, is there any way to judge genocide and terrorism as bad? I think that there is, and I would now like to outline the directions of my own thinking on this matter. To do this I will first introduce the notion of a "relationship-canceling conversation" and second suggest that this is the standard against which we can evaluate various individual and organizational actions.

If I sound a bit Habermassian here, this is appropriate (see Habermas, 1984). We both share an interest in securing a basis for judging the quality of actions within the context of communication. My central assumption, however, is that conversations that are relationship canceling undermine the very conversations of which they are a part and so undo the very home base of intelligibility and world construction that requires such conversations in the first place.

RELATIONSHIP-CANCELING CONVERSATIONS BETWEEN TWO DIFFERENT FORMS OF LIFE

The constructionist model is concerned with language and the various conversations we hold that both construct and sustain the world in which we live. These conversations emerge from a particular form of life and, by their existence, generally help sustain it. Without the commonsense terms of individual psychology, for example, including such concepts as courage and wisdom, we could not live for long in our own social world. Psychological talk, then, does not refer to something that is independent of our world but rather to something that is very real and essential for us to function effectively in that world as it is currently constituted. Without these psychological conversations we would live in a very different world; we could not live in our own.

Consider another example of this same point, one that will lead us further into my argument about relationship-canceling conversations. The example involves the Tewa people's story of their origins versus the scientific account (Ortiz, 1991). When a Tewa elder was presented with current scientific thought on the origins of his people, he listened respectfully. He was told that based on their expert analysis of carbon-dated geological and archeological records, scientists now believed that his people originated in Asia and, when an ice bridge made the journey possible, crossed by land to North America, settling finally in their pueblos in what is known today as New Mexico.

The Tewa elder thought these ideas were interesting, but they were not convincing to him or his people. He knew that his people had originated very differently. It was in a distant time and place, at a lake far to the north. That is where they first emerged from the lower world. Yes, they did take a journey; at least that part of the scientific story was correct. But theirs was not a journey to be measured in centuries or miles, as the scientists believed, but was as much a journey of the spirit as a migration of a people.

From the Tewa elder's perspective the scientific account was not really helpful: it did not tell his people what they needed to know to live as human beings. On the other hand, as the elder put it, the Tewas' own story tells them who they are; where they came from; what the boundaries of their world are; what kind of order exists within that world; how suffering, evil, and death came into it; and what is likely to happen to them when they die.

And so we have two rather different conversations about origins. Our own inclination may be to side with the scientific account, because for us it is correct, while the Tewas' account is quaint but not informed by the truth. But constructionism urges a different approach.

First, we are asked to note that there are two different conversations about origins, stemming from two rather different forms of life: one scientific, the other indigenous.

Next, we are asked to note that the scientific form, of which even the natives are now quite aware, while convincing to us, does not serve the same purposes for them as does their own account. The scientific story does not help them deal with the everyday problems they encounter, nor can it direct, guide, or sanctify their actions. Only their formulations accomplish these purposes.

Rather than choosing between discourse A, the scientific, and discourse B, the native, we are asked now to probe more deeply into each in order to see the forms of life and social relationships that each helps to sustain. At this point we can see how sterile is the scientific account in terms of sustaining the Tewas' form of life and how nurturant is their own account. But we would also have to note that their account is not useful for sustaining the scientific form of life. The streets here go both ways.

I should add that a similar argument can be made for us as well: how useful is the scientific account of humanity in giving direction and meaning to our lives, compared to religious and spiritual conversations?

Returning to the Tewa example, for us to adopt the Tewas' view would require a change in science as we know it. To phrase this point somewhat differently (and in a way that is essential to understanding my next point), we might say that the Tewas' conversation undermines the very form of life that the scientific account upholds, and vice versa. There is a kind of relationship-canceling quality as well as a relationship-sustaining quality to both accounts. Each would cancel out the relationships of its other, even while sustaining its own forms of relationship.

I am not saying that one account is correct while the other is in error. I am simply observing that each account comes from a different form of life and nurtures that form of life. But I am also saying that if for some reason either science or the Tewas began to accept the other version, it would undermine their own form of life, transforming them and their understanding in perhaps dramatic ways. This is not to claim that a Tewa could not consider both accounts, but rather that one nurtures and one undermines his existing way of life. And much the same can be said for scientists.

RELATIONSHIP-CANCELING CONVERSATIONS WITHIN A SINGLE FORM OF LIFE

The preceding example illustrates how *different* forms of life may engender incompatible conversations. My next question asks if there are certain conversations within a *single* form of life that undermine the very form of life in which they are both embedded (that is, that are relationship canceling). Consider people you may know who act in a self-defeating or self-sabotaging manner, in ways detrimental to their own maintenance, or couples or families who similarly illustrate this relationship-canceling quality.

Much the same point was made by John Shotter (1990) when he observed that by its very use, counterfeit coinage undermines its own value as currency. Obviously he was referring not simply to actual coinage but also to the metaphorical currency of our conversations, whose value is debased through counterfeit use. This is what I mean by a relationship-canceling conversation: a conversation that requires a particular form of life in order to appear in the first place and not only fails to sustain that form of life but also effectively cancels it out, ultimately destroying the very form of life from which it derives its meaning and existence.

It is not too difficult to think of human relationships that have this relationship-canceling quality. Some years ago, R. D. Laing (1970) wrote a book, *Knots,* that illustrated relationship-canceling exchanges. Here is one of the many knotted examples he presented:

JILL: I'm upset you are upset.

JACK: I'm not upset.

JILL: I'm upset that you're not upset that I'm upset you're upset.

JACK: I'm upset that you're upset that I'm not upset that you're upset that I'm upset, when I'm not [p. 21].

DIALOGUES AND MONOLOGUES

The next step in my analysis of relationship-canceling conversations builds on three related ideas:

1. From Habermas (1984) comes the idea that certain ideal conditions provide us with a standard for evaluating actual communications between people.

2. From social constructionism comes the idea that our everyday reality is an ongoing accomplishment of conversations.

3. From my own previous works (for example, Sampson, 1993), based especially on the ideas of Bakhtin (1981), comes the idea that conversations are inherently dialogic, occurring between a person and an other.

Combining these three leads me to suggest that any actions that undermine the otherness of dialogic partners serve to undermine the possibility for conversation to take place at all and are thus relationship canceling. A conversation is itself relationship canceling to the extent that it undermines otherness, turning dialogue into monologue.

Acts can systematically destroy another person, either directly as through genocide or indirectly as through denying the other recognition (see Taylor and Gutmann, 1994) or a distinct voice. Either eliminates the other as a partner in a dialogic conversation. Although such relationship-canceling acts may not literally snuff out a life, they snuff out otherness and so cancel the possibilities for a relationship, which requires self and other.

It is my contention that no society can be sustained nor can any relationship persist that is built on the destruction or denial of otherness, whatever form this destruction or denial might take.

My argument is based on these three ideas:

1. The minimal conditions necessary for a conversation to take place are dialogic: at a minimum, a person and an other are essential. This is the Habermassian moment.

2. Furthermore, because the creation of an intelligible social world is achieved through conversations, anything that minimizes the realization of a dialogue undermines the social order and its intelligibility. This is the constructionist moment.

3. Thus a conversation that systematically eliminates otherness undermines the very basis that is requisite for a conversation to take place at all. This is the dialogic moment.

Genocide seeks to eliminate otherness and in this manner is relationship canceling: it eliminates the possibility for conversations to take place by canceling out the very conditions of otherness that are required.

But genocide is not the only means whereby such relationship cancellation occurs. All forms of domination that seek to reduce the other to the same as the speaker, that fail to recognize or grant a separate voice to the diversity of otherness, are similarly relationship canceling and result in monologues, not dialogues. And, in the end, monologues cave in on themselves, because dialogic otherness is essential to maintaining the very fabric of relationship on which all conversations minimally depend. Without the other, there can be no conversation. Destroying the other, by whatever means, undermines the very conditions necessary to hold a conversation, which in turn is the heart and soul of the community in which people are embedded.

The point, then, is not that genocide is evil because it violates some universal ethic of humanity but that it is evil because it destroys the very fabric of the community that is essential for any actions to be sustained and intelligible in the first place. Any silencing of otherness eventually undermines the intelligibility of the social world, because that world requires otherness.

THE MESSAGE FOR ORGANIZATIONS

Let me now pull together the various threads of my argument. I have suggested that insofar as a wide variety of actions are subsumed under the terms *courageous* and *wise,* these cannot serve as useful guidelines for decisions or as ideals toward which persons or organizations should be encouraged to move. What is necessary, rather, is to probe the forms of life and social relationships that are sustained or undermined by a given conversation. Although we may disagree with a given form of life and think it horrible, immoral, and so forth, this all too readily breaks down into "our way of life versus their way of life," with no ready means of choosing between them other than to insist that our way is to be preferred. But this is precisely the story of humankind's efforts to impose one way on the world, and it ends with the horrors that are all too familiar to us.

And so I have argued that relationship-canceling conversations that undermine the very conditions necessary for any conversations to be held in the first place—that, in short, eliminate otherness, or diversity—offer us a useful guidepost for evaluating human actions. The reason that relationship-canceling conversations eventually fail is that they implode into themselves. They are not intrinsically bad; rather, their problem is that they eliminate the conditions necessary for maintaining even themselves and thus undermine the very intelligibility of the social world, which is dialogically constructed.

What individuals and organizations must be taught to do, then, is not to seek either wisdom or courage but rather to evaluate the degree to which they destroy the very otherness that they require to engage in conversation. How is the structure of power and authority maintained? How are decisions reached, and by whom? What are the various devices that are employed to encourage or discourage otherness and diversity?

Our task, then, is to evaluate the conditions that encourage (and those that discourage) dialogue within couples, families, organizations, communities, and nations. In the end, relationship-canceling conversations are self-canceling and undermine the conditions under which any intelligibility can be maintained.

REFERENCES

Bakhtin, M. M. *The Dialogic Imagination.* Austin: University of Texas Press, 1981.

Burleigh, M., and Wippermann, W. *The Racial State: Germany, 1933–1945.* Cambridge, England: Cambridge University Press, 1991.

Chalk, F., and Jonassohn, K. *The History and Sociology of Genocide: Analyses and Case Studies.* New Haven, Conn.: Yale University Press, 1990.

Gergen, K. J. *Realities and Relationships: Soundings in Social Constructionism.* Cambridge, Mass.: Harvard University Press, 1994.

Goldhagen, D. J. *Hitler's Willing Executioners: Ordinary Germans and the Holocaust.* New York: Knopf, 1996.

Habermas, J. *The Theory of Communicative Action.* Vol. 1: *Reason and the Rationalization of Society.* Boston: Beacon Press, 1984.

Hilberg, R. *Perpetrators, Victims, Bystanders: The Jewish Catastrophe, 1933–1945.* New York: HarperCollins, 1992.

Howell, S., and Willis, R. *Societies at Peace: Anthropological Perspectives.* New York: Routledge, 1989.

Laing, R. D. *Knots.* New York: Pantheon Books, 1970. Copyright © 1970 by R. D. Laing. Reprinted by permission of Pantheon Books, a division of Random House, Inc.

Milgram, S. "Some Conditions of Obedience and Disobedience to Authority." *Human Relations,* 1965, *18,* 57–75.

Ortiz, A. "Through Tewa Eyes: Origins." *National Geographic,* 1991, *180,* 6–13.

Rose, P. L. *German Question/Jewish Question: Revolutionary Anti-Semitism from Kant to Wagner.* Princeton, N.J.: Princeton University Press, 1990.

Sampson, E. E. *Celebrating the Other: A Dialogic Account of Human Nature.* Boulder, Colo.: Westview Press, 1993.

Shotter, J. *Knowing of the Third Kind.* Utrecht, The Netherlands: University of Utrecht, 1990.

Smith, M. B. "Selfhood at Risk: Postmodern Perils and the Perils of Postmodernism." *American Psychologist,* 1994, *49,* 405–411.

Taylor, C., and Gutmann, A. *Multiculturalism: Examining the Politics of Recognition.* Princeton, N.J.: Princeton University Press, 1994.

U.S. Holocaust Memorial Museum. *Historical Atlas of the Holocaust.* Old Tappan, N.J.: Macmillan, 1996.

White, G. M., and Kirkpatrick, J. *Person, Self, and Experience: Exploring Pacific Ethnopsychologies.* Berkeley: University of California Press, 1985.

7

THE RELATIONAL REBIRTHING OF WISDOM AND COURAGE

Mary M. Gergen and Kenneth J. Gergen

LET US BEGIN WITH A STORY from our recent past:

It was a Tuesday in September, about 9:30 A.M., at the Pennsylvania State University campus in State College. Students were strolling to and from classes, conversing with friends and laughing and enjoying the sunny autumn day, which was fresh from an overnight rain. Meanwhile a nineteen-year-old woman, who was not a student but had attended the local high school and now lived alone near campus, spread out a tarp on the damp grass under a crab apple tree on a hill overlooking the student union. She read for a while and then removed a high-power rifle from her duffel bag. Shouldering the loaded weapon, she took aim at the strolling students below and then began firing. With her first shot she hit one of them in the back; the student fell to the ground, dead. The next shot hit another student in the stomach; he lay on the ground, severely injured but alive. A third student felt the jolt of a bullet piercing his backpack. Several shots lodged in nearby tree trunks. As the woman stopped to reload, a twenty-two-year-old engineering student who had seen smoke rising from behind the bushes ran to where she was hidden and wrestled the rifle from her. Briefly disarmed, she thrust her hand into her duffel bag, extracted a knife with a seven-inch blade, and lunged at him. He evaded her, and in the ensuing struggle she stabbed herself in the leg; the wound bled profusely. The engineering student, who now had possession of

both weapons, removed his raincoat belt and fashioned a tourni-
quet to curtail her bleeding as she lay, now quietly, on the ground.
He remained with her until the police and ambulances arrived on
the scene. When he asked her why she did it, she responded that she
did not know. Later, when reporters asked him about his actions, he
claimed that he acted spontaneously, without any thought to the
consequences.

At the outset this story suggests that there is little to be said about
courage and wisdom. That is, acts of courage and wisdom are among
the rare and wonderful occurrences in society. At one time or another
most people are the beneficiaries of exceptional individuals who have
acquired or been endowed with wisdom and courage; we stand in
appreciation and sometimes in awe of such people, and wherever possible we give them recognition and praise. Case closed.

But consider this: what if the sniper had managed to reload and
shoot our hero dead? Would we then consider him courageous?
Perhaps we would say that he had courage but lacked wisdom. And
when someone simply acts spontaneously, as he admitted, are we to
credit his acts to courage? Can one be called courageous who, without
understanding the situation, bolts headlong into the jaws of danger?
What does *foolhardy* mean but this? The sniper acted, it seems, with
similar spontaneity; yet we surely would not call her actions courageous. There is more to courage than mindless action. Courage
requires more specificity than we have yet defined. As for wisdom, can
people be wise when they do not understand the multiple consequences
of their actions? These twin graces are enigmas deeply in need of expli-
cation.

In what follows we enter into dialogues, bringing together fragments
from heterogeneous domains of discourse. As authors, we do not speak
in a single voice or even in two separate ones; rather, our voices
emanate from the many relationships we have had throughout our
lives. We hope that through these conversations we will enhance our
readers' understanding and enlarge the possibilities for community.

Our discussion is divided into three parts. First we look critically at
prevailing views of courage and wisdom, with particular emphasis on
some of the ethical and political implications of our current understandings of these concepts. Then we explore some of the potential
benefits of "rebirthing"—that is, of redrawing our understandings to
compensate for some of the shortcomings in our traditions. We will
contrast various meanings of *courage* and *wisdom* as they are embedded in conversations and interpersonal activities. Finally, we turn back

to consider where these reflections have taken us, as well as to open the discussion to a broader array of concerns.

WISDOM AND COURAGE AS SOCIAL CONSTRUCTIONS

As social constructionists, we do not consider courage and wisdom to be features of the natural world that are available for scientific exploration. Rather, *wisdom* and *courage* are first and foremost words, constituents of the common vernacular with rich and lengthy histories. *Wisdom* is said to have been part of the English language since before 1,000 A.D., and a parallel word first appeared around 3,000 B.C. in the world's oldest book, by Ptah-hotep, an Egyptian *vizier,* or wise man. From a social constructionist view, words, such as *wisdom* and *courage,* are created and sustained by human communities in relation to some agreed-upon events. Approaching the topic from this perspective brings three major issues into central focus: the multiplicity of possible constructions, the significance of social negotiation, and the social utility of words in practice. Let us consider each in turn.

First, because language is not fixed by the world it attempts to describe, a variety of possible constructions can exist. We must be sensitive to differing cultural, historical, and political contexts and the ways in which various conceptions are embedded within them (for examples of this diversity, see Gergen and Gergen, 1984; Graumann and Gergen, 1996; Josselson and Lieblich, 1993; Kappeler, 1986; Lieblich and Josselson, 1994; Moraga and Anzaldua, 1983; Shotter and Gergen, 1989). Thus we in the present era have inherited a plethora of conceptions of courage and wisdom, each emerging from differing cultural conversations over the course of history.

To illustrate, let us consider the range of accounts of wisdom articulated in a recent book on psychology edited by Robert Sternberg (1990). Although Sternberg's analysis is confined to wisdom, a similar investigation could be applied to any abstract construct—friendship, violence, democracy, and so on. A close examination of this edited volume demonstrates that even within a relatively narrow sphere of scholarship, highly differentiated definitions of wisdom coexist. How is wisdom defined? Let us count the ways. Wisdom is variously described as

- A cognitive process:

  A holistic way of thinking

  An advanced stage of intellectual development

A metacognitive outlook

An awareness of the fallibility of knowing

Technological knowing

A balanced dialogue between the logical and the subjective

A detection of asymmetry in the face of evidence implying symmetry and equilibrium

A score on the Reflective Judgment Interview Scale

- A valuational process:
Emotional control and mastery

An ability to sense problems of fundamental importance

A preference for certain conceptual directions over others

A preoccupation with questions rather than answers

- A moral process:
A virtue providing a compelling guide to action

A personal good (that is, as an intrinsically rewarding attribute)

The result of an attempt to achieve closer harmony with the laws of the physical universe

A dialectical integration of one's soul with one's agency in the world

A grounding mythos, a close identification between the self and the object of thought

It is interesting to note that many of these definitions of wisdom vary considerably from the six major dictionary definitions of the concept: reasoning ability, sagacity, learning from ideas and the environment, judgment, expeditious use of information, and perspicacity. Given this variety of conceptions of wisdom, each nurtured within different cultural quarters, people's capacity to socially negotiate meaning becomes of central interest. The same action may be identified as wise or foolish, courageous or callow, depending on how one understands these terms. The labeling, as we have suggested, is not determined by the action itself. Rather, as ethnomethodologists have noted, the understanding of an action requires a certain amount of relational work to negotiate meaning (see Garfinkel, 1967, for a detailed discussion of this process). The major point, one to which we shall return later in our discussion of conceptual rebirthing, is that identification of wisdom and courage in social groups, such as organizations, is ultimately dependent on the concerted engagement of active participants in relational processes that eventuate in a consensus on their meaning.

The third major emphasis growing from a constructionist perspective is that of social utility. If language does not gain its meaning directly from the world as it is but through social relationships, our attention is drawn to the value of various usages for various groups. How do the various conceptions of wisdom and courage function within various subcultures and, more specifically, within various conversations? It is this concern that serves as a necessary prolegomenon to our arguments for the relational rebirthing of courage and wisdom.

THE POLITICS OF WISDOM AND COURAGE

What patterns of cultural life are rationalized, sustained, obscured, or obstructed by the differing usages of *wisdom* and *courage*? Let us here adopt a critical posture in which the political and moral implications of our discursive choices are foregrounded. Much has been implied in the preceding account concerning what most would consider the positive potential of these two terms. They are generally regarded as terms of praise and value that function to communicate part of the culture's vision of what is good. To praise one for acts of courage is also to pay homage to the values that such actions sustain. It is courageous to risk one's life in the service of the common good, for example. However, given the unquestioned value associated with these terms, in what follows we want to give voice to the margins of meaning making. That is, we want to consider the underside of existing visions of courage and wisdom from the standpoint of otherwise unheralded communities. For example, how is it *not* courageous to risk one's life in the service of the common good?

INDIVIDUALISM AND COMMUNALISM

In virtually all of the examples cited above, wisdom and courage are considered attributes of individual actors, in line with the long-standing individualist tradition of Western culture. These terms contribute to a cultural ethos in which individual agents serve as the fundamental atoms of society, the components that make up all relationships—family, community, organizational, state, and so on. They are also part and parcel of the "psychological" view of human behavior, a view that regards individual thought, emotion, intention, motivation, moral values, and the like as critical determinants of social action. Words such as these also sustain patterns of organizational life in which individuals are rewarded and punished, rise or fall. The sniper in our introductory narrative was held for psychiatric review and judicial proceedings; the "hero" was heralded in international news stories and honored by the university.

In these ways the traditional discourse concerning courage and wisdom has contributed to an ideology Edward Sampson (1977) has termed "self-contained individualism." It is this tradition that many critics feel to be inimical to communal life. While we need not review all of the many critiques of self-contained individualism launched by Sampson (1988), Bellah and others (1985), Gergen (1994), and many others, it is instructive to observe that the concepts of courage and wisdom function as social wedges. They distinguish between individuals as moral agents, drawing particular attention to their differences. Further, within organizations, attributions of courage and wisdom contribute to hierarchies of the good, in which a select few are singled out as leaders and the remainder delegated to the ranks of the followers. At Penn State the engineering student was distinguished as a courageous hero. As a result our eyes were diverted from all those who might have wisely taken cover, warned others of the gunfire, ran to find help, ministered to the wounded, or helped to reduce the outbreak of panic. And we did not see the links that connected the seemingly solitary hero to other significant persons in his life. For example, we were not reminded of those relationships within his family, Boy Scout troop, or karate class that helped him to acquire whatever was necessary for him to undertake these actions.

Besides narrowing our focus to the inner strengths and weaknesses of single actors, there are other shortcomings to the tradition of explaining heroic actions on the individual level. Those who do not achieve wisdom or courage in the eyes of their peers may feel unworthy: "How am I inadequate?" "What are my deficiencies?" "Why don't I have 'the right stuff'?" In their soul-searching they are thrown back to deliberate on their own interior "failings." "Why didn't I stop the sniper?" Each may ask the question and fall silent. What is wrong with this rumination? Our answer is not only that one's web of relationships is diminished in salience by an emphasis on individual qualities but also that a stress on individual courage and wisdom indirectly devalues the significance of the broader community.

There are many hidden costs for the "hero" as well. A hero learns that in times of difficulty one must rely on oneself. Others cannot be counted on, because they are now defined as inferior. Many a captain, manager, coach, or husband has gone down to defeat for "doing it my way" and resisting the resources to be found within the bonds of relationships. In traditional hierarchical systems such dynamics are commonplace. As a consequence, subordinates often simply do as they are told, acting to realize the missions of those individuals defined as superior. The vast majority of the management literature encourages such an attitude. Consultants goad managers with challenges: "Let us teach you how to inspire, lead, motivate, and instill courage and wisdom in 'your people.'" The consultant takes up the mantle of the individual guru and then offers to pass along his or her wisdom to the chosen few managers, who will use it to change their subordinates, much as they have been coopted by the consultants.

COURAGE AND WISDOM IN A FEMINIST FRAME

Feminists have been active critics of those notions of courage and wisdom that have negatively affected gender relations. The most clear-cut objection is related to the gender bias seen in who is labeled wise and courageous within society. Prime examples are heads of state; military leaders; leaders of civil rights struggles; world-renowned scientists, inventors, explorers, and entrepreneurs; and certain philosophers, artists, and visionaries who have carved out realms in the mind, in outer space, and in the spiritual world. From Abe to Zoro, thousands of famous names populate our cultural histories. They are almost always the names of men. Narratives of the hero, central to the cultural constructions of wisdom and courage, shape our culture's notions of reality and frame the organization of authority in society.

The vast majority of all histories primarily record political and military events and credit selected leaders associated with certain outcomes with courage and wisdom. More recently economic histories—focusing on money, natural resources, markets, the labor force, and the distribution of resources—have offered another resource for cultural studies. We recognize the names Rockefeller, Ford, Getty, Trump, and, more recently, Gates and Greenspan. One means of righting this masculine bias is to recognize those women who have served the culture with courage and wisdom as they have been traditionally defined. Women have been a part of the grand events of history, but historians have been notoriously lax about telling the stories of any group but influential, upper-class males. The contributions of women, minority groups, immigrants, lower-class men, and slaves have been virtually absent or minimized in all of these stories. Yet even as other neglected groups have made their claims to glory, the general absence of women from most histories has been ignored.

Even if gender equity were stressed among historians, parity between men and women would not be achieved in the number of military, political, and economic heroes discussed. It is instructive to imagine how impossible it is for a woman to play out the traditional heroic role noted in the monomythic headlines of history. If we read our history well we will discover that, in the main, women have been positioned as either saints or sinners. And even women of virtue have been portrayed, at best, as auxiliary figures alongside the (male) heroes. Less admirable roles for women have included that of spy, siren, slave, prisoner, or victim, but never the main character. There are no "heroinic" (as opposed to "heroic") stories to parallel the hero sagas. To re-create an individualistic feminist monomyth replete with courage and wisdom would require an extensive resuscitation of women as active players in wars, politics, and economic events, and the rewriting of our entire history. This is highly unlikely.

Perhaps it would be easier instead to create new stories of cultural import that laud different *actions* as courageous and wise. By broadening our definitions of these terms we might also undermine the traditional association of courage and wisdom with actions that are conflictual, aggressive, violent, or cruel. Pacifists have rarely been considered courageous or wise in American culture, though warriors often have been. Presidents who lead the country into war are more often considered heroic than those who keep the peace. A president who would try at all costs to avoid bloodshed by cooperating or communicating with the enemy would be reviled. Those who prefer to use peaceful means, dialogue, compromise, and common civility in addressing situations that might lead to warfare are unlikely to be called courageous. The association between the heroic and the violent is so close that one can scarcely think of a heroic figure without thinking of struggle, conflict, and the use of force. The feminist "turn" here is focused on the cultural binary that categorizes human qualities by gender. Men are associated with physical violence, whereas women tend not to be. The traditional model of the courageous and wise leader, feminists argue, promotes violence as necessary. Men are encouraged to solve the problems of the world through physical force, and they are strongly discouraged from expanding their repertoire for dealing with conflict to include "feminine" modes of conduct, which are by default "not courageous" and "not wise" (Elam, 1994; Flax, 1990; Grosz, 1994; Root, 1996).

More generally, we should move toward a full enrichment of the terms *courage* and *wisdom*. If, for example, *courage* refers to spontaneous, uncalculated, selfless, and life-preserving acts, then many of women's ordinary everyday actions are apt candidates. It could be regarded as courageous to give birth, to protect and care for one's children, to rescue fellow workers in emotional distress, to plan a benefits package that will give an organization a strong and secure safety net, or to evaluate subordinates with openness and charity. Why are such acts not regarded as courageous? Redefining these terms to encompass everyday activities would produce a more gender-inclusive account of courage (and, similarly, of wisdom).

Although moving toward more mundane definitions of *courage* and *wisdom* that include men's and women's daily activities would certainly militate against feminist critiques of the current usage of these terms, even this expansion of meaning continues to vest these qualities in single individuals. As such this solution for eliminating the sexist bias in the use of *courage* and *wisdom* continues to leave intact the centrality of the individual as the font of social behavior.

THE REBIRTHING OF WISDOM AND COURAGE AS RELATIONAL CONCEPTS

We have now recognized an array of critical voices and called into question the traditions sustained by and sustaining common conceptions of wisdom and courage. At the same time, we, the authors, speak with many voices—not all of them so critical. We are drawn now to the possibility of redefining wisdom and courage. Rather than simply erasing these concepts, let us recognize the positive dimensions they represent. After all, the American tradition of individualism encouraged the development of our institutions of democracy, public education, and social justice. And without the heroic imagination, the landscape of the dramatic arts and literature would be quite impoverished. Further, we must recognize the continuing rhetorical power of these terms and the ways in which they motivate and reward actions that society deems worthy or honorable—at times even essential. If wisdom and courage are vital social constructions, then as action-oriented scholars, can we not *re*construct them? Specifically, are there means of resituating these terms within alternative discourses in such a way that their negative implications are diminished and their positive potential realized? In what follows we wish to explore two primary modes of such a reconstitution.

WISDOM AND COURAGE AS CONDITIONS OF CONVERSATION

First, it is instructive to consider Janis Bohan's discussion (1993) of essentialism, as opposed to constructionism. In reference to gender, the essentialist orientation speaks of the feminine and the masculine as internal traits of the individual. From the constructionist perspective, in contrast, actions may be coded as feminine or masculine, but there is no warrant for the conclusion that such actions are produced by inner traits. This distinction between constructionist and essentialist views can also be applied to courage and wisdom. According to the constructionist view, acts (not persons) are courageous or wise, depending on whether the culture values or devalues them. However, molded by the essentialist tendencies in our cultural tradition, we come to view actors as inherently courageous or wise. The student who wrestled the weapons from the sniper performed a courageous act and was thus referred to as courageous. The trait then superseded the action in people's perceptions, and they expected it to remain a part of his personality for the foreseeable future. Similarly, the sniper may well have been judged criminally insane, and this label will also be hers for a long time, possibly for life.

The labeling of wisdom and courage as essential traits is quite compatible with a social constructionist viewpoint (compare to Sarbin and Kitsuse, 1994). It also helps us appreciate the significance of wisdom and courage in everyday conversation in our culture. However, rather than tracing such actions to origins within the individual, let us inquire here into the antecedent social conditions out of which such individual actions are defined. By bringing social conditions into focus rather than individual personalities, we can gain in our attempts to foster wisdom and courage within the organizational sphere. Here we propose that the originating social conditions behind these concepts lie within different forms of social connection, one favoring courage and the other, wisdom.

To appreciate the contrast between these different conditions, consider the traditional tension between the ways _wisdom_ and _courage_ are used in conversation. Even in folk myths there is evidence of this tension: courage is typically traced to the heart (the French word _coeur_) and wisdom to the intellect (the German word _Weisheit_). Consider La Rochefoucault's maxim, "The steadfastness of the wise is but the art of keeping their agitation locked in their hearts," and Lord Chesterfield's, "The wisest man sometimes acts weakly, and the weakest sometimes wisely." In sum, wisdom is more often associated with taking account of all contingencies and acting with careful sagacity born of a long life, whereas courage is more often conceptualized as a spontaneous, impulsive burst of action, often characteristic of youth.

In this context we may ask, What are the conditions of social connection that favor the latter as opposed to the former—the spontaneous as opposed to carefully modulated action? In order to be courageous, we suggest, one must experience a set of relationships in which there is substantial agreement on what is real and good and on the virtue of protecting these stakes. Opposing logics and values may be recognized, but their importance is diminished in comparison to the dominant reality. If realities are socially constituted, then an individual's steadfast singularity of purpose must be traced to the nature of an originative community. It is within this community that the commanding understanding is molded.

Apposite here is Tololyan's study (1989) of Armenian terrorism. As his work suggests, terrorist activity, according to the terrorists' own community, is not the work of madmen or sociopaths but of courageous heroes. Terrorists are "believers" in a given form of reality that is valued by their community (which is typically presumed to be under some threat from an opposing community). Further, in the case of the Armenians, the terrorists' understandings are often based on ancient tales of heroism, courage, and self-sacrifice that are treasured within the culture.

Let us consider further the conditions of dialogue necessary to sustain acts of courage. First we must presume that such dialogue continues to play an active role in the daily life of the individual. This salience need not imply that the dialogists are always physically present; indeed, the courageous individual may be carrying on an internal conversation with a "social ghost"—a heroic figure from an ancestral past, for example (Gergen, forthcoming). Second, the courageous action serves as a symbolic means of valuing one's dialogic companions. It is essentially an act of allegiance or dedication; it honors relationships, community, and history. Finally, the result of such action may often be a sense of personal value. "I risk myself in this action," one implies, "and thus secure recognition from these significant others." To be courageous, then, is to remain steadfast within the bosom of those relationships from which one's sense of personal esteem and identity are derived.

Let us contrast these conditions supporting courage with those favoring wisdom. Rather than a community where a single construction of reality is shared, consider one in which competing realities are in play and conflicts among them are apparent. The myriad contingencies inherent in such a community confront the conflicting needs and values in each individual's deliberations. In terms of constructed realities, the wise person is one who is conversant with multiple understandings. We must further suppose that such individuals acknowledge their participation within a polyphony of multiple relationships. In terms of the modes of relating, experiences with wisdom pay respect not to a single history of connection but to many. And in doing so those experiences defer ultimate allegiance to any particular relationship.

When they are considered in this way we can also see more clearly the tension between courage and wisdom. Members of street gangs, militia groups, "cult" religions, and military organizations demonstrate courage through their loyal and committed actions. Yet this form of loyalty appears constrained and ignorant from the standpoint of the wise. In contrast, those who are wise may appreciate their richness of vision and their capacity for broad empathy and understanding. Yet, for the courageous, the wise exhibit a flabby relativism, an incapacity for sustained and committed action, and even a tendency for duplicity or false consciousness with respect to their beliefs.

How might these distinctions be applied to contemporary organizational life? In general this context appears to be one of polyvocalization, marked by high information density, rapid and often chaotic change, and multicultural investments. This is a context that should foster "wise" decisions but suppress courage. Elsewhere we have described the characteristics of the "relational leader" within this postmodern environment and argued the merits of relational leadership in organizational life (Gergen and Gergen, 1995). Relational leadership requires wisdom. The relational leader attempts to integrate the multiple voices within the organization, recognizes the legitimacy of multiple and competing values, and acts as an interpreter among multiple organizational subcultures. Further, the relational leader attempts to reduce the boundary between the organization and the outside world. The attempt is to bring into the organization the many voices within the outside culture, not only to enrich the organization's internal dialogues and enable it to adjust to the climate of opinion and value without but also to enable the organization's internal voices to inform the surrounding community.

In elevating wisdom within this conceptualization we have failed to take into account the values of courage. It would appear that a new form of courage, a relational courage that coalesces after the informational flood has receded, needs to be developed. One possibility at this juncture would be to manifest relational leadership ourselves and place the issue into the laps of our readers. Our task as authors is not, then, to offer a unilateral rationality but to remain open and sensitive to surrounding voices and to search for integration, coordination, and innovation. Yet another option at this juncture is to listen to the voice of courage within our own histories. For we have been very much constituted by cultural investments in courage. Would we be able to join in this volume if it were not for the courage of our forebears—in wars, immigrant waves, crashing economies, and domestic tensions of all stripes? So let us proceed to outline a means of reconciliation—of having it both ways, or almost so.

In the textual moves just made we suggest the importance of reasserting the virtues of courage. Courage is one mode of life that must be given its due. However, to allow it full sway is to undo the advantages of wisdom. We do not wish to readmit the full virtues of courage—that is, prizing one tradition above all and deriving from it a solid raison d'être. However, we are able through this incorporation to admit the significance of a singular relationship. In effect, while a courageous commitment can scarcely tolerate wisdom, an informed wisdom can supply the grounds for courageous action.

Yet, this conceptual move does not terminate our conversation. We have contrasted two modes of dialogic existence: one honors dedication, and the other, flexibility; one values tradition and fosters trust and security, and the other honors mobility, fluidity, and coordination. In our typically American way, we want it all. And while this may seem possible conceptually, we fail to appreciate the complexities of such tensions within the daily life of the organization. How can we simultaneously be true and untrue, dedicated and free, resolute and nonconflictual? On the level of concrete relations, these questions deserve far more consideration.

COURAGE AND WISDOM AS ORGANIZATIONAL PROPERTIES

Although we are excited by the potential of relational leadership outlined in the preceding discussion, it must be admitted that more than a jot of individualism and hierarchy remain integral to this analysis. Let us follow, then, another conceptual path, one that attempts to envision courageous and wise actions as features of entire groups or organizations. This move, from the individual to the group as the fundamental unit, follows from a profoundly relational standpoint in which all intelligible actions are seen as the outcome of interdependency. There are precedents for expanding our understanding in such a direction. Mary Douglas (1986) has proposed that we cease thinking of intelligence and rationality as residing in the heads of single managers and consider it as being distributed throughout an organization. In this way we can speak of rational and intelligent organizations and work groups. Similar movements toward reconceptualizing otherwise psychological traits as relational are found in work on communal memory (Middleton and Edwards, 1990), emotional scenarios (Gergen and Gergen, 1988), and relational responsibility (McNamee and Gergen, forthcoming). In these analyses what have traditionally been viewed as psychological states are treated instead as social phenomena.

As suggested earlier, the preconditions of such a move to a relational organization requires a suppression of the notion of individual heroes and wizards. When a "mentality of scarcity" is created, in which only a few, highly gifted people are seen to have extraordinary virtues (and get rewarded accordingly), the efficacy of the group may be decreased.

What kinds of conditions might be created within an organization so that its members will share a positive sense of contributing to courageous or wise organizational action? We have no handy three-step program at this point. Again, broader discussion is needed. However, we offer the following incitements to dialogue and action:

- Develop opportunities for communication within the organization as well as among all stakeholders so that wisdom may be accumulated and decisions and actions based on ignorance avoided. Courageous action may be enhanced by communication networks that allow the development of unified concerns.

- Evaluate the efficacy, morale, resources, priorities, responsibilities, and rewards of groups, as opposed to those of individuals. Provide continuous feedback on the efficacy of various group actions. Indicators of merit should be widespread and should recognize all who are part of any activities that garner success: hourly workers, service support people, and others who often work very hard for group goals but are sidelined when recognition time comes around.

- Generate cooperative relationships among various groups in the organization. Competition among coordinating units is problematic, as it encourages face-saving, hoarding of information and resources, jealousy, deception, spiteful retaliations, and "free riding." Blur the boundaries in such a way that cooperation is appropriate among a wider array of entities, including those that are usually regarded as competitors (Brandenberger and Nalebuff, 1996).

• Plan for recursive, reflexive elements in the organization that are sensitive to means-ends relationships (that is, sensitive to the processes as well as the outcomes of activities). How does the work get done? Especially important are the level of engagement and satisfaction of the various groups. While forms of hierarchies, pay differences, and other status indicators are valued in today's organizations, care would have to be taken that differences are deemed fairly distributed.

• Locate exemplars of group success. Courage and wisdom as relational phenomena can be seen in the workings of ad hoc groups self-organized to solve a particular problem or design a special event. Task forces are particularly apposite. People in such groups are pulled together by some common threat or interest and produce outcomes that are sometimes exceptionally creative. Being a part of such a group is an exhilarating experience; business as usual pales in comparison. Members of athletic teams, teams working during natural disasters, even teams in combat can recall the joy of genuine and total involvement and commitment to a group goal.

• Reduce the hierarchical structure of the organization by developing workplace democracy (Deetz, 1992). When organizational participants can express their views and are acknowledged and integrated into the decision-making process, the grounds are established for a sense of ownership of organizational outcomes. If the organization succeeds, it is "we" who have succeeded.

• Create flexibility in forms of decision making. Encouraging an informal organizational culture could make a positive contribution to the organization's wisdom and courage. Organizations should avoid commitments to "one way" of solving problems, setting goals, making decisions, and the like. In this way there will be increased dependence on local, spontaneous synergy among involved parties. Strong informal bonds also encourage the kind of loss of self-consciousness that is necessary to sense the significance of "we."

Is it possible to build such an organization? This question is offered as a challenge for us all. The relational views presented here conflict with the traditional corporate culture that worships the "Lone Ranger" leader, as well as with much of the conventional wisdom in leadership theory. Some organizational theorists are advancing perspectives that lend support to a relational standpoint, however (see Boje, Gephart, and Thatchenkery, 1996; Heckscher and Donnellon, 1994; Hosking, Dachler, and Gergen, 1995). To build an atmosphere in which these transformations can take place may require significant effort. Approaches such as appreciative inquiry (Hammond, 1996)—in which people share in envisioning projects in coordinated ways to assess resources, opportunities, and skills—are helpful, as are educational development programs and new forms of incentives for changing organizational structures. The payoffs for engaging in the development of a relational organization should be both in the process and in ultimate productivity.

REFLEXIVE MOMENTS

The title of this chapter, "The Relational Rebirthing of Wisdom and Courage," puns on the notion of giving new life to words long familiar. It also suggests the reberthing of a vessel, from one pier to another, as we bring old words into new discursive contexts. In so doing we subtly change the action implication of the words. As we shift to new frameworks, we enter new forms of relationship. Yet, to apprehend the contours of the new position we must necessarily step outside its confines. In this final section we move from the reality spaces created in the preceding sections to join other conversations. Specifically, as we listen to other voices within ourselves, to the intelligibilities of other relationships of which we are a part, what do we hear? Let us share a cache of connections:

•

In our second attempt to reconceptualize wisdom and courage as organizational phenomena, we have succeeded in removing the single individual as the bounded unit of analysis. In this way we can move toward a communal as opposed to an individualist conception of courage and wisdom. However, we fear we have done so at the cost of establishing yet another bounded unit: the organization. In speaking of courageous and wise organizations, we fall prey to our critique of the individualist conception, only with a larger unit of analysis in focus. Thus we not only fail to take into account the context within which organizations may be recognized as wise or courageous and the debt they owe to others in achieving such status, but also, more seriously, we imply a world in which organizations are isolated, alienated, and ultimately compete for their survival. Despite these limits, we believe that the conversation must continue. In terms of our own political interests, we prefer to locate means of understanding wisdom and courage in a context of full relatedness. We wish not only to make intelligible the ways in which any individual or group action is inextricably entwined with the full societal complex of relationships but also to see these actions in terms of their embeddedness within historical trajectories that forever unite us with previous generations. Further, if we were fully successful we might be able to understand these concepts in the context of our environment and the ways in which we as humans are inextricably entwined with the natural and possibly even the cosmic conditions. If a vital consciousness of connection may enhance the human and environmental condition, then the challenge is fully worth the effort.

●

The preceding revisions of organizational wisdom and courage celebrate relatedness, interdependence, dialogue, joint action. Yet if we scan the con/text against which these formulations are figured, we discover subtle tendencies to the contrary. We find submerged in these discussions assumptions of subject versus object, controller versus controlled, powerful versus weak. Worse still, we locate a nostalgia, if not a subtle desire, for occupancy of the former positions. Or, in short, if postmodernism is a celebration of interconnections and emergence, we find remainders here of the modernist love of singularity and control. How is this so? In both these revisionings an unspoken assumption is that wisdom and courage can be constructed. This is the case not only in terms of our authoring the concepts in hopes that they may be taken up by others but also in terms of their invitation to others to achieve wisdom and courage in the organizational setting. The subtle subtext is that people can change, effect, act upon, control, influence, or otherwise move others to action—whether it is authors changing readers or managers changing organizations.

In a broader sense this issue speaks to our hopes that change will occur. We fear that the blatant message is "We want to change others"—we want to have others do the right thing by *our* standards, to become us. If we are fully committed to a dialogic orientation, then is our aim not better served by joining in dialogues with others everywhere and under all conditions? Again, the conversation must continue.

●

We place a strong emphasis on relationships, but what sort of relationship does our writing encourage with you, our reader? Is the selection of a monologue not already a way of positioning the reader as silent? Even in our polyvocalism we retain control over the text, its directions and outcomes. We keep you at a distance, without touch, without passion, without intimacy. In our reliance on academic formalisms we suppress many alternative argots—street languages, visual displays, intimate expressions, spiritual forms. We exclude at every turn. How can means of your inclusion be located?

But perhaps we are unwise in overestimating our readership's passivity. You may well have reconstructed these words in ways that would yield our version unrecognizable to us. Surely you have constructed some new reality for our words. We are not so powerful after all.

REFERENCES

Bellah, R. H., and others. *Habits of the Heart.* Berkeley: University of California Press, 1985.

Bohan, J. S. "Regarding Gender: Essentialism, Constructionism, and Feminist Psychology." *Psychology of Women Quarterly,* 1993, *17,* 5–21.

Boje, D. M., Gephart, R. P., Jr., and Thatchenkery, T. J. (eds.). *Postmodern Management and Organization Theory.* Thousand Oaks, Calif.: Sage, 1996.

Brandenberger, A. M., and Nalebuff, B. J. *Co-opetition.* New York: Doubleday, 1996.

Deetz, S. *Democracy in an Age of Corporate Colonization.* Albany: State University of New York Press, 1992.

Douglas, M. *How Institutions Think.* Syracuse, N.Y.: Syracuse University Press, 1986.

Elam, D. *Feminism and Deconstruction.* New York: Routledge, 1994.

Flax, J. *Thinking Fragments, Psychoanalysis, Feminism and Postmodernism in the Contemporary West.* Berkeley: University of California Press, 1990.

Garfinkel, H. *Studies in Ethnomethodology.* Englewood Cliffs, N.J.: Prentice Hall, 1967.

Gergen, K. J. *Realities and Relationships: Soundings in Social Construction.* Cambridge, Mass.: Harvard University Press, 1994.

Gergen, K. J., and Gergen, M. M. (eds.), *Historical Social Psychology.* Hillsdale, N.J.: Erlbaum, 1984.

Gergen, K. J., and Gergen, M. M. "Narrative and the Self as Relationship." In L. Berkowitz (ed.), *Advances in Experimental Social Psychology.* Orlando: Academic Press, 1988.

Gergen, K. J., and Gergen, M. M. "What Is This Thing Called Love? Emotional Scenarios in Historical Perspective." *Journal of Narrative and Life History,* 1995, *5,* 221–238.

Gergen, M. M. *Improvisations in Psychology: Feminist/Social Constructionist Practices.* Thousand Oaks, Calif.: Sage, forthcoming.

Graumann, C. F., and Gergen, K. J. (eds.), *Psychological Discourse in Historical Perspective.* New York: Cambridge University Press, 1996.

Grosz, E. *Volatile Bodies, Toward a Corporeal Feminism.* Bloomington: University of Indiana Press, 1994.

Hammond, S. A. *The Thin Book of Appreciative Inquiry.* New York: S. A. Hammond, 1996.

Heckscher, C., and Donnellon, A. (eds.). *The Post-bureaucratic Organization: New Perspectives on Organizational Change.* Thousand Oaks, Calif.: Sage, 1994.

Hekman, S. *Gender and Knowledge; Elements of a Postmodern Feminism.* Boston: Northeastern University Press, 1990.

Hosking, D., Dachler, P., and Gergen, K. J. (eds.). *Management and Organization: Relational Alternatives to Individualism.* Aldershot, England: Avebury Press, 1995.

Josselson, R., and Lieblich, A. (eds.). *The Narrative Study of Lives.* Thousand Oaks, Calif.: Sage, 1993.

Kappeler, S. *The Pornography of Representation.* Minneapolis: University of Minnesota Press, 1986.

Lieblich, A., and Josselson, R. (eds.). *Exploring Identity and Gender: The Narrative Study of Lives.* Thousand Oaks, Calif.: Sage, 1994.

McNamee, S., and Gergen, K. J. *Relational Responsibility.* Thousand Oaks, Calif.: Sage, forthcoming.

Middleton, D., and Edwards, D. (eds.). *Collective Remembering.* Thousand Oaks, Calif.: Sage, 1990.

Moraga, C., and Anzaldua, G. *This Bridge Called My Back: Writings by Radical Women of Color.* New York: Kitchen Table Press, Women of Color Press, 1983.

Root, D. *Cannibal Culture: Art, Appropriation, and the Commodification of Difference.* Boulder, Colo.: Westview Press, 1996.

Sampson, E. E. "Psychology and the American Ideal." *Journal of Personality and Social Psychology,* 1977, *35,* 767–782.

Sampson, E. E. "The Debate on Individualism." *American Psychologist,* 1988, *43,* 15–22.

Sarbin, T. R., and Kitsuse, J. I. (eds.). *Constructing the Social.* Thousand Oaks, Calif.: Sage, 1994.

Shotter, J., and Gergen, K. J. (eds.). *Texts of Identity.* Thousand Oaks, Calif.: Sage, 1989.

Sternberg, R. J. (ed.). *Wisdom, Its Nature, Origin and Development.* New York: Cambridge University Press, 1990.

Tololyan, K. "Narrative Culture and the Motivation of Terrorism." In J. Shotter and K. Gergen (eds.), *Texts of Identity.* Thousand Oaks, Calif.: Sage, 1989.

PART THREE

AIMING HIGHER

*Disciplines for the Development of
Wisdom and Courage*

8

THORNY GLORY: TOWARD ORGANIZATIONAL GREATNESS

Pradip N. Khandwalla

OVER THE YEARS, inquiries into what constitutes excellence and what causes it have been distinguishing features of the organizational and management literature. A narrow, instrumentalist view of organizations has tended to limit these inquiries to organization-centered excellence, however, with their concern primarily being excellence or effectiveness vis-à-vis organization-centered goals like profitability, growth rate, efficiency, productivity, target fulfillment, employee and customer satisfaction, and so on. While there is some literature on the role organizations and their management play in society (Berle and Means, 1934; Burrell and Morgan, 1979; Chandler, 1977; Galbraith, 1972; Perrow, 1979), rarely, if ever, has there been an inquiry into the architecture of organizational greatness and its implications for human evolution.

At first glance, organizational greatness is perceived to have two essential components: excellent performance and exalted conduct or beneficial contributions to society. Although there is generally no acknowledgment of greatness without excellent performance, excellence itself does not confer greatness. Greatness requires an exalting contribution to society or the commitment of some sacred attribute like wisdom, courage, or dedication to a noble cause. Thus, although being the most profitable corporation in a competitive industry may merit a rating of excellent, to earn the appellation "great" a corporation must, for example, succeed by catering to the neediest in a society rather than to those with the greatest purchasing power, embody a level of integrity rare in the commercial world, or work to further a great social cause. Such greatness redefines social standards of excellence, alters mind-sets stuck in self-centered grooves, and increases people's perception of the feasibility of exalted striving.

Greatness consists mostly of striving. In the next section I survey some of the literature on performance excellence to identify what kinds of striving can help an organization achieve performance excellence, especially in competitive contexts. In the section after that, several potential ennobling paths are briefly discussed based on the literature on stakeholder theory, corporate social responsibility, strategic development, institution building, organizational morality and ethics, organizational justice, radical humanism, organizational altruism, and organizational spirituality.

APPROACHES TO THE STUDY OF PERFORMANCE EXCELLENCE

There seem to be five broad approaches to the study of organizational performance. One approach is to uncover environmental determinants of organizational performance. Another approach seeks to identify strategic choices that result in excellent performance. The third seeks to identify organizational traits that differentiate high-performance from low-performance organizations. The fourth approach seeks to identify positive synergies between organizational variables. The fifth seeks to identify "good fits" between contextual and organizational variables.

Environmental Determinants of Performance

Microeconomics, population-ecology, and resource-dependence approaches tend to see an organization's operating environment, rather than anything the organization does, as the primary determinant of its survival and performance. Microeconomics describes several different types of ideal market environments (Samuelson, 1992). Under assumptions of organizational rationality and a given cost structure, a firm's profitability is strictly determined by the market structure in which it operates. It is likely to earn, at best, normal profits in a competitive market and supernormal profits in a monopolistic niche. Evidence does suggest a positive relationship between industry concentration (a surrogate for monopoly power) and profitability (Scherer, 1970). But the variation among firms in profitability in almost every industry (even declining ones) is so high (Hall, 1980) that market structure becomes suspect as the sole arbiter of profitability.

The population-ecology perspective (Hannan and Freeman, 1977) assumes a level of organizational rigidity that makes it impossible for organizations to adjust to major shifts in their operating environments. The purpose of this theoretical perspective is to shed light on the birth and death rates of organizations in a domain or niche (Singh, 1990). However, it conspicuously fails to explain massive performance differences within a single domain, spectacular performance improvement in a sick organization from intense management action (Bibeault, 1982; Khandwalla, 1992b; Slatter, 1984), and quantum changes in organizational strategy, structures, style, and so on (Miller and Friesen, 1984).

The resource-dependence perspective (Pfeffer and Salancik, 1978) also gives primacy to the environment as a controlling factor vis-à-vis performance. Where dependence on external resources is very high, the dispensers of those resources are likely to dictate what actions the organization may take and thereby substantially determine its performance. Regulated environments may also diminish the latitude of organizations and thus control their performance (Mahon and Murray, 1981; Smith and Grimm, 1987), although empirical research has pointed to the adoption of alternative strategies, even in highly regulated environments, and thus by implication to management's ability to influence performance (Hrebeniak and Joyce, 1985; Tan and Litschert, 1994). In contrast to regulated environments, expansive environments may raise organizational performance (McDougall, Covin, Robinson, and Herron, 1994).

Strategic-Choice Perspective

In sharp contrast to the environmental determinism of the performance approach, the strategic-choice perspective gives primacy to those strategic initiatives on the part of management that have long-term, organization-wide effects (Child, 1972; Hrebeniak and Joyce, 1985). These include diversification and various related strategies; internationalization; mergers and acquisitions; and major changes in corporate philosophy, technology policy, and so on. One fairly constant finding in different social contexts is that, on the whole, related diversifiers tend to outperform unrelated diversifiers (George, 1984; Haveman, 1992; Rumelt, 1974), possibly because of the advantage of greater familiarity with the market or technology and synergies with existing businesses.

This advantage is retained when diversification is achieved through acquisition of related companies (Shelton, 1988; Singh and Montgomery, 1987). Also, when refocusing is attempted to reduce excessive diversification, there is generally an improvement in performance (Markides, 1992). Similarly, there is growing evidence from various different societies that internationalization of operations aids organizational performance (Khandwalla, 1992a; Roth and Ricks, 1994), possibly because of the bootstrapping effect of having to match international quality and cost standards.

Both diversification and internationalization of operations extend the organization into partly familiar, partly unfamiliar and challenging domains. Their great merit is that the core competence of the organization (Prahalad and Hamel, 1994) is harnessed for relatively easily attainable extensions of operations. In the process the organization consolidates its strengths and adds to them by tackling moderately unfamiliar processes.

Management-Attributes Approach

Many studies have sought to identify the management determinants of organizational performance. Studies in several organizational settings indicate that participative management, especially at upper levels, is associated with superior organizational performance. These studies include Likert's analyses of branches of an American company and of voluntary organizations (Likert, 1961), Pearce and Zahra's study (1991) of the functioning of the boards of large American industrial and service corporations, and Khandwalla's studies of corporate turnarounds in many countries (Khandwalla, 1992b) and of Indian corporate management styles (1995). Similarly, studies in several cultural settings have indicated that formal corporate planning is associated with superior organizational performance. These include several American studies (Bracker and Pearson, 1986; Rhyne, 1986; Thune and House, 1970), Miller's study (1987) of small- and medium-sized firms in Quebec, studies of state-owned enterprises in India (Bhatt, 1985) and East Africa (Jorgensen, 1990), and a study of planning in Japanese corporations (Kono, 1992).

The type of supervision also seems to have a significant effect on organizational performance, especially at operating-group levels. Several studies in various settings have suggested that caring but exacting supervision (which emphasizes task achievement but is also nurturing, high on consideration and structure, and oriented toward employees) is associated with superior performance of organizational groups. These include the Bowers and Seashore study (1966) of departments in an American life insurance company, studies by Sinha (1990) of diverse managerial groups in India, Ahiauzu's study (1989) of the Efako work system in Africa, and studies of Japanese management (Editors of *World Executive's Digest*, 1981). Studies in different settings suggest that transformational leadership is also associated with superior organizational performance. These include the Bennis and Nanus study (1985) of American organizational leaders, the Singh and Bhandarkar study (1990) of Indian corporate leaders, and Khandwalla's study (1992b) of the management of innovative turnarounds in many countries.

The emphasis in the management literature on general efficacy in planning, participative management, supportive but exacting supervision, and transformational leadership suggests that these may be especially effective integrative mechanisms for organizations that are highly differentiated, both vertically and horizontally (Lawrence and Lorsch, 1967). Such organizations tend to divide up work, especially at lower levels, into narrow specializations, and this often makes work tedious. Routinization further depresses the human spirit. Task-oriented but caring supervision brings to the workplace a human touch that makes routine work bearable, and visionary, dynamic, empowering, transformational leadership makes work worthwhile. These four dimensions of management may be efficacious for many kinds of formal organizations; indeed, one may speculate that the more formally structured an organization gets, the more efficacious they become.

An elaboration of the traits approach is the search for clusters of attributes that characterize high-performance organizations. For example, Peters and Waterman (1982) identified eight traits of "excellent" American companies. The pioneering management identified in a study of Indian companies (Khandwalla, 1985, 1987) was also marked by eight characteristics, though they differed substantially from those identified by Peters and Waterman. Successful Japanese management (Editors of *World Executive's Digest*, 1981) also seems to have several distinctive traits. Differences between these clusters of traits possibly reflect differences in cultural and institutional environments (North, 1990). The management style identified by Peters and Waterman is quintessentially American in several respects: bias toward action, customer orientation, respect for the individual, flexibility, hands-on management, spirit of innovation. These traits seem to make sense in the hypercompetitive, turbulent U.S. market. The Japanese style likewise seems quintessentially Japanese in its paternalism and its stress on cooperation, adaptation, and a hard work ethic. The Indian style reflects the imperatives of a rapidly developing, modernizing society in its emphasis on innovation, technological sophistication, and pioneering entrepreneurship. An interesting point is that none of these styles emphasize ethics, social responsibility, altruism, justice, or spirituality. In addition, each style displays not only cultural coherence but also certain balancing and compensating mechanisms. For example, the American style emphasizes innovation and entrepreneurship (risk taking) but also stresses "sticking to one's knitting" (risk aversion); likewise, it values decentralization (organizational differentiation) but also emphasizes core shared values (organizational integration). The paternalism and job security characteristic of Japanese organizations—which can both breed indolence—are offset by the powerful emphasis on the work ethic in Japanese culture. The higher risk characteristic of much business in India is balanced by seeking novel, technologically sophisticated market niches in which there is considerable, sometimes prolonged protection from the competitive pressures unique to the Third World.

Internal Synergy Approach

Following Chandler's study (1962) of the relationship between corporate diversification and division, various attempts have been made to uncover relationships between organizational variables that positively influence performance. Several studies in different settings have indicated that a balance or alignment between certain classes of organizational variables is a predictor of organizational performance. For example, Lawrence and Lorsch (1967) showed that integration carried out in proportion to required differentiation separates high- from low-performing manufacturing organizations. A more recent study of firms in two American manufacturing industries (Powell, 1992) also found that a balance between differentiation and integration is associated with higher organizational performance. Khandwalla's study (1973) of American manufacturing firms indicated that balance between uncertainty reduction, differentiation, and integration mechanisms was correlated with corporate profitability. In a study of North American and Australian companies, Miller and Friesen (1984) found that synchronized changes in uncertainty reduction, differentiation, and integration variables were associated with high organizational performance.

Some studies have shown synergies between management styles or modes. For example, Khandwalla's study (1977) of Canadian corporations indicated a positive synergy between analytical, technocratic, participative modes of management and risk-taking, organic modes of management. Covin and Slevin (1988), too, found that entrepreneurial organizations achieved positive results when they had organic rather than mechanistic structures, as did Naman and Slevin (1993).

Several North American studies have sought to trace relationships between strategy and structure. Some have focused on one or more of the Miles and Snow (1978) strategies, such as the study by Golden (1992), in which relationships were identified between different kinds of autonomy and the "prospector" and "defender" strategies. Several others have sought relationships between competitive strategies and management structures and systems, such as the Thomas, Clark, and Gioia (1993) study of hospitals, the Zahra and Covin (1993) study of manufacturing firms, and the Govindrajan and Fisher (1990) study of the strategic business units of Fortune 500 companies. Some studies have sought relationships between the mode of strategy making and organizational structure (Miller, 1987).

These studies indicate the likely high prevalence of relationships between strategic choices and organizational arrangements. Thus how a strategy is executed may be as important—possibly more important—than the strategic choice itself (Venkatraman and Camillus, 1984).

Contingency Fit Approach

One interesting line of research is the attempt to identify effective responses to various contingencies faced by organizations. This line of inquiry was triggered by Thompson's argument (1967) that different operating environments may produce different contingencies, each requiring a distinctive adaptive response, and by the Burns and Stalker (1961) argument for the appropriateness of the organic management mode for organizations operating in fluid, dynamic, unstable environments and the mechanistic mode for those operating in stable environments.

Empirical work on this topic has ranged widely since these studies. It suggests that effective organizational responses to such major contingencies as environmental uncertainty, turbulence, variability, hostility, expansiveness, complexity, and deregulation are quite distinctive. For instance, Lawrence and Lorsh (1967) reported that relatively high levels of organizational differentiation and integration contribute to high performance in an uncertain, variegated environment, while

Khandwalla's study (1973) of American manufacturing firms indicated a strong relationship between uncertainty in a firm's technological and economic environments and relatively high use of uncertainty-reduction, differentiation, and integration mechanisms. In another study (of Canadian companies) he found a good fit between environmental turbulence and an entrepreneurial mode of management (Khandwalla, 1977), a finding that has been replicated by Naman and Slevin (1993). Child's studies of British manufacturing organizations (1974, 1975) indicated that an organic structure and selective centralization of authority may be associated with a high growth rate in a variable, changeable operating environment. Thus a complex structure and an entrepreneurial management style may be required in a fluid operating environment.

Industry deregulation brings in its wake new competitive pressures and also new opportunities. A study of Chinese electronics firms (Tan and Litschert, 1994) suggests a "defender" strategy—consisting of attempts at greater efficiency—as an effective response. In a study of deregulated savings and loan associations, related diversification was found to be an appropriate response (Haveman, 1992). Jennings and Seaman (1994) found that for savings and loans that had broadened their legitimate domains, a prospector strategy and an organic structure gave the best results; however, for organizations that stuck close to their earlier domain, a defender strategy and a mechanistic structure worked best. Much may depend on how a deregulated environment is interpreted by management. If it is seen as more threatening than before, the effective response may be a defender-type response aiming at greater efficiency, competitiveness, and related diversification. If it is seen as more rich in opportunity, the most effective response may be a prospector-type, entrepreneurial one.

Environmental complexity (diversity, constraints, technological sophistication) also requires complex responses. Khandwalla (1977), in a study of Canadian firms, saw a good fit between environmental complexity and an analytical-cum-participative mode of management that combined organizational differentiation (more functional and role specialization) with integration (more planning and participative decision making). Nohria and Ghoshal (1994) found that for multinational corporations operating in a variety of national environments, it makes sense to decentralize the company's control structure among its subsidiaries but to offset this differentiation by emphasizing shared values and informal communications between headquarters and the subsidiaries.

A Syncretic Model of Performance Excellence in Competitive Domains

The increasing pervasiveness of market economies and democracy indicates that most operating domains are, or are likely to become, competitive (Khandwalla, 1981). For excellence in competitive domains, two sets of organizational responses may be needed: essential responses, for becoming or remaining viable; and discretionary, hard-to-match, but appropriate responses, to confer competitive advantage. These essential responses are likely to become institutionalized (that is, widely practiced) and therefore confer no competitive advantage. Thus, for larger corporations all over the world, such structural features as specialization, division of labor, rules, standard operating procedures, hierarchies, decentralization, management information systems, and so on may still be indispensable, but they will confer no competitive advantage because "everyone" has them by now. These corporations must look for relatively distinctive and hard-to-imitate mechanisms for performance excellence in a competitive domain.

Some examples may illustrate the above point. Miller and Friesen (1984) sought archetypes of corporate response in different contexts, such as appropriate adaptive responses to moderate as well as extreme challenges in the operating environment. The appropriate response to a moderate challenge consisted of a defender strategy–type attempt to cut costs; incremental strategic change; a functionally organized, centralized decision-making structure with a "charismatic" chief executive; personal information processing and informal control; an intuitive-cum-analytical type of decision making; and a focus on the efficiency of production and marketing. The appropriate response to a moderate threat appears to consist of not only a defender strategy and tighter management (likely to be commonplace) but also hard-to-imitate elements of entrepreneurial management (a charismatic, larger-than-life, bright chief executive) and professional management (analytical decision making superimposed on intuitive decision making) that are ideologically inconsistent with traditional management but appropriate in the circumstances. The successful response to an exceptionally challenging environment was found to be a prospector-type strategy; bold innovations; use of new technologies; emphasis on R&D and engineering; an organic, differentiated, but integrated structure; emphasis on environmental scanning; reliance on committees; open internal communication; and an analytical, planning-orientated, yet entrepreneurial mode of decision making. Notice the far greater complexity of the successful response to extreme challenge, and the conflation of entrepreneurship, innovation, flexibility, technological sophistication, opportunity seeking, professionalized decision making, and structural complexity—a really hard to match but appropriate concoction.

Another example of effective necessary-and-discretionary responses to a specific context is from research on corporate turnarounds. Khandwalla (1992b) examined sixty-five corporate turnarounds reported in several Western as well as Third World countries. He found that some elements—changes in top management, diversification, product-line rationalization or expansion, better marketing, restructuring for greater decentralization and accountability, cost reduction, and plant modernization for greater efficiency, product quality, and productivity—were common elements in most turnarounds. None of these, however, was significantly correlated with the rate of improvement in profitability, a variable criterion for turnaround effectiveness. When the turnarounds were sorted into two types—surgical and nonsurgical—a fairly clear picture emerged. On average the nonsurgical turnarounds improved company profitability at nearly twice the rate as surgical turnarounds (Khandwalla, 1992b). But within each type, analysis also indicated two subtypes that differed substantially on the variable criterion. Compared to the low-performance subtype, the high-performance subtype was far more complex. In surgical turnarounds, the high-performance subtype exhibited four more instances of turnaround management than did the low-performance subtype, and in the nonsurgical turnarounds, the high-performance subtype had as many as seven more turnaround management elements compared to the low-performance subtype. The high-performance nonsurgical turnaround was by far the best performer among all four subtypes, and it also had the largest number of turnaround management elements.

Even in a competitive domain, many contingencies and constraints can be ignored (Hirschman, 1970; Metcalfe, 1981). But there are some potent contingencies that must be addressed, and how they are addressed can make a great difference in organizational performance. If these contingencies are not addressed they can threaten viability, as per the population-ecology perspective. If they are addressed in a widely practiced manner, as per the contingency-theory perspective, viability may be protected, but the organization is unlikely to achieve performance distinction. If they are addressed in an uncommon but appropriate manner and without sacrificing viability-protecting responses, as per the strategic-choice and synergy perspectives, the organization may achieve performance excellence.

Implicit in the above formulation is the importance of organizational learning and innovation. Failure to learn is perilous. Commonplace learning and innovation only lessen mortality. But they also prepare a platform of new organizational competencies that can enable the organization to venture further. If these new competencies are harvested by a resort to uncommon, hard-to-imitate organizational responses, then only performance glory becomes possible. An implication of this model is that in a competitive domain, new contingencies will tend to increase organizational complexity. Indeed, even relatively hard to imitate or unfamiliar organizational responses may gradually become institutionalized, so that the quest for performance excellence in a competitive domain becomes practically unending. Thus over time such widely hailed nostrums as participative management, planning, transformational leadership, and considerate but demanding supervision are likely to lose their performance-related potency in particular competitive domains, and past findings of their efficacy may become increasingly irrelevant. The same fate may befall the current panaceas of benchmarking, Total Quality Management, downsizing and delayering, the fractal corporation, networking, and the virtual corporation.

To sum up, performance excellence in a competitive domain requires both wisdom and courage: in choosing critical contingencies to respond to, in making essential strategic and systemic adaptive responses and learning new competencies from them, and in using this learning to choose and implement uncommon but high-potential discretionary responses that fit with the contingency or strategic choice *and* give a comparative advantage to the organization.

PATHS TO ORGANIZATIONAL EXALTATION

Like individuals, organizations too can rise above their bread-and-butter concerns. They may be able to do so in several different ways. For example, they may adopt an enlightened-self-interest stance and extend their accountability beyond their owners or managers to other stakeholders like employees, customers, suppliers, financiers, governments, communities, and so on. A bolder, more ambitious route to exaltation is corporate social responsibility, the notion that an organization must not only look after the interests of its specific stakeholders but also satisfy various obligations to the societies in which it operates. A special, more focused form of corporate social responsibility is the commitment to help the domain wherein an organization operates to grow and develop. Institution building is a related road to glory. It is the process by which an organization integrates into its activities those core values that enable the organization to be seen as a role model by others.

Besides the above four relatively sociocentric paths to exaltation there are several others. In the ethical path the organization learns to ask persistently whether its acts are good or bad, moral or immoral, and to heed the answers it finds. A related path concerns fairness and justice—how justly the organization evaluates and rewards stakeholders, and how justly it responds to the grievances of its stakeholders. Altruism or helping behavior by the organization and within the organization is still another avenue to glory. A more turbulent path is that of radical humanism, which seeks, in the organizational context, to liberate people working in organizations from their occupational as well as psychic prisons. Finally, the most elusive of all trails is that of organizational spirituality, the effort to dissolve interpersonal strife by recognizing the spiritual fraternity of all beings and to mitigate intrapersonal stress by seeing work as worship, a divine calling, an offering to God.

In market economies the dominant paradigm of performance excellence amounts to winning in a competitive domain. Often it degenerates into winning at all costs—costs to others as well as to organizational stakeholders. The nine alternative paths to glory are costly and painful. Their agonies are different from those of the competitive domain, and they pose fundamental challenges to this dominant paradigm. The management of greatness is very substantially the effective management of the creative tension between the organization's flesh needs and its soul needs. Each of these nine paths to potential glory is briefly reviewed below.

Stakeholder Orientation

One influential stream of thinking on corporate management has stressed that the only stakeholder in a corporation is the owner. The rest are mere "factors of production," or agents of the owner, and therefore the only duty of management is to maximize the owner's earnings. The ethical foundation of this maxim is the inference of neoclassical economic theory that the only principle that maximizes customer welfare and ensures equity in payments to factors of production in a competitive market economy is the single-minded pursuit of maximal profits (subject to compliance with legal requirements) (Friedman, 1970). However, when markets are imperfect or there are gross market failures (Kapp, 1971), there are also gross inequalities and injustices and potentially large negative effects from corporate actions. Profit maximization as a principle can then degenerate into an opportunistic, get-rich-quick mind-set that does not, either in the short run or the long run, necessarily lead to Pareto optimality (Grant, 1991; Reilly and Kyj, 1990; Sen, 1987).

In contrast to the logic of profit maximization is the notion of multiple corporate stakeholders. A stakeholder is a group or individual who can significantly affect or is affected by an organization's performance. Freeman (1984) described the possible impacts of a firm's relationship with a number of stakeholders. If such stakeholders as suppliers, employees, customers, or the government have positive relationships with an organization, then it can achieve its objectives more fully and with greater ease. If the relationship with an important stakeholder is negative, it can endanger the organization's goal attainment and sometimes its very survival.

Proponents of stakeholder theory have argued that effectively managing the interface with each stakeholder increases the competitive advantage of an organization (Jones, 1995). Attention to the principles of trust, trustworthiness, and cooperativeness in dealing with stakeholders can lower operating costs. Short-term profit maximization may involve high costs resulting from top-heavy control structures, large transaction costs, and poor team cooperation in situations where no one's contribution can be accurately measured or differentially rewarded. Emphasis on corporate morality, trust, and cooperation, even if it results in some abuses, can strengthen relations with stakeholders, reduce drastically the costs of profit maximization, and lead to long-term higher profits.

Effective stakeholder management incorporates ideas from several management disciplines (Freeman and Reed, 1983). One is participation of stakeholders in organizational decision making (Dill, 1975)—including participation of adversarial groups such as Nader's Raiders. Another is to treat each stakeholder as a customer, to understand the stakeholder's needs and design programs, services, and products that fulfil them. From political science comes the idea of understanding the political nature of the relationships with and between stakeholders by applying such tools as coalitional analysis, conflict management, and unilateralism. From economics comes the idea of allocating organizational resources to stakeholders in proportion to the degree of importance of their claims to the organization. The involvement of stakeholders in corporate governance is likely to make such governance more democratic, since forums need to be created (such as stakeholder councils) to give voice to stakeholders' interests and suggestions. The corporate board, in particular, may need to be restructured to reflect stakeholders' concerns and to harness their cooperation.

Two examples from research on turnarounds (Khandwalla, 1992b) may illustrate the choices involved in stakeholder management. British Steel and the Steel Authority of India, Ltd. (SAIL) were both sick organizations in the late seventies and early eighties, and both were successfully turned around in the early and mid eighties. Both were large, with staffs in excess of two hundred thousand; both were overmanned, and both were dominant firms in the steel industry in their respective countries. Both were state-owned enterprises. But in one turnaround, that of British Steel, the costs to stakeholders were frightful: Britain's national steel-making capacity was practically halved, a debt of £3,500 million was written off to the British government, and the company shed nearly 80 percent of its workforce. There were no such costs to stakeholders in the recovery of SAIL: no debts were written off, there was no reduction in capacity, no one lost his or her job (although a few thousand did opt for voluntary retirement), price rises were kept below inflation, energy costs were reduced, and production and productivity were raised at a very healthy rate. The SAIL turnaround was an act of faith—in the creative capacity of people when they are empowered. It was engineered by a vast communication, retraining, and participative decision making exercise and a huge investment in human resource development and modernization.

Corporate Social Responsibility

Davis (1973) conceived of corporate social responsibility as the obligation of firms to work for the betterment of society and to pursue social benefits along with economic gains. These obligations arise because corporations are, according to this view, citizens in a complex, interdependent world that have responsibility for the good of the larger society that gave them birth and sustained them with supportive infrastructures, institutions, resources, and facilities (Aram, 1989; Preston and Post, 1975). In addition, since corporations are institutions with vast power and very little accountability (Berle and Means, 1934; Galbraith, 1972), inculcating a social conscience within them is a way of bridging this gap.

Corporate social responsibility involves various obligations (Carroll, 1979): economic obligations, which extend to being productive and profitable and to meeting the needs of customers; legal obligations, which include doing business within the limits of the law; ethical obligations, to incorporate the codes, norms, and values of society in the organization's daily business; and philanthropic or discretionary obligations, which involve contributing to social causes.

There have been attempts to determine what business leaders regard corporate social responsibility to be. In a study of 203 deans of U.S. business schools and 116 CEOs, there was much agreement with such statements as "responsible corporate behavior can be in the best economic interest of the stakeholders," "involvement by business in improving its community's quality of life will also improve long-run profitability," and "social problems such as pollution control sometimes can be solved in ways that produce profits from the problem solution" (Ford and McLaughlin, 1984, Table 1). Agreement was low on statements such as "since businesses have such a substantial amount of society's managerial and financial resources, they should be expected to solve social problems" and "other social institutions have failed in solving social problems, so business should try." The pattern of agreements and disagreements suggests that the business establishment in the United States favors that form of corporate social responsibility that is in the best long-term economic interests of business or offers opportunities for profits, not the one that stems from purely ethical or moral compulsions or social necessity. Both the CEOs and the deans agreed that the American business community's support for socially responsible activities has risen over the past decade and is likely to rise further in the future. Research by Aupperle, Carroll and Hatfield (1985) on 241 U.S. CEOs also indicated that the economic dimension of corporate social responsibility was considered most important, followed by the legal, ethical, and philanthropic dimensions. (Indeed, the economic dimension was inversely correlated with the three.)

Whether socially responsive behaviors are indeed associated with corporate financial performance has been probed. Extant U.S. research does not suggest any strong relationship between the two. In a study of 241 CEOs of sizeable companies, no significant relationship was found between profitability and any of the measures of corporate social responsiveness (Aupperle, Carroll, and Hatfield, 1985). A study of 131 U.S. firms described a fairly strong positive correlation between certain past (1977–1981) measures of financial performance and *Fortune*'s rating of "socially responsible" in 1983, and it found a fairly strong negative correlation between financial precariousness and social responsibility (McGuire, Sundgren, and Schneeweis, 1988). Thus corporate social responsibility may be a consequence rather than a cause of positive financial performance.

As a refinement and concretization of corporate social responsibility, corporate social performance stresses actions and outcomes (Wartick and Cochran, 1985; Wood, 1991). Wood's model of corporate social performance encompasses principles of corporate social responsibility, processes of corporate social responsiveness, and outcomes of corporate behavior at the institutional (business as a whole), organizational, and managerial levels. For example, at the institutional level the principle of legitimacy (Davis, 1973) implies that businesses must avoid abusing their power. At the organizational level it implies that organizations must take public responsibility for their negative externalities (for example, pollution). At the managerial level it implies that managers must try to ensure socially responsible outcomes through specific actions and performance goals. Various processes of corporate social responsiveness can be harnessed, such as environmental assessment, stakeholder management, and issues management, and several outcomes can be expected, including social impacts, social programs, and social policies. This sort of conceptualization can lead to the development of socially responsible corporate policies such as "produce only ecologically sound products," "use low-polluting technologies," and "cut costs with recycling" and to charitable investments that actually help solve social problems. Several environmentally responsive corporate policies have been proposed, such as the Valdez Principles (Sanyal and Neves, 1991) and "greening" policies aimed at profitably protecting the environment (Shrivastava, 1996).

Shrivastava (1996) provides an interesting example of a medium-sized U.S. company, the ice cream maker Ben & Jerry's, that has grown quickly, become very profitable, and thrived using greening policies. The company buys its materials from "organic" sources that are eco-friendly or preserve local lifestyles. For example, it buys wild blueberries from an Indian reservation and nuts harvested by natives of the Amazonian rain forest. It has an active, eco-friendly waste management program, recycling its packaging, stationery, copier paper, plastic materials, and so on. For this a "Green Team," headed by a manager for natural resources, brainstorms periodically about environment-related issues and executes energy conservation projects, sometimes in collaboration with the company's energy team. Energy conservation is achieved through energy audits, the use of low-watt bulbs, occupancy sensors that turn off lights in empty rooms, the generation of energy from waste, use of cold winter air for refrigeration, use of solar energy, and so on. The company's resource conservation program involves recycling and reuse of production and other wastes. For example, egg yolks, a waste product, is fed to pigs, and spilled ice cream is used to sweeten manure pits. The company sponsors community projects and campaigns for promoting environmental awareness, and it is a signatory to the Valdez Principles. It contributes 7.5 percent of its profits to various social causes, including an institution dedicated to diverting military spending to the pursuit of global peace.

Few organizations in India can match the corporate social responsibility record of the House of Tatas (Lala, 1981). It is India's largest business and also one of its most diversified. Its growth and financial performance has been enviable. But it is also famous for the social responsiveness its companies display, its integrity, its emphasis on product quality and quality of life, and its contributions to education, research, and the alleviation of suffering. Tata Steel, its flagship company, has been managing the city of Jamshedpur (where its plant is located) in an exemplary manner. Its welfare agencies provide medical facilities and other aid to hundreds of thousands of tribal people and other poor persons living around its plants. It has had an astonishing record of good personnel practices. It pioneered the eight-hour work day in India in 1912, and before the Second World War it introduced such staff welfare measures as free medical aid, schooling facilities for children, a works committee to handle grievances, leave with pay, a workers' provident fund or retirement fund, profit-sharing bonuses, retirement gratuities, and so on. The House of Tatas also administers many charities. It has funded the higher studies of thousands of bright but disadvantaged Indians. It has set up outstanding institutions for fundamental research, cancer research, energy research, social sciences work, and the performing arts.

Strategic Domain-Development Orientation

During the twentieth century, a good deal of socioeconomic development of poor, "developing" societies has been accomplished through strategic developmental organizations (SDOs) (Khandwalla, 1988; 1990). The SDO can come in many forms, including apex governmental organizations; industry, trade, or sector associations; state-owned and even private sector enterprises; cooperative societies; not-for-profit institutions; developmental programs; and volunteer organizations. But the distinguishing characteristic of the SDO in all its various forms is its commitment to the strengthening and long-term development of some aspect or other of its domain of activities. While the concept of corporate social responsibility in the First World has emphasized such good citizenship behaviors as equal opportunity, environmental protection, community action, and control of pollution, the SDO goes well beyond these, actually transforming its domain through strategic action. Depending upon the nature of the SDO, its domain can consist of markets, sectors, client systems, or beneficiaries.

Several examples of SDOs illustrate their exalted missions and achievements. Japan's Ministry of International Trade and Industry, for example, masterminded Japan's industrial strategy; coordinated industry and governmental action; created Japan, Inc.; and catalyzed the economic superpower status of Japan (McMillan, 1985). The Philippine Rice Development Programme, following a devastating rice shortage in the Philippines in the early seventies, launched the Masagana-99 program for increasing the productivity of rice cultivation. Due largely to its efforts, by 1979 the Philippines had not only wiped out its rice deficit but also could export sizeable quantities of rice (Paul, 1982). The Grameen Bank of Bangladesh has been able to alleviate the poverty of half a million rural households, in spite of charging commercial rates of interest (Gibbons, 1988), and the Self-Employed Women's Association of India has been able to organize over thirty thousand very poor unemployed or self-employed women and give them productive work, protection, skills, services, and dignity (Self-Employed Women's Association, 1988).

Bharat Heavy Electricals, Ltd. (BHEL), owned by the government of India and specializing in producing and marketing power-generating equipment, played a major role in India's ability to increase its power-generating capacity forty times in as many years. From 1975 to 1985, BHEL supplied 90 percent of the power-generating equipment installed in India (Bhasin, 1988), often in competition with domestic and foreign suppliers. Although its main business was in producing equipment for conventional power plants, it invested large amounts in research and development of nonconventional renewable energy sources (solar, wind, biogas, and so on). It helped India develop significant technological capabilities through collaboration agreements with about twenty-five international giants in the West, Japan, and the Soviet Union. From 1975 to 1985 it nurtured some two thousand small-scale units as ancillaries, took over and turned around two medium-sized sick public enterprises, and set up two management development institutions for training and research as well as a welding research institute. During these ten years it tripled its profits and increased its exports ten times.

SDOs face many special pressures (Khandwalla, 1988). Many SDOs are either owned by the government or depend on it for resources and so are subjected to the onerous pressures of bureaucratic and political systems. When they operate in competitive domains, as several do, they must balance their domain commitments while remaining viable. When they operate in hostile environments, as some of the more radical, social-change- and social-justice-oriented SDOs (D'Souza, 1984) do, they need to fend off hostile acts from vested interests by forming coalitions and engaging in other political behaviors. Such are their daunting missions and difficult operating domains that they need to master organic as well as mechanistic, entrepreneurial as well as professional management modes, and management failures can be very costly—not only to the organizations themselves but also to their domains (Khandwalla, 1988). They need to pursue distinctive compliance strategies, learning strategies, innovation diffusion strategies (within the domain), and autonomy strategies (Khandwalla, 1990). These include setting up specialized institutions for domain development, coopting leading elements of the domain into the SDO's decision-making processes, and withdrawing from activities not because they have turned into "dogs" but because the domain-development mission has been substantially achieved.

Since SDOs pursue domain-development missions, the primary criteria appropriate for assessing their performance go beyond conventional indicators to measure the extent to which the SDOs have pioneered or innovated products, services, methodologies, or processes that yield positive externalities for their domains; strengthened (and not merely exploited) underdeveloped client systems (Mehta, 1988; Tandon and Brown, 1981); networked and collaborated with other organizations to further social goals (Brown, 1988, 1993); promoted social change and awareness about alternative, more autonomous, more value-based lifestyles; and inculcated in themselves and their domains a culture of social achievement, democratic and collaborative functioning, and positive innovation (Khandwalla, 1988).

The strategic developmental role can be played by almost any organization in any domain. Even in the wealthiest societies, most domains may be grossly deformed in relation to what they may be a hundred years hence (or even now) in terms of quality-of-life indicators. Any organization can play an SDO role if it has a vision of excellence for its domain and conceptualizes the strategic role the organization can play in transforming its domain.

Institution Building

The concern with institution building became acute during an altruistic phase of American foreign policy following the Second World War, when the United States provided developmental assistance to many poor countries. Somehow the organizations that were set up to channel this developmental assistance did not function well, and so the question arose, How can formal, artificially created organizations designed to optimize technical efficiency be turned into proactive, adaptive organizations that respond to social needs and pressures and internalize the aspirations of the communities they serve (Selznick, 1957)? These institutions were intended to have a strong normative orientation and a strong commitment to performing socially valued functions and services (Esman, 1972). This implies that their internal structures, systems, and processes would be impregnated with positive social norms and values and that they would affect their environment in positive ways (Pareek, 1981). Institution-building organizations play role-model and positive-change-agent roles, and the test of normative institutionalization for them is not how profitable or efficient they are but how socially relevant their activities are, how values-driven their operations are, and how positive their social impact is. Although institution building has an obvious synergy with the SDO role, its relevance extends to any organization with a social conscience.

The literature on institution building suggests that the key components of an effective institution-building organization may be its leadership, the doctrine or ideology it espouses, its program of action for delivering services, the resources it needs, and the internal structure and processes established for operating and maintaining it. Meeting social needs effectively makes it almost obligatory for the organization to network with others and develop various kinds of linkages (Pareek, 1981). These linkages include those with entities on which the organization depends for resources (enabling linkages), those with entities performing functions or providing services that are complementary in an input-output or production sense to those provided by the organization (functional linkages), and those with entities that incorporate norms and values relevant to the doctrine and program of the organization (normative linkages). Institution building may proceed in cycles: formulation of a fresh idea, concretization into programs and activities, review and consolidation, multiplication of impact through innovation diffusion, networking, and so on (Pareek, 1981).

Various institution-building processes and mechanisms have been identified (Ganesh, 1979). Effectively managed processes and mechanisms contribute to the movement toward institutionalization; ineffectively managed processes impede it (Ganesh, 1980). These processes and mechanisms include birth, start-up, development-related, renewal, and institutionalization processes. Some of the more interesting subprocesses are choice of form (corporate versus, say, cooperative), choice of a role-model organization, early leadership selection, initial resource and support mobilization, culture creation and boundary management, choice of decision-making processes and control mechanisms, choice of leadership style (openness, innovation orientation, and so on), building up a distinctive organizational identity, change in leadership, creation of internal mechanisms for voicing dissent or new perspectives, mission redefinition, communicating with organizational stakeholders, and such environmental-impact processes as knowledge or expertise dissemination. Effective institution building may be evidenced by three criteria (Ganesh, 1980): the extent of the organization's capability development, the extent of its innovative thrusts or unique contributions, and its domain penetration.

Institution building may require the organization's leadership to perform several distinctive tasks (Pareek, 1981), such as identity creation, development of various kinds of resources, identification of synergies between various resources and various activities, balancing staff compliance with staff creativity, external networking, envisioning the future and preparing the organization to adapt to it, conceiving and implementing the organization's (positive) social-impact strategy, and providing superordination to organizational members (for example, by articulating and promoting a mission for the organization). *How* these tasks are performed may be as important as whether or not they are achieved. Trust, collaboration, self-dispensation, and concern for people and their growth become key ingredients of leadership (Ganesh, 1979; Ganesh and Joshi, 1985; Pareek, 1981). The motives that can sustain such behavior may be a desire for power not for its own sake but for increasing the influence of the organization (McClelland, 1961); concern for people, the organization, and society (Pareek, 1968); and a desire for creativity, pioneering, and innovation (Khandwalla, 1994). Institutional managers—that is, managers that develop their organizations or build business empires—seem to score relatively high on measures of psychosocial maturity, be more organization-centered than self-centered, like to work hard, be willing to sacrifice for the welfare of their organization, and have a keen sense of justice (McClelland and Burnham, 1976).

The Institute of Engineering and Rural Technology (IERT) at Allahabad in Northern India offers an interesting example of institution building in a relatively uncongenial climate (Gupta and Kalra, n.d.). This is a much-sought-after polytechnic institute that offers engineering diploma courses in some fifteen areas and nonengineering diploma courses in management, rural technology, and management of rural development. It runs a "technical hospital"—a training-and-production center that provides real-life learning situations and produces wooden and steel furniture, plastic products, sewing machines, farm equipment, biogas plants, windmills, various consumer products, rural industrial equipment, and so on. It also develops and markets curricula and educational aids for educational programs in India and abroad. It has set up a center for the development of rural technology and a wind-energy research center, and it offers a course in hotel management. In a region where the prevailing ethic is characterized by indolence, corruption, intrigue, dirty politics, casteism, and nepotism, this institute stands out as a beacon of the exaltation of the mundane. How did this institution grow? Researchers have identified several mechanisms. These included members' being aware of the institute's history and taking pride in it, a shared vision of development through technology, and a norm that stresses training practitioners to produce results with minimum resources. At the daily morning meeting the faculty discusses current issues and arrives at consensus solutions. IERT's early leaders set an example for self-sacrifice, staff empowerment, the encouragement of innovation and flexibility, risk taking, and practical applications of expertise. Its leadership style, institutionalized even at lower levels, is nurturing and supportive but also demanding of excellence. There is a strong emphasis on working on real-life problems, on involving staff in designing and implementing new ventures, on hiring the best and the brightest, and on inviting outside experts to visit IERT and contribute to its initiatives. IERT avoids punishment and instead emphasizes fun, freedom, and autonomy as major motivators. It employs a matrix structure, with various interdisciplinary committees, and activity centers with high autonomy (although their activities are periodically reviewed by the head of IERT). The faculty is encouraged to offer consulting services and to grow professionally by acquiring higher qualifications, attending conferences, going abroad for exposure, and so on. The pay scales are higher than standard polytechnic-institute grades, and IERT also provides many staff benefits. Although IERT takes government money, it wards off bureaucratic and political interference by means a number of devices: getting many VIPs to visit its campus, organizing high-profile seminars and workshops, getting funds from industry and various governments, earning money through marketing its products and services, networking with like-minded organizations in India and abroad, and displaying credible performance.

Organizational Ethics

Every decision involves choices, and almost all choices may have moral implications, even if these are frequently overlooked. Thus all humans and their institutions are moral entities and at some time or other have to confront issues of good and bad and right and wrong. Hosmer (1994) has listed ten frequently cited ethical principles. Besides the Friedman (1970) rule of maximizing profits (subject to legal constraints), they are as follows: avoid actions that

- Are not in one's long-term interests
- Are not transparently honest
- Are not kind and compassionate and do not build a sense of community and shared goals
- Are illegal
- Result in greater social harm than good (the utilitarian rule)
- One would not like similarly placed individuals to take (the Kantian categorical imperative)
- Abridge the legitimate rights of others
- Harm the least powerful (the Rawls rule)
- Interfere with the right of individuals for self-development and self-fulfillment (based on Maslow's self-actualization norm)

Such a plethora of proscriptions is likely to paralyse decision making, because of conflicts between principles or difficulties in interpreting them in particular situations. Human beings must therefore search for and adopt those moral principles or heuristics that resonate with their core convictions and values. This is also true of organizations and other institutions that humans build.

Schwartz (1983) has argued that humans want to discharge their moral obligations, and people vary in terms of the potency of this desire. Whatever embryonic moral motive may be there at birth may become vastly elaborated through socialization processes, and there may be several stages of moral development in humans (Kohlberg, 1964). Analogically, organizational scholars have attempted to conceptualize stages of the moral development of business organizations. Reidenbach and Robin (1991) have indicated five ascending stages, with illustrative examples. The base stage is the amoral organization. It seeks to win at any cost and with any means, including, for example, exposing workers to life-threatening substances, in violation of safety codes, for the sake of profits. The next higher stage is the legalistic stage, consisting of abiding by the letter of the law. An example may be Ford's recall of the unsafe Pinto car only after it was ordered to do so by the U.S. National Highway Traffic Safety Administration. The third stage is the responsive organization, which goes somewhat beyond profitability and legalistic concerns and attempts to strike a balance between making a profit and doing the right thing. As an example, rather than wait for government orders, Procter & Gamble withdrew its Rely tampon when it was confronted with nonconclusive evidence of harm it might do to users.

The next stage is characterized by the "emergent ethical" organization, in which there is a much greater tilt toward ethics, based on the recognition on the part of management of a social contract between business and society. Such organizations adopt codes of conduct that are elaborated in handbooks and policy statements, in committees, by ombudsman, in ethics training programs, and so on. For example, General Mills has developed guidelines for ethically dealing with competitors, customers, and vendors, and in its recruitment decisions it looks for ethical values in job applicants. Johnson & Johnson not only has a lofty credo but acted quickly and at great cost ($80 million) in recalling Tylenol during the tampering scare of the 1980s. The fifth and highest stage is that of the ethical organization, which is characterized by organization-wide acceptance of a common set of ethical values that permeate all organizational actions. A possible example is the Alacrity Foundation, a private sector company in the business of building urban housing (Karnad, 1990). In India this industry is notably corrupt. Alacrity's core value is completely ethical business practices, which it follows routinely. For instance, in one housing project there was great customer dissatisfaction due to uncontrollable delays resulting from government sanctions. Most construction firms do nothing in such cases. However, Alacrity voluntarily made cash payments to its customers to compensate them. In another housing project the customers complained that the water supplied to them was unfit for use. Alacrity arranged to supply good water by tanker for five years. In a third project a government department threatened to disconnect the sewer line on a technicality, possibly to extort a bribe. Alacrity offered to relay an entire sewer line at its own cost. Alacrity acquired such a strong reputation for ethics that in several cases the government dropped legal proceedings related to apartments built by Alacrity.

A wide variety of shapers of ethical behavior in organizations have been identified (Stead, Worrell, and Stead, 1990). These include employees' early socialization, background, and personalities; the organization's management philosophy; the behaviors the organization reinforces; the context in which the organization operates, and so on. Identification of these factors has led to several suggestions for institutionalizing ethical behavior in organizations. These include example setting by managers, especially the chief executive; screening of potential employees for their ethical credentials and orientation; development of a code of ethics; training employees in ethics by exposing them to various sorts of ethical dilemmas and the ethical decision-making heuristics they could use; rewarding of ethical behaviors, including whistle-blowing; punishment of unethical behaviors; and the creation of roles and structural mechanisms, such as an ethics monitoring committee or a code of ethics committee, to deal with ethics issues. A further mechanism that indirectly reinforces ethical behavior is an emphasis on professionalism and participative, consensus-based decision making, since professionalism involves at least some indoctrination into professional ethics, and consensus-based, participative decision making is likely to increase the probability that ethical concerns will be voiced and considered.

Ethical behavior is not only an end unto itself; it can also have practical consequences for organizational effectiveness. Obviously, in a society that values ethics, an ethical organization is likely to enjoy a privileged position and social goodwill. This may lower its operating costs (Williamson, 1975) and lower the costs of attracting and retaining human and other resources. In a predominantly pragmatic and utilitarian society, however, ethical stances may create handicaps for organizations by constraining their options.

The different value systems of different people may buttress different systems of ethical behavior in organizations (Etzioni, 1988; Musser and Orke, 1992; Rokeach, 1973). Rokeach distinguishes between terminal (that is, end-states-related) and instrumental (that is, means-related) value types. Further, he conceives both to be either socio-centric (society-centered, interpersonal) or self-centric (self-centered, intrapersonal, concerned with personal competence). Musser and Orke used this fourfold categorization to develop a typology of organizational moral systems. A terminal socio-centric and instrumental self-centric competence value system was termed the value system of the "Effective Crusader"; a terminal socio-centric and instrumental self-centric moral value system was called that of the "Virtuous Advocate"; a terminal self-centric and instrumental competence-oriented value system was called that of the "Independent Maximizer"; and a terminal and instrumental self-centric moral value system was called that of the "Honorable Egoist." Musser and Orke's data indicated that the Independent Maximizer type tended to have the highest score on Machiavellianism (deception, manipulation, deceit), while the Honorable Egoist type tended to have the lowest score on Machiavellianism, closely led by the Virtuous Advocate type. An implication of these findings seems to be that the neoclassical economic system idealized by Friedman and his followers may rest on or result in a Machiavellian value system in which organizational ethics may be discounted.

Organizational Justice

Rawls (1971) claimed justice to be the prime virtue of social institutions. Just organizational systems may increase identification with the organization and thus increase organizational effectiveness; unjust systems, by contrast, may be alienating. The major ingredients of organizational justice appear to be distributive justice and procedural justice (Greenberg, 1990). Distributive justice relates to the question of fairness in paying or rewarding various categories of stakeholders (particularly employees), and procedural justice relates to fairness in the processes used to resolve issues and conflicts (Aram and Salipante, 1981). Several principles of distributive justice have been adumbrated (Reidenbach and Robin, 1991), such as equal shares for all and the distribution of shares based on need, rights, effort, social contribution, or merit. Empirical work suggests that, in terms of performance appraisals, the main elements of procedural justice in U.S. organizations are solicitation of input from those being evaluated prior to making a judgment, two-way communication during the evaluation process, facility in challenging and rebutting evaluations, evaluators' familiarity with the work of persons being evaluated, and consistent application of standards of evaluation (Greenberg, 1986a, 1986b). In

Greenberg's study, subjects' perception of distributive justice in their organizations appeared to be related to their receiving ratings based on their actual performance and emoluments and promotion recommendations based on fair and objective criteria. In the United States, procedural justice measures seem to be related to such aspects of organizational effectiveness as trust in management, job satisfaction, and organizational commitments (Alexander and Ruderman, 1987; Folger and Konovsky, 1989), and distributive justice measures seem to be related to pay satisfaction and satisfaction with verdicts (Folger and Konovsky, 1989; Tyler, 1984).

Organizational Altruism

Organizational altruism has to do with helping behavior in and by organizations. It may be rooted in the biological need of mammals to nurture their young, or possibly in an instinct for symbiosis, which makes us want to help others out of enlightened self-interest (Sherrington, 1964). Some scholars have postulated an altruistic motive in humans that goes beyond instinctual nurturance and cooperation, however (Hoffman, 1981; Kanungo and Conger, 1993; Pareek, 1968; Rushton, 1984). As Kanungo and Conger point out, altruistic behavior requires a conception of an extended self, one that incorporates the interests of others besides oneself in one's priorities. Indeed, some economists have postulated that humans have dual utility functions—one relating to priorities for oneself and the other to those for the group, community, or society one belongs to—and suggested the possibility of trade-offs between the two (Margolis, 1982). Pareek (1968) has postulated an extension motive in people, one that impels them to be concerned for the well-being and development of others. Mehta (1982) has identified and measured a social achievement motive—that is, a motive to get a collectivity (like one's organization or community) to perform excellently. Extension and social achievement motives may be critically important in promoting liberation movements, human development, and socioeconomic transformations, and they may play a critical role in organizations' commitment to social responsibility, domain development, and institution building.

Kanungo and Conger (1993) have defined altruistic behavior in organizations as any work-related behavior that benefits others regardless of any benefits to the self. Altruism is the basis of what has been called prosocial behavior in the organizational context. Prosocial behavior is behavior that a person engages in voluntarily to benefit others, without expecting material or social rewards in return (Brief and Motowidlo, 1986). It is disinterested helping behavior. Brief and Motowidlo list several specific kinds, such as assisting coworkers with job-related and personal matters; providing services, products, or personal services to customers even when this collides with the interests of the organization; suggesting various work-related improvements; objecting to improper orders, policies, or procedures; contributing extra effort; volunteering for additional assignments; and staying with the organization despite hardships. It has been suggested that organizations with strong reciprocity norms (Gouldner, 1960), responsibility norms (Berkowitz and Daniels, 1963), altruistic role models, leadership styles, and organizational climates promote prosocial behavior among their members (Brief and Motowidlo, 1986). An organization in which prosocial behavior has become a way of life may well exhibit prosocial behavior in its domain.

Several examples of organizational—specifically, corporate—altruism are available. In the United States, corporations like Montgomery Ward and Westinghouse have funded large programs for training the hard-core unemployed; IBM and Xerox have given paid leaves to executives to allow them to contribute their time to socially beneficial projects; and the National Alliance of Businessmen has found jobs for hundreds of thousands of young persons (Moch and Seashore, 1981). In India, too, several corporations have distinguished altruistic records (Khandwalla, 1995). For example, Hindustan Lever has adopted an orphanage in which its managers and their family members make contributions in their spare time, and it runs a rural development project in Northern India.

Radical Humanism

Radical humanism seeks to emancipate humans from repressive social, occupational, and ideological conditions and bring them to the center stage in the affairs of the systems they inhabit (Alvesson and Wilmott, 1992). Theoretically, such emancipation leads to the fuller development and articulation of human consciousness and greater autonomy in personal, organizational, and social life.

Strongly influenced by the concept of alienation propounded by Marx, one form of radical humanism offers, through the application of critical theory, a powerful critique of profit-oriented functionalism in corporate management. This functionalism results in unilateral power to make decisions and allocate resources in the hands of management;

fragmentation of work and overspecialization, which makes work meaningless; the absence of dialogue and opportunities for self-expression at work; dishonesty toward employees; the objectification of human beings; narrow economism and utilitarianism; and so on (Aktouf, 1992; Burrell and Morgan, 1979; Clegg and Dunkerley, 1977; Freire, 1983). While "bourgeois" humanism is all right as far as it goes (in terms of such "top-down" managerial tools as limited participative management, human relations, transformational and visionary leadership, the total quality movement, and so on), what is really worth pursuing is the struggle for individual and collective self-determination (Alvesson and Wilmott, 1992), ownership of organizations by their workers, industrial democracy (Emery and Thorsrud, 1969; Rhenman, 1968), and empowerment of employees (Block, 1987).

Aktouf (1992) has provided an example of what may be close to a radical-humanist theory of management. Cascades, Inc., a billion-dollar pulp and paper multinational based in Quebec, was started almost from scratch in 1963 by three brothers and their father in a small Quebec town. Aktouf found that the company had no organizational charts and almost no official positions, job descriptions, time sheets, supervisory control, and so on. The structure was relatively flat, with just three or four "symbolic" levels of hierarchy. There was "self-management" in everything through self-management teams, and there were direct, informal relations and frank exchanges at all levels. There was an open-book policy concerning all information, including financial information; access to executive offices for all employees; profit sharing by all employees (unrelated to individual productivity), and so on. Employees apparently reported that they were cared for and respected. In spite of (or because of) this nonhierarchical, organic mode of management, Cascades apparently had consistently achieved profitability levels that compared favorably with industry standards, and it weathered recessions better than most of its competitors.

Radical humanism need not derive its inspiration solely from Marx. It can also be inspired by Freudian and Maslowian perspectives (respectively, the promise of liberation from internal oppressors, resulting in mental health, and fulfillment of higher-order needs for self-actualization). Organizational (or, indeed, social) oppressors include not only the "objective" technological and economic conditions of work but also a repressive, authoritarian culture that condemns human beings to suffer neuroses, stunted personalities, psychoses, and so on (Argyris, 1956; Maslow, 1954). Management practices can exact a fearful toll in terms of human sickness. In one U.S. study of thirteen thousand employees of sixteen subsidiaries of a large corporation, some 20 percent of the variations on an index of aggregate health symptoms were accounted for by such variables as perceived lack of management concern for individuals' needs, perceived ill treatment of employees, and perceived discrimination (on the basis of race, gender, and so on) (Smith, Kaminstein, and Makodok, 1995). Suggested remedies have included approaches that take into account not only technological and economic considerations but also psychological considerations in designing systems (Trist and Bamforth, 1952), job enrichment to make work more interesting (Herzberg, 1966), organizational development interventions (Golembiewski, 1988), participative redesign of work (Kanawaty and Thorsrud, 1981), and the empowerment of subordinates by supervisors (Block, 1993; Greenleaf, 1987, Sergiovanni, 1992).

Organizational Spirituality

Spirituality refers to the experience of the divine, the underlying unity of all things and beings, an ineffable bliss that is beyond any mundane, sensory pleasure (James, 1960). Saints have commonly considered the quest for spirituality to be the ultimate human journey. Can organizations, usually set up and operated to achieve mundane goals such as making profits, conducting elections, healing patients, or educating people, be spiritual? If so, what is the nature of organizational spirituality?

Organizations can, of course, have spiritual goals, as do religious organizations in the business of salvation. A larger number can employ or try to employ spiritual means in their mundane work, a pursuit that is not as paradoxical as it sounds. Almost the entire message of the *Bhagavad Gita* (the "Song of God") amounts to being spiritual in worldly matters, doing one's duty as an offering to God, and working without the expectation of reward. The ascetic Protestant Ethic also seems to be close to this idea (Weber, 1958). Singer's studies of South Indian entrepreneurs (1982) indicate that the commitment to create wealth without coveting it (because wealth creation is the special calling of the businessman) is not a sham but a living tradition that enables the entrepreneur to be a shrewd, even callous industrialist but also enables him or her to be religious and charitable. In the West, "Christian businesses" apparently are quite widespread (Ibrahim, Rue, McDougall, and Greene, 1991). While these companies are profit oriented, they also engage in the proselytization of their employees, customers, and suppliers and support Christian organizations and charities.

Gandhi's concept of trusteeship (Dantwala, 1991) is a refinement of organizational spirituality. It is not enough to create wealth without coveting it; the businessman must also administer wealth as a trustee for society, especially workers and other stakeholders. While management must be efficient, spirituality is manifest in the utilization of profits and wealth. Gandhi also advocated purity of means, so that spirituality is manifest as well in the running of the business.

Chakraborty has strongly advocated spirituality in management (1985, 1993, 1995). A trenchant critic of self-centered individualism and of the greed and selfishness that characterizes the corporate order in India today, he has sought to trace the evils of contemporary Indian business organizations—such as interpersonal and interdepartmental conflicts, corruption, waste, lethargy, money-mindedness, opportunism, unfair competition, and so on—to godlessness. If only decision makers would become aware that they share with all others the same immanent divinity, if only they could experience the fraternity of the universal Self, then their pettiness would fall away, and they would be able to tackle with far greater equanimity and selflessness the pressing problems of their organization. A more wholesome mind-set would prevail, and through a contagion effect others too would become more spiritual and ethical, and the problems that arise from pettiness and selfishness would thus subside.

The journey toward spiritual management begins with the individual manager. In the Indian tradition, through yoga, meditation, faith in God and in one's own intrinsic divinity, and introspection, a pure mind receptive to wholesome values can be achieved. These values include selfless work, work as a calling, and commitment to discharge one's obligations rather than assert one's rights. Chakraborty has reported that several Indian corporations have organized values-based workshops for their managers. Results suggest that these workshops enhance managers' relationships at work, ethical sensitivity, ability to cope with stress, creativity, personal life, and domestic life (Chakraborty, 1993).

Chakraborty (1995) has castigated contemporary models of leadership as "dealership." As alternatives he offers "wisdom leadership" and the *rajarshi* leader, who embodies truth, order, justice, and goodness and induces the eternal order of the cosmos (*rita*) into the logos of society. This eternal order is to be grasped intuitively by stilling the mind and anchoring it within the Self, the "state of quiescent unconditional awareness" (p. 209). It is this Self that provides guidance in all matters. Deep breathing, cleaning the mind of egotism, introspection, meditation, concentration, hunger for accessing the all-pervasive intelligence, prayer, and so on facilitate this stilling and anchoring. The *rajarshi* leader is free from fear, insecurity, and narcissistic power hunger. He promotes goodness rather than pleasantness. He sees at once, and clearly, the whole reality rather than comprehending reality in fragments and through successive approximations (compare to Simon's bounded rationality [1960]). He comprehends the working of the cosmic order in everything and gives primacy to detached performance of his duty and appointed role over self-interest and other distortions. The *rajarshi* is not one who shirks action but rather one who acts wisely.

The Swadhyay (meaning self-study and self-development) Movement in India provides a remarkable example of an organization that uses spiritual means to pursue spiritual goals and in the process generates amazingly good mundane consequences (Prakash, 1996; Srivastava, 1986). The mission of this movement, which was founded in the fifties, is spiritual development of individuals and society. Its main inspiration is Hindu philosophy concerning the universal immanence of God. The movement seeks to demonstrate its practical utility. Its core values stress the spiritual fraternity of all humans, reliance on the force of one's conscience for solving life's problems, the dignity of lowly work, reform of ossified cultures to revitalize them, love, knowledge, effort without expectation of reward as a foundation of individual and social development, and full involvement in life rather than escaping from it. The basic discipline is one of transcending egotism through *bhakti,* or devotion to God, and self-purification to release *nipunata* ("expertise") as an offering to God. The movement seeks social transformation through spiritual self-transformation rather than through social engineering (formal education, planned development, "conscientization," and the like) (Freire, 1983). The chief methodology adopted by the movement is *bhakti pheri,* or trips of devotion and love by adherents to local communities. In these trips the adherents neither preach nor seek converts nor accept any food or hospitality. Instead they simply talk about the divine brotherhood of humans, their personal experiences of self-transformation, and their unconditional acceptance of others. But this seemingly simple methodology has spawned creative new activities like *krushibhakti,* or devotion to God, through farming and collective cultivation; collective fishing, as an offering to God, whose profits are distributed to the needy: construction of collective places of worship: collective planting of trees on barren lands: setting up of youth, educational, training, and research institutions related to spirituality, and so on. The movement's management is highly informal and decentralized, but it does have a charismatic and highly innovative founder-head.

The social impact of the Swadhyay Movement has been so remarkable that it has been described by some social scientists as an alternative to conventional models of socioeconomic development (Srivastava, 1986). As of 1996 it reportedly had an active membership of about two hundred thousand and a presence in eighty thousand villages (15 percent of Indian villages). In those communities in which it has been active, mainly low-caste and rural communities, caste barriers have been eroded, and drinking, gambling, thieving, smuggling, and wife beating have disappeared. Conducting the marriage ceremony, traditionally reserved for only the highest caste (the Brahmins), has been opened to lowest-caste women. Hygiene and cleanliness, never strong in India, have been institutionalized. There has been a highly perceptible improvement in living standards and quality of life. Over three thousand collectively farmed plots are in operation, and over nine thousand wells and dry lakes have been recharged by Swadhyay engineers and technicians, with local participation and without financial assistance from the government.

CONCLUSION

It is the thesis of this chapter that organizational greatness ascends on two legs. One leg is conventionally defined performance excellence, especially in a competitive context, as measured by the usual indicators for the type of organization in question. The other is exalted striving, in terms of some ethic, social concern, ideal, or exalted state.

A number of approaches to performance excellence have been discussed in this chapter—notably, the environmental selection or determination model associated with economics and population ecology, the strategic choice perspective, the organizational attributes approach, synergy between organizational elements, and the contingency fit approach. These approaches have been integrated into an organizational model based on a competitive domain. Several alternative paths of exaltation have been briefly discussed as well. These are stakeholder orientation, corporate social responsibility, strategic-domain development orientation, institution building, organizational ethics, organizational justice, organizational altruism, radical humanism, and organizational spirituality. These do not exhaust the possible paths to organizational exaltation. Others have been suggested, including love and joyous celebration (Upadhayaya, 1995), but the nine described here are relatively well researched and likely to be tenable in organizational contexts. Each of these nine paths involves an enlargement of organizational concerns and a sharpening of organizational responsiveness to human and social needs and moral and spiritual promptings. Embedded in these paths of exaltation are strategic choices of as much import as the better-known conventional strategic choices. Table 8.1 summarizes the core meaning, values, and instrumentalities of each of the nine paths of exaltation.

An interesting question is this: How feasible is it to fuse the mundane with the sublime? In a competitive domain, in which it takes a great deal of competence just to survive and the margin for "frills" is so small, can organizations afford the "luxury" of an ethical, spiritual, altruistic, or socio-centric posture? There is no easy answer to this question. But the numerous examples given here of organizations that have seemed to be able to successfully blend the mundane with the exalted do suggest that it is feasible, and possibly advantageous, to pursue the sublime along with the worldly.

Each path of organizational exaltation can be pursued at several levels. At a low level, most organizations need to comply with legal requirements or strong social expectations about moral, altruistic, or socially responsive conduct. At a modest level, most of these paths can be adapted to make them instrumental for competitive excellence. Thus, for example, keeping stakeholders happy can yield a competitive advantage, since stakeholder cooperation can provide lower coordination and transaction costs. Similarly, some demonstration of organizational ethics, social responsibility, justice, altruism, domain development, radical humanism, or spirituality can build up a positive image for the organization and therefore facilitate access to scarce resources and insulate the organization from market pressures, which in turn could help the organization in its competitive battles (Ford and McLaughin, 1984; Kanungo and Conger, 1993) and possibly inspire the staff to be more productive (Block, 1987). At a moderate level, the paths can be aspects of organizational functional rationality, subject to analysis of their incremental costs and benefits.

But beyond this point of easy synergy with conventional performance excellence, each path is clearly a thorny one, for walking hard on any of these paths *could* require sacrifices in terms of profitability, growth, market dominance, and other traditional management goals. Ethical qualms could rule out many shady but profitable ventures. A strong stakeholder orientation could sharply attenuate the imperative to maxi-

Table 8.1. Paths of Organizational Exaltation

	Core Meaning	Core Values	Some Instrumentalities
1. Stakeholder orientation	The organization's well-being is contingent on the cooperation of many stakeholders besides the owners, and therefore the organization is obligated to act in the interests of all of its stakeholders.	Enlightened self-interest; service to stakeholders.	1. Participation of stakeholders in organizational decision making (e.g. stakeholders' council(s)). 2. Application of "market orientation" to stakeholders to understand their needs. 3. Coalitional analysis of stakeholders, management of conflict between stakeholders. 4. Allocation of organizational resources to stakeholders in proportion to their contributions and legitimate demands.
2. Corporate social responsibility	The organization is a creature of society and therefore has a responsibility for the well-being of society. A sense of corporate social responsibility can temper the power of the larger, dominant organizations.	Reciprocity vis-à-vis society based on social contract. Subservience of the organization's narrowly defined interests to the social good.	1. Use of indicators of corporate social performance to assess the organization. 2. Enunciation and pursuit of corporate social policies vis-à-vis, such areas as environment, safety, employment of disadvantaged persons, pollution control, community action, etc.
3. Strategic domain development orientation	The organization's contributions to the development of the domain in which it operates, especially in societies in which domains of activity are poorly developed.	The organization as an instrument of socio-economic transformation of an under-developed society/sector; primacy to the development of its domain over its own narrowly defined interests; patriotism.	1. Assess strategic developmental organizations on criteria that emphasize externalities, social impact of their innovations and interventions, extent of strengthening of client systems, promotion of social change, and contribution to the emergence of a pro-active, demo-cratic, collaborative culture in the domain. 2. Distinctive domain compliance, learning, innovation diffusion, autonomy seeking strategies.

Table 8.1. (*continued*)

	Core Meaning	Core Values	Some Instrumentalities
4. Institution building	The processes by which an organization acquires internal and external legitimacy which enables it to play an effective social change agent role and be regarded as a model organization.	Commitment to a vision of societal excellence and to such core values as concern for social relevance of activities, democratic decision making, collaboration, and dignity and growth of individuals and groups.	1. Organization's social change ideology, program of action, and values-based internal systems and processes. 2. Networking with like-minded groups or complementary organizations for multiplying social impact. 3. Robust birth, start-up, growth-related, renewal, and institutionalization processes. 4. Assessment in terms of capability development, innovative thrust, and domain penetration. 5. Leadership that stresses superordinate goals, empowerment of stakeholders, self-dispensing role, mobilization of resources, creating synergies and links, building a unique organization.
5. Organizational ethics	Subjecting organizational choices to the test of whether they are right or wrong from a moral viewpoint.	Accountability, caring, conscientiousness, fairness, integrity, loyalty, promise-keeping, respect, etc.	1. Create a checklist of moral "do's" and "dont's" to guide decision making. 2. Institutionalize a code of organizational ethics and publicize it. 3. Provide training in ethical management. 4. Select ethical personnel. 5. Reward ethical actions and punish unethical ones. 6. Set up an ethics monitoring committee. 7. Emphasize professionalism and participative management so as to give voice to ethical concerns.

6. Organizational justice	Justice, fairness, transparency.	Emphasis on fairness in the internal and external dealings of the organization and observation of canons of justice in these dealings.	1. System of distributive justice in the organization for rewards-related decisions. 2. System of procedural justice in the organization for reaching staff evaluation decisions.
7. Organizational altruism	Enlightened self-interest; being one's brother's keeper.	Helping behavior by the organization and helping behavior in the organization regardless of benefit to the helper.	1. Recognition and reward for prosocial or helping behaviors within the organization. 2. Strengthening of altruistic, reciprocity, and responsibility norms in the organization. 3. Reinforcement of organizational citizenship behaviors like conscientiousness, courtesy, and sportingness. 4. Promotion of stewardship in the organization, that is, leader as servant, and the primacy of service over self-interest. 5. Empowerment, and more egalitarian distribution of resources within the organization.
8. Radical humanism	Centrality of the human and of the human's autonomy in all matters.	Emancipation of humans from repressive social, work-related, and ideological bonds, to enable them to develop and articulate fully their consciousness and experience greater autonomy.	1. Design of socio-technical systems. 2. Job enrichment. 3. OD. 4. Participative redesign of work. 5. Industrial democracy and empowerment of the workforce.
9. Organizational spirituality	Purity of means; self-control; surrender to God; detachment and inner calm; trusteeship and selflessness	Spiritual conduct at work: working without being attached to the fruits of action; work as an offering to the divine; perception of the divine in self and others and living experience of the fraternity of godliness; decisions influenced by spiritual considerations.	1. Spiritual transformation of the individual manager through yoga, prayer, meditation, etc. 2. Values examining workshops. 3. Wisdom leadership. 4. Attempt to integrate the organization with the cosmic order by letting the divine self guide decisions. 5. Reliance on trust and love as principles of interaction rather than mistrust and self-interest. 6. Proselytization of stakeholders besides owners and staff.

mize profits. A stringent domain-development orientation may require persistence in an activity that brings financial losses but yields positive externalities, or withdrawal from a highly lucrative initiative that yields no such externalities. A passion for institution building can require giving primacy to the process of *making* decisions over the decisions themselves and playing the role of social change agent instead of exploiting every market niche. A relentless pursuit of organizational justice can erode management prerogatives. Impassioned radical humanism can erase power and status differences between managers and workers. The achievement of organizational spirituality can sow profound doubts about the materialistic goals and means of the organization.

How might an organization tackle these thorns on its path to exaltation? Each of these nine paths is strongly normative and therefore capable of affecting pervasively the way an organization operates. A strong commitment to exaltation by the organization's management tends to introduce multiple discourses or mind-sets within the organization, greater diversity in the organization's goals, and, therefore, an increase in the organization's operating complexity. A necessary adaptive response to this increased complexity may be more differentiated strategies, structures, know-how, operating norms, and rules. But without more complex or uncommon forms of integration, superior performance on conventional as well as exaltation goals are unlikely in a competitive domain. Such integrators could include the development of a dedicated cadre of managers to pursue the full goal set, indoctrination of rank-and-file workers in an ideology and value system congruent with the new goal set, a recruitment and reward system that stresses progress toward achieving the full goal set, periodic reflection by organizational stakeholders on the implications of the enlarged goal set, an information system that disseminates to stakeholders information on the performance of the organization and its subunits vis-à-vis the full goal set, and a conflict resolution system that utilizes credible sages as mediators, conciliators, or judges. What is more, since the acceptance of a path toward exaltation implies much initial failing and learning, the organization must strive even harder to create slack (Cyert and March, 1963; Singh, 1986) to cushion these initial failures. This implies more creative, imaginative, and better-planned strategy formulation and implementation and more proactive and participative management styles. It may also imply vigorous networking with like-minded organizations and institutions, both for accelerated learning from common experiences and for mutual support during times of adversity or failure.

Finally, why organizational greatness? Contemporary society is profoundly shaped by organizations. Organizational greatness is desirable because of the boost it gives to the emergence of a more humane, ethical, and spiritual civilization. Civilization's future is clouded by crass materialism and epidemics of violence. A sophisticated id has been let loose in the global marketplace; it needs to be checked and sublimated for our collective good. Organizational goodness can restrain this id. The pursuit of normative organizational excellence is also desirable because attempts at fusing the mundane with the sublime may well provide a vast new impetus to management innovation and new organizational forms, which in turn can sustain managerial creativity in the coming decades.

In much of the world the Zeitgeist favors organizational exaltation. Will organizational researchers rise to the occasion and build a paradigm of organizational greatness? Will they show wisdom and courage?

REFERENCES

Ahiauzu, A. "The 'Theory A' System of Work Organization for the Modern African Workplace." *International Studies of Management and Organization,* 1989, *19*(1), 6–27.

Aktouf, O. "Management and Theories of Organization in the 1990s: Toward a Critical Radical Humanism." *Academy of Management Review,* 1992, *17*(3), 407–431.

Alexander, S., and Ruderman, M. "The Role of Procedural and Distributive Justice in Organizational Behavior." *Social Justice Journal,* 1987, *1,* 177–198.

Alvesson, M., and Wilmott, H. "On the Idea of Emancipation in Management and Organization Studies." *Academy of Management Review,* 1992, *17*(3), 432–464.

Aram, J. "The Paradox of Interdependent Relations in the Field of Social Issues in Management." *Academy of Management Review,* 1989, *14,* 266–283.

Aram, J., and Salipante, P., Jr. "An Evaluation of Organizational Due Process in Resolution of Employee/Employer Conflict." *Academy of Management Review,* 1981, *6,* 197–204.

Argyris, C. *Personality and Organization.* New York: HarperCollins, 1956.

Aupperle, K., Carroll, A., and Hatfield, J. "An Empirical Examination of the Relationship Between Corporate Social Responsibility and Profitability." *Academy of Management Journal,* 1985, *28*(2), 446–463.

Bennis, W., and Nanus, B. *Leaders: The Strategies for Taking Charge.* New York: HarperCollins, 1985.

Berkowitz, L., and Daniels, L. "Responsibility and Dependency." *Journal of Abnormal and Social Psychology,* 1963, 66, 429–437.

Berle, A., and Means, G. *The Modern Corporation and Private Property.* Old Tappan, N.J.: Macmillan, 1934.

Bhasin, M. *Inflation Accounting in Public Enterprises.* New Delhi: Amol, 1988.

Bhatt, K. *Research Report on Corporate Planning in Public Enterprises.* Hyderabad, India: Institute of Public Enterprises, 1985 (photocopied).

Bibeault, D. *Corporate Turnaround: How Managers Turn Losers into Winners.* New York: McGraw-Hill, 1982.

Block, P. *The Empowered Manager.* San Francisco: Jossey-Bass, 1987.

Block, P. *Stewardship: Choosing Service over Self-interest.* San Francisco: Berrett-Koehler, 1993.

Bowers, D., and Seashore, S. "Predicting Organizational Effectiveness with Four-Factor Theory of Leadership." *Administrative Science Quarterly,* 1966, *11*(2), 238–263.

Bracker, J., and Pearson, J., "Planning and Financial Performance of Small, Mature Firms." *Strategic Management Journal,* 1986, *7,* 503–522.

Brief, A., and Motowidlo, S. "Prosocial Organizational Behaviors." *Academy of Management Review,* 1986, *11,* 710–725.

Brown, D. "Private Voluntary Organizations and Development Partnerships." In P. Khandwalla (ed.), *Social Development: A New Role for the Organizational Sciences.* Thousand Oaks, Calif.: Sage, 1988.

Brown, D. "Development Bridging Organizations and Strategic Management for Social Change." In P. Shrivastava, A. Huff, and J. Dutton (eds.), *Advances in Strategic Management.* Greenwich, Conn.: JAI Press, 1993.

Burns, T., and Stalker, G. *The Management of Innovation.* New York: Tavistock, 1961.

Burrell, G., and Morgan, G. *Sociological Paradigms and Organizational Analysis.* Portsmouth, N.H.: Heinemann, 1979.

Carroll, A. "A Three-Dimensional Conceptual Model of Corporate Social Performance." *Academy of Management Review,* 1979, *4,* 497–505.

Chakraborty, S. *Human Response in Organizations: Towards the Indian Ethos.* Calcutta: Vivekananda Nidhi, 1985.

Chakraborty, S. *Management Transformation by Values: A Corporate Pilgrimage.* Thousand Oaks, Calif.: Sage, 1993.

Chakraborty, S. "Wisdom Leadership: Leading Self by the Self." *Journal of Human Values,* 1995, *1*(2), 205–220.

Chandler, A. *Strategy and Structure.* Cambridge, Mass.: MIT Press, 1962.

Chandler, A. *The Visible Hand.* Cambridge, Mass.: Harvard University Press, 1977.

Child, J. "Organizational Structure, Environment, and Performance: The Role of Strategic Choice." *Sociology,* Jan. 1972, pp. 2–22.

Child, J. "Managerial and Organizational Factors Associated with Company Performance. Part 1." *Journal of Management Studies,* 1974, *11*(3), 175–189.

Child, J. "Managerial and Organizational Factors Associated with Company Performance. Part 2." *Journal of Management Studies,* 1975, *12*(1), 12–27.

Clegg, S., and Dunkerley, D. *Critical Issues in Organizations.* New York: Routledge, 1977.

Covin, J., and Slevin, D. "The Influence of Organization Structure on the Utility of an Entrepreneurial Top Management Style." *Journal of Management Studies,* 1988, *25*(3), 217–234.

Cyert, R., and March, J. *A Behavioral Theory of the Firm.* Englewood Cliffs, N.J.: Prentice Hall, 1963.

Dantwala, M. "Trusteeship: An Alternative Ideology." *IASSI Quarterly,* 1991, *10*(1), 179–211.

Davis, K. "The Case for and Against Business Assumption of Social Responsibilities." *Academy of Management Journal,* 1973, *16,* 312–322.

Dill, W. "Public Participation in Corporate Planning: Strategic Management in a Kibitzer's World." *Long-Range Planning,* 1975, *8*(1), 57–63.

D'Souza, K. "Organizations as Agents of Social Change." *Vikalpa,* 1984, *9,* 233–247.

Editors of *World Executive's Digest. Management Japanese Style.* Bombay: India Book House, 1981.

Emery, F., and Thorsrud, E. *Form and Content in Industrial Democracy.* New York: Tavistock, 1969.

Esman, M. "The Elements of Institution Building." In J. Eaton (ed.), *Institution Building and Development.* Thousand Oaks, Calif.: Sage, 1972.

Etzioni, A. *The Moral Dimension: Toward a New Economics.* New York: Free Press, 1988.

Folger, R., and Konovsky, M. "Effects of Procedural and Distributive Justice on Reactions to Pay Raise Decisions." *Academy of Management Journal,* 1989, *32,* 115–130.

Ford, R., and McLaughlin, F. "Perceptions of Socially Responsible Activities and Attitudes: A Comparison of Business Deans and Corporate Chief Executives." *Academy of Management Journal,* 1984, *27,* 656–674.

Freeman, E., and Reed, D. "Stockholders and Stakeholders: A New Perspective on Corporate Governance." *California Management Review,* 1983, *15*(3), 88–106.

Freeman, R. *Strategic Management: A Stakeholder Approach.* New York: Ballinger, 1984.

Freire, P. *Pedagogy of the Oppressed.* Harmondsworth, England: Penguin, 1983.

Friedman, M. "The Social Responsibility of Business Is to Increase Its Profits." *New York Times Magazine,* Sept. 13, 1970, pp. 32 and following.

Galbraith, J. *The New Industrial State.* (2nd ed.) Boston: Houghton Mifflin, 1972.

Ganesh, S. "From Thin Air to Firm Ground: Empirical Guidelines for a General Process Model of Institution Building." *Human Relations,* 1979, *32*(9), 751–779.

Ganesh, S. "Performance of Management Education Institutions: An Indian Sampler." *Higher Education,* 1980, *9,* 239–253.

Ganesh, S., and Joshi, P. "Institution Building: Lessons from Vikram Sarabhai's Leadership." *Vikalpa,* 1985, *10*(4), 399–413.

George, P. "Diversified Indian Companies: A Study of Strategies and Financial Performance." Unpublished doctoral dissertation, Indian Institution of Management, Ahmedabad, India, 1984.

Gibbons, D. (ed.) *The Yunus Reader, Part II.* Selangor: Amanah Ikhtiar Malaysia, 1988.

Golden, B. "SBU Strategy and Performance: The Moderating Effects of the Corporate-SBU Relationship." *Strategic Management Journal,* 1992, *13,* 145–158.

Golembiewski, R. "OD Applications in Non-affluent Settings: Four Perspectives on Critical Action Research." In P. Khandwalla (ed.), *Social Development: A New Role for the Organizational Sciences.* Thousand Oaks, Calif.: Sage, 1988.

Gouldner, A. "The Norm of Reciprocity: A Preliminary Statement." *American Sociological Review,* 1960, *25,* 161–178.

Govindrajan, V., and Fisher, J. "Strategy, Control Systems, and Resource Sharing: Effects on Business-Unit Performance." *Academy of Management Journal,* 1990, *33*(2), 259–285.

Grant, C. "Friedman Fallacies." *Journal of Business Ethics,* 1991, *10,* 907–914.

Greenberg, J. "Determinants of Perceived Fairness of Performance Evaluations." *Journal of Applied Psychology,* 1986a, *71,* 340–342.

Greenberg, J. "The Distributive Justice of Organizational Performance Evaluations." In H. Bieroff, R. Cohen, and J. Greenberg (eds.), *Justice in Social Relations.* New-York: Plenum, 1986b.

Greenberg, J. "Organizational Justice: Yesterday, Today, and Tomorrow." *Journal of Management,* 1990, *16*(2), 399–432.

Greenleaf, R. *Servant Leadership: A Journey into the Nature of Legitimate Power and Greatness.* Mahwah, N.J.: Paulist Press, 1987.

Gupta, R., and Kalra, S. *Educational Innovations in the Backyard: An Organizational Study of Institute of Engineering and Rural Technology (IERT), Allahabad.* Lucknow, India: Indian Institute of Management, n.d. (photocopied).

Hall, W. "Survival Strategies in a Hostile Environment." *Harvard Business Review,* Sept.-Oct. 1980, pp. 75–85.

Hannan, M., and Freeman, J. "The Population Ecology of Organizations." *American Journal of Sociology*, 1977, *82*, 929–964.

Haveman, H. "Between a Rock and a Hard Face: Organizational Change and Performance Under Conditions of Fundamental Environmental Transformation." *Administrative Science Quarterly*, 1992, *37*, 48–75.

Herzberg, F. *Work and the Nature of Man*. Cleveland: World, 1966.

Hirschman, A. *Exit, Voice and Loyalty*. Cambridge, Mass.: Harvard University Press, 1970.

Hoffman, M. "Is Altruism Part of Human Nature?" *Journal of Personality and Social Psychology*, 1981, *40*, 121–137.

Hosmer, L. "Strategic Planning as if Ethics Mattered." *Strategic Management Journal*, 1994, *15*, 17–34.

Hrebeniak, L., and Joyce, W. "Organizational Adaptation: Strategic Choice and Environmental Determinism." *Administrative Science Quarterly*, 1985, *30*, 336–349.

Ibrahim, N., Rue, L., McDougall, P., and Greene, R. "Characteristics and Practices of 'Christian-Based' Companies." *Journal of Business Ethics*, 1991, *10*, 123–132.

James, W. *The Varieties of Religious Experience*. London: Colins, 1960.

Jennings, D., and Seaman, S. "High and Low Levels of Organizational Adaptation: An Empirical Analysis of Strategy, Structure, and Performance." *Strategic Management Journal*, 1994, *15*, 459–475.

Jones, T. "Instrumental Stakeholder Theory: A Synthesis of Ethics and Economics." *Academy of Management Review*, 1995, *20*(4), 404–439.

Jorgensen, J. "Organizational Life-Cycle and Effectiveness Criteria in State-Owned Enterprises: The Case of East Africa." In A. Jaeger and R. Kanungo (eds.), *Management in Developing Countries*. New York: Routledge, 1990.

Kanawaty, G., and Thorsrud, E. "Field Experiments with New Forms of Work Organizations." *International Labour Review*, 1981, *120*, 263–277.

Kanungo, R., and Conger, J. "Promoting Altruism as a Corporate Goal." *Academy of Management Executives*, 1993, *7*(3), 37–48.

Kapp, K. *The Social Costs of Private Enterprise*. New York: Schocken Books, 1971.

Karnad, A. "Value-Based Management." *Vikalpa*, 1990, *15*(3), 3–15.

Khandwalla, P. "Viable and Effective Organizational Designs of Firms." *Academy of Management Journal*, 1973, *16*, 481–495.

Khandwalla, P. *The Design of Organizations*. Orlando: Harcourt Brace, 1977.

Khandwalla, P. "Properties of Competing Organizations." In P. Nystrom and W. Starbuck (eds.), *Handbook of Organizational Design*. Vol. 1: *Adopting Organizations to Their Environments*. New York: Oxford University Press, 1981.

Khandwalla, P. "Pioneering Innovative Management: An Indian Excellence." *Organization Studies*, 1985, *6*(2), 151–169.

Khandwalla, P. "Generators of Pioneering-Innovative Management: Some Indian Evidence." *Organization Studies,* 1987, *8*(1), 39–59.

Khandwalla, P. "OB for Social Development: A Position Paper." In P. Khandwalla (ed.), *Social Development: A New Role for the Organizational Sciences.* Thousand Oaks, Calif.: Sage, 1988.

Khandwalla, P. "Strategic Developmental Organizations: Some Behavioural Properties." In A. Jaeger and R. Kanungo (eds.), *Management in Developing Countries.* New York: Routledge, 1990.

Khandwalla, P. *Organizational Designs for Excellence.* New Delhi: Tata McGraw-Hill, 1992a.

Khandwalla, P. *Innovative Corporate Turnarounds.* Thousand Oaks, Calif.: Sage, 1992b.

Khandwalla, P. "The PI Motive: A Resource for Socio-economic Transformation of Developing Societies." In R. Kanungo and M. Mendonca (eds.), *Work Motivation: Models for Developing Countries.* Thousand Oaks, Calif.: Sage, 1994.

Khandwalla, P. *Management Styles.* New Delhi: Tata McGraw-Hill, 1995.

Kohlberg, L. "Development of Moral Character and Moral Ideology." In L. W. Hoffman (ed.), *Review of Development Research.* New York: Russell Sage Foundation, 1964.

Kono, T. *Long-Range Planning of Japanese Corporations.* Hawthorne, N.Y.: Walter de Gruyter, 1992.

Lala, R. *The Creation of Wealth.* Bombay: IBH, 1981.

Lawrence, P., and Lorsch, J. *Organization and Its Environment.* Cambridge, Mass.: Harvard University Press, 1967.

Likert, R. *New Patterns of Management.* New York: McGraw-Hill, 1961.

Mahon, J., and Murray, E. "Strategic Planning for Regulated Companies." *Strategic Management Journal,* 1981, *2,* 251–262.

Margolis, H. *Selfishness, Altruism and Rationality: A Theory of Social Choice.* Cambridge, England: Cambridge University Press, 1982.

Markides, C. "Consequences of Corporate Refocusing: Ex Ante Evidence." *Academy of Management Journal,* 1992, *35*(2), 398–412.

Maslow, A. *Motivation and Personality.* New York: HarperCollins, 1954.

McClelland, D. *The Achieving Society.* New York: Van Nostrand Reinhold, 1961.

McClelland, D., and Burnham, D. "Power Is the Great Motivator." *Harvard Business Review,* 1976, *54*(2), 100–110.

McDougall, P., Covin, J., Robinson, R., Jr., and Herron, L. "The Effects of Industry Growth and Strategic Breadth on New Venture Performance and Strategy Content." *Strategic Management Journal,* 1994, *15,* 537–544.

McGuire, J., Sundgren, A., and Schneeweis, T. "Corporate Social Responsibility and Firm Financial Performance." *Academy of Management Journal,* 1988, *31*(4), 854–872.

McMillan, C. *The Japanese Industrial System.* (2nd ed.) Hawthorne, N.Y.: Walter de Gruyter, 1985.

Mehta, P. *Manual for Personal Achievement, Social Achievement and Influence Motivation.* New Delhi: Participation and Development Centre, 1982.

Mehta, P. "Organizing for Empowering the Poor." In P. Khandwalla (ed.), *Social Development: A New Role for the Organizational Sciences.* Thousand Oaks, Calif.: Sage, 1988.

Metcalfe, L. "Designing Precarious Partnerships." In P. Nystrom and W. Starbuck (eds.), *Handbook of Organizational Design.* Vol. 1: *Adopting Organizations to Their Environments.* New York: Oxford University Press, 1981.

Miles, R., and Snow, C. *Organizational Strategy, Structure, and Process.* New York: McGraw-Hill, 1978.

Miller, D. "Strategy Making and Structure: Analysis and Implications for Performance." *Academy of Management Journal,* 1987, *30,* 7–32.

Miller, D., and Friesen, P. *Organizations: A Quantum View.* Englewood Cliffs, N.J.: Prentice Hall, 1984.

Moch, M., and Seashore, S. "How Norms Affect Behaviors in and of Corporations." In P. Nystrom and W. Starbuck (eds.), *Handbook of Organizational Design.* Vol. 1: *Adopting Organizations to Their Environments.* New York: Oxford University Press, 1981.

Musser, S., and Orke, E. "Ethical Value Systems: A Typology." *Journal of Applied Behavioral Science,* 1992, *28*(3), 348–362.

Naman, J., and Slevin, D. "Entrepreneurship and the Concept of Fit: A Model and Empirical Tests." *Strategic Management Journal,* 1993, *14,* 137–153.

Nohria, N., and Ghoshal, S. "Differentiated Fit and Shared Values: Alternatives for Managing Headquarters—Subsidiary Relations." *Strategic Management Journal,* 1994, *15,* 491–502.

North, D. *Institutions, Institutional Change and Economic Performance.* Cambridge: Cambridge University Press, 1990.

Pareek, U. "A Motivational Paradigm of Development." *Journal of Social Issues,* 1968, *2,* 115–122.

Pareek, U. *Beyond Management: Essays on Institution Building Processes.* New Delhi: IBH, 1981.

Paul, S. *Managing Development Programs: The Lessons of Success.* Boulder, Colo.: Westview Press, 1982.

Pearce, J., II, and Zahra, S. "The Relative Power of CEOs and Boards of Directors: Associations with Corporate Performance." *Strategic Management Journal,* 1991, *12,* 135–153.

Perrow, C. *Complex Organizations: A Critical Essay.* New York: Random House, 1979.

Peters, T., and Waterman, R. *In Search of Excellence: Lessons from America's Best-Run Companies.* New York: HarperCollins, 1982.

Pfeffer, J., and Salancik, G. *The External Control of Organizations: A Resource-Dependence Perspective.* New York: HarperCollins, 1978.

Powell, T. "Organizational Alignment as Competitive Advantage." *Strategic Management Journal,* 1992, *13,* 119–134.

Prahalad, C., and Hamel, G. *Competing for the Future.* Boston: Harvard Business School Press, 1994.

Prakash, A. "The Bloodless Revolution." *Outlook,* Apr. 3, 1996, pp. 74–75.

Preston, L., and Post, J. *Private Management and Public Policy: The Principle of Public Responsibility.* Englewood Cliffs, N.J.: Prentice Hall, 1975.

Rawls, J. *A Theory of Justice.* Cambridge, Mass.: Harvard University Press, 1971.

Reidenbach, R., and Robin, D. "A Conceptual Model of Corporate Moral Development." *Journal of Business Ethics,* 1991, *10,* 273–284.

Reilly, B., and Kyj, M. "Economics and Ethics." *Journal of Business Ethics,* 1990, *9,* 691–698.

Rhenman, E. *Industrial Democracy and Industrial Management.* New York: Tavistock, 1968.

Rhyne, L. "The Relationship of Strategic Planning to Financial Performance." *Strategic Management Journal,* 1986, *7,* 413–436.

Rokeach, M. *The Nature of Human Values.* New York: Free Press, 1973.

Roth, K., and Ricks, D. "Goal Configuration in a Global Industry Context." *Strategic Management Journal,* 1994, *15,* 103–120.

Rumelt, R. *Strategy, Structure and Economic Performance.* Boston: Harvard Business School Press, 1974.

Rushton, J. "The Altruistic Personality: Evidence from Laboratory, Naturalistic and Self-Report Perspectives." In E. Staub, D. Bar-Tal, J. Karylowski, and J. Reykowski (eds.), *Development and Maintenance of Prosocial Behavior: International Perspectives on Positive Morality.* New York: Plenum, 1984.

Samuelson, P. *Economics.* (14th ed.) New York: McGraw-Hill, 1992.

Sanyal, R., and Neves, J. "The Valdez Principles: Implications for Corporate Social Responsibility." *Journal of Business Ethics,* 1991, *10,* 883–890.

Scherer, F. *Industrial Market Structure and Economic Performance.* Skokie, Ill.: Rand McNally, 1970.

Schwartz, H. "A Theory of Denotic Work Motivation." *Journal of Applied Behavioral Science,* 1983, *14,* 204–214.

Self-Employed Women's Association. *SEWA in 1988.* Ahmedabad, India: Self-Employed Women's Association, 1988.

Selznick, P. *Leadership in Administration.* New York: HarperCollins, 1957.

Sen, A. *On Ethics and Economics.* Cambridge, Mass.: Blackwell, 1987.

Sergiovanni, T. *Moral Leadership: Getting to the Heart of School Improvement.* San Franscisco: Jossey-Bass, 1992.

Shelton, L. "Strategic Business Fits and Corporate Acquisition: Empirical Evidence." *Strategic Management Journal,* 1988, *9*(2), 279–287.

Sherrington, C. "Altruism." In C. Sherrington (ed.), *Man on His Nature*. New York: Mentor, 1964.

Shrivastava, P. *Greening Business: Profiting the Corporation and the Environment*. Cincinnati: Thomson Executive Press, 1996.

Simon, H. *Administrative Behavior*. Old Tappan, N.J.: Macmillan, 1960.

Singer, M. "Industrial Leadership, the Hindu Ethic, and the Spirit of Socialism." In N. Sheth (ed.), *Industrial Sociology in India*. New Delhi: Allied, 1982.

Singh, H., and Montgomery, C. "Corporate Acquisition Strategies and Economic Performance." *Strategic Management Journal*, 1987, *8*, 377–386.

Singh, J. "Performance, Slack, and Risk Taking in Organizational Decision Making." *Academy of Management Journal*, 1986, *29*, 562–585.

Singh, J. (ed.). *Organizational Evolution: New Directions* Thousand Oaks, Calif.: Sage, 1990.

Singh, P., and Bhandarkar, A. *Corporate Success and Transformational Leadership*. New York: Wiley, 1990.

Sinha, J. "A Model of Effective Leadership Styles in India." In A. Jaeger and R. Kanungo (eds.), *Management in Developing Countries*. New York: Routledge, 1990.

Slatter, S. *Corporate Recovery: Successful Turnaround Strategies and Their Implementation*. Harmondsworth, England: Penguin Books, 1984.

Smith, K., and Grimm, C. "Environmental Variation, Strategic Change and Firm Performance: A Study of Railroad Deregulation." *Strategic Management Journal*, 1987, *8*, 363–376.

Smith, K., Kaminstein, D., and Makodok, K. "The Health of the Corporate Body: Illness and Organizational Dynamics." *Journal of Applied Behavioral Science*, 1995, *31*(3), 328–351.

Srivastava, R. "Swadhyaya Movement: Its Meaning and Message." Paper presented at a seminar of the U.N. University at Rome, September 1986.

Stead, W., Worrell, D., and Stead, J. "An Integrative Model for Understanding and Managing Ethical Behavior in Business Organizations." *Journal of Business Ethics*, 1990, *9*, 232–242.

Tan, J., and Litschert, R. "Environment-Strategy Relationship and Its Performance Implications: An Empirical Study of the Chinese Electronics Industry." *Strategic Management Journal*, 1994, *15*, 1–20.

Tandon, R., and Brown, L. "Organization Building for Rural Development: An Experiment in India." *Journal of Applied Behavioral Science*, 1981, *17*(2), 172–189.

Thomas, J., Clark, S., and Gioia, G. "Strategic Sensemaking and Organizational Performance: Linkages Among Scanning, Interpretation, Action and Outcomes." *Academy of Management Journal*, 1993, *36*(2), 239–270.

Thompson, J. *Organizations in Action*. New York: McGraw-Hill, 1967.

Thune, S., and House, R. "Where Long-Range Planning Pays Off." *Business Horizons*, 1970, *13*(4), 81–87.

Trist, E., and Bamforth, K. "Some Social and Psychological Consequences of the Longwall Method of Coal Mining." *Human Relations,* 1952, *4,* 3–38.

Tyler, T. "The Role of Perceived Injustice in Defendants' Evaluation of Their Courtroom Experience." *Law and Society Review,* 1984, *18,* 51–74.

Upadhayaya, P. "The Sacred, the Erotic and the Ecological: The Politics of Transformative Global Discourses." *Journal of Organizational Change Management,* 1995, *8*(5), 33–59.

Venkatraman, N., and Camillus, J. "Exploring the Concept of 'Fit' in Strategic Management." *Academy of Management Review,* 1984, *9*(3), 513–525.

Wartick, S., and Cochran, P. "The Evolution of the Corporate Social Performance Model." *Academy of Management Review,* 1985, *10,* 758–769.

Weber, M. *The Protestant Ethic and the Spirit of Capitalism.* London: Unwin, 1958.

Williamson, O. *Markets and Hierarchies: Analysis and Antitrust Implications.* New York: Free Press, 1975.

Wood, D. "Corporate Social Performance Revisited." *Academy of Management Review,* 1991, *16*(4), 691–718.

Zahra, S., and Covin, J. "Business Strategy, Technology Policy and Firm Performance." *Strategic Management Journal,* 1993, *14,* 451–478.

9

SOCIETAL LEADERSHIP:
THE WISDOM OF PEACE

Nancy J. Adler

WHY NOT HAVE PEACE in the twenty-first century? Would not wise leaders declare peace instead of continuing to resolve the world's conflicts through violence? Is this naively idealistic? Yes. Well, no; such wisdom only becomes naive from the parochial perspective of the last seven thousand years.

As Riane Eisler (1987) and others have observed, there have always been legends and writings about an earlier, more harmonious and peaceful age.[1] The Bible, for example, tells us of the Garden of Eden. But many, if not most, people assume that these are only idyllic fantasies, expressions of universal yearnings for seemingly impossible goals. Only now, thanks to new discoveries and new scientific dating methods, are archaeologists exposing the actual facts of our distant past (see Gimbutas, 1991).

New excavations reveal that these supposed legends derive from folk memories, not mere idealistic fantasies, about real flesh-and-blood people who organized their societies along very different lines from our own. For example, at Çatal Höyük and Hacilar, both located in modern-day Turkey, archaeologists date communities to 7,000 B.C., or ninety centuries ago. These communities were located in the middle of fertile plains, not in defensible positions against stone cliffs or atop mountains. Moreover, they were not surrounded by moats, stone walls, or other defense systems.

In addition, their art—which was plentiful given their easy access to food on the fertile plain—showed no sign of either individual- or community-level violence and only minimal indications of hierarchy.

Just as Columbus's discovery that the world was not flat made it possible to "find" a world that had been there all along, the archaeologists' new findings allow us today to rediscover communities that were organized peacefully and cooperatively with their neighbors. Their recent findings allow us to ground supposedly unattainable idealism in the reality of history. Perhaps not coincidentally, these communities were largely led by women.

IS A PEACEFUL WORLD POSSIBLE AGAIN?

What would it take to remarry such idealism with contemporary reality? First, we would need to again believe that peace is possible, that humanity is capable of living in peace. To that end, the archaeologists' findings are critical. Second, we would need to believe that change is possible, that society could move from a world organized around war to one organized around peace. Third, we would need to believe in the efficacy of nonmilitary solutions to societal problems. And fourth, we would need to move from the contemporary belief that a single country or army can "win" a war (while only their designated enemy loses) to the twenty-first-century truth that either all of humanity will win or no one will win; that is, we would need to move from discrete, open-system, international thinking to integrated, closed-system, global thinking. Finally, to embrace each of these beliefs needed for peace we would need new, wiser leaders and a style of leadership radically different from that of the last seventy centuries.

Where are we to find wise leaders to guide us toward such beliefs, which differ so markedly from those of the present? While many people in search of models for twenty-first-century global leadership continue to review men's historical patterns of success, few have even begun to appreciate the historical and potential contributions of women leaders (Adler, 1996). My personal search for leaders outside of twentieth-century paradigms has led me to review the voice that the world's women leaders are bringing to society. Let me briefly describe today's women leaders and then explain why the symbolism of their leadership and their actual approaches to leading may be a more likely source of the kind of leadership that will return us to peace.

The myth, of course, is that there are few global women leaders and that their assumption of power is not only rare but also sporadic.[2] One international survey, for example, concluded that less than .005 percent of the world's political leaders are women (Blondel, 1987). Although women presidents and prime ministers are still rare, twenty-seven women have held these offices in their country in recent years. Moreover, the number of women who hold the highest political office in their country is rapidly increasing, with half having come to power since 1990 (see Table 9.1 and Adler, 1996).[3] Given the current numbers, just over 5 percent of all nations currently have a woman as head of state. Although the public knows much too little about these women political leaders as a group, the question "Can a woman be a global leader?" is no longer salient. Clearly, these twenty-seven women presidents and prime ministers, along with their counterparts in business, have already definitely answered that question.[4]

THE SYMBOLISM OF WOMEN LEADERS: CHANGE IS POSSIBLE

Do societies believe that the fundamental ways in which they operate, especially in such crucial areas as war and peace, can change? Not usually; however, women's assumption of elite political office brings with it the symbolic possibility of fundamental societal change. The combination of women's becoming insiders at senior leadership levels previously completely controlled by men and of their beating the electoral odds produces powerful public imagery about the possibility of broad-based change in society. As "firsts," women in positions of political power bring change by definition.[5] Many are not only the first woman political leader in her country but also the first in her region.

If a woman can win high public office where no other woman has ever won before and few people think she can win, then other national changes become believable. Bookies gave Mary Robinson only a one-in-one-thousand chance of winning her first presidential election in Ireland (O'Neill, 1994). She won, and today she enjoys more than a 90 percent approval rating from the electorate (O'Neill, 1994). In her presidential acceptance speech she coupled the unique event of a woman's being elected president with the possibility of national change: "I was elected by men and women of all parties and none, by many with great moral courage who stepped out from the faded flags of Civil War and voted for a new Ireland. And above all by the women of Ireland—Mna na hEireann—who instead of rocking the cradle rocked the system, and who came out massively to make their mark on the ballot paper, and on a new Ireland" (quoted in Finlay, 1990, p. 1).

Table 9.1. Global Women Leaders: A Chronology.

Country	Name	Office	Date
Sri Lanka	Sirimavo Bandaranaike	Prime Minister	1960–1965, 1970–1977, 1994–1997*
India	(Indira Gandhi)	Prime Minister	1966–1977, 1980–1984
Israel	(Golda Meir)	Prime Minister	1969–1975
Argentina	(Maria Estela [Isabel] Martínez de Perón)	President 1974–1976	
Central African Republic	Elizabeth Domitien	Prime Minister	1975–1976
Portugal	Maria de Lourdes Pintasilgo	Prime Minister	1979
Great Britain	Margaret Thatcher	Prime Minister	1979–1990
Dominica	Mary Eugenia Charles	Prime Minister	1980–1995
Iceland	Vigdís Finnbógadottir	President	1980–1996
Norway	Gro Harlem Brundtland	Prime Minister	1981, 1986–1989, 1990–1996
Yugoslavia	Milka Planinc	Prime Minister	1982–1986
Netherland-Antilles	Mary Liberia-Peters	Prime Minister	1984, 1989–1994
The Philippines	Corazon Aquino	President	1986–1992
Pakistan	Benazir Bhutto	Prime Minister	1988–1990, 1993–1996
Lithuania	Kazimiera-Danute Prunskiene	Prime Minister	1990–1991
Haiti	Ertha Pascal-Trouillot	President	1990–1991
Myanmar (Burma)	Aung San Suu Kyi	Opposition Leader†	1990

Ireland	Mary Robinson	President	1990–1997*
Nicaragua	Violeta Barrios de Chamorro	President	1990–1996
Bangladesh	Khaleda Zia	Prime Minister	1991–1996
France	Edith Cresson	Prime Minister	1991–1992
Poland	Hanna Suchocka	Prime Minister	1992–1993
Canada	Kim Campbell	Prime Minister	1993
Rwanda	(Agatha Uwilingiyimana)	Prime Minister	1993–1994
Turkey	Tansu Çiller	Prime Minister	1993–1996
Sri Lanka	Chandrika Bandaranaike Kumaratunga	Executive President and Prime Minister	1994–1997*
Switzerland	Ruth Dreifuss	State Councilor‡	1995–1997*
Bangladesh	Hasina Wajed	Prime Minister	1996–1997*

( ) = No longer living.

*Still in office in 1997.

†Party won 1990 election but prevented by military from taking office; Nobel Prize laureate.

‡Switzerland governed by Council of (7) Ministers, rather than a president or prime minister.

Source: Adapted from Adler, 1996.

People see Robinson "as a representative of a changing Ireland" (Opfell, 1993, p. 186).

Similarly, commentators viewed Çiller's election as prime minister of Turkey as a sign and a confirmation of change. Because few women have played a major role in Turkish politics, Çiller's ascendancy was welcomed as a sign of Turkey's modernity (Lazerges, 1993), as a sign of change. This was particularly important at the time of Çiller's election, when Turkey, a predominantly Muslim country, was trying to communicate its modernity to the Christian countries of Europe in its bid to gain acceptance into the European Union.

When a woman first gains a nation's highest office, it symbolizes change simply because it is new, because women have not held that office before. It is perhaps not coincidental that a disproportionate number of the women who have achieved such an office—two-thirds of the twenty-seven women presidents and prime ministers on Table 9.1—have led countries experiencing major change. Nine led countries struggling to establish their independence,[6] and another nine led countries either attempting to reunite following a civil war or experiencing other forms of major societal upheaval, often including instituting new forms of government.[7]

A BACKGROUND BEYOND WAR

As noted previously, ancient history reveals that peace is possible. Countries selecting women for the first time as their president or prime minister reveal that change is possible. But why might we believe that, once in office, women are more likely than their male predecessors to bring peace? Why might women leaders be more likely to attempt to resolve world conflicts in ways other than through military intervention and war? The most immediate clue is that none of the world's current women leaders have a military background. In contrast with the majority of their male counterparts, none of the women leaders have had either military training or military experience prior to assuming office. If, even at the most minimal level, leaders draw on their personal experience in governing, then women must draw on personal resources other than familiarity with military strategies. As Burma's Aung San Suu Kyi (1995) described in her keynote address to the Beijing Conference on Women,[8]

> For millennia women have dedicated themselves almost exclusively
> to the task of nurturing, protecting and caring for the young and

the old, striving for the conditions of peace that favour life as a whole. To this can be added the fact that, to the best of my knowledge, no war was ever started by women. But it is women and children who have always suffered most in situations of conflict. Now that we are gaining control of the primary historical role imposed on us of sustaining life in the context of the home and family, it is time to apply in the arena of the world the wisdom and experience thus gained in activities of peace over so many thousands of years. The education and empowerment of women throughout the world cannot fail to result in a more caring, tolerant, just and peaceful life for all.

This is not to say that women leaders have not sent their countries into war; they have. However, given their backgrounds, their tendency to resort to military intervention is considerably less pronounced than that of their militarily trained male counterparts. When asked if she had ever killed anyone, Israel's former prime minister Golda Meir, who clearly knew the exigencies of war, described her very personal responsibility for war and death: "No. . . . I've learned to shoot, of course, but I've never happened to kill anyone. I don't say it as consolation—there's no difference between killing and making decisions by which you send others to kill. It's exactly the same thing. And maybe it's worse" (quoted in Fallaci, 1976, p. 122).

Nicaragua's president Violeta Chamorro symbolized her rejection of military solutions by having the guns she collected from both sides in Nicaragua's civil war thrown into an open pit and covered with cement. She then dropped roses, a symbol of life, on top of the entombed armaments (Saint-Germain, 1993).

Although she doubted she would see peace in her own lifetime, Golda Meir did believe that humanity's aspirations to move beyond war would one day be fulfilled: "War is an immense stupidity. I'm sure that someday all wars will end. I'm sure that someday children in school will study the history of the men who made war as you study an absurdity. They'll be astonished, they'll be shocked, just as today we're shocked by cannibalism. Even cannibalism was accepted for a long time as normal. And yet today, at least physically, it's not practised any more" (quoted in Fallaci, 1976, p. 95). Change is possible; peace is possible.

Burma's Aung San Suu Kyi underscores the necessity of changing not just the gender and stated goals of our leaders but also our fundamental perspective on the efficacy of material, military, and institutional solutions, before society can achieve any form of essential well-being, including peace:

The quintessential revolution is that of the spirit, born of an intellectual conviction of the need for change in those mental attitudes and values which shape the course of a nation's development. A revolution which aims merely at changing official policies and institutions with a view to an improvement in material conditions has little chance of genuine success. Without a revolution of the spirit, the forces which produced the inequities of the old order would continue to be operative, posing a constant threat to the process of reform and regeneration. A people who would build a nation in which strong, democratic institutions are firmly established as a guarantee against state-induced power must first learn to liberate their own minds from apathy and fear" [personal communication, 1996].

ONE WORLD, INDIVISIBLE

To create a world based on peace we must fully appreciate that the world we live in is indivisible and that therefore peace is for everyone or for no one. In the lingo of economics, peace is an externality. From the perspective of systems thinking, the world has shifted from an open to a closed system. Peace can only be created in the twenty-first century if it respects the dynamics of the closed global system in which we now live.

Global, Closed Systems Versus International, Open Systems

In 7,000 B.C. communities viewed themselves as local; that is, they saw themselves as discrete, closed systems. What people did only affected people living in their own community. As history unfolded, explorers and then businesspeople and armies began to voyage beyond the boundaries of the local community, beyond the parochial boundaries of previously closed systems. The ancient closed-system perspective was thus replaced by open-system, frontier thinking. By the nineteenth and twentieth centuries people regularly exported their ideas, ideologies, products, and, unfortunately, pollution beyond their local communities to all corners of the world. Only in the last few decades (from an environmental perspective) or years (from an economic perspective) have we begun to realize that we are again living in a closed system; not the local, community-based closed system of 7,000 B.C. but rather the global closed system of our planet. Anything we do in one part of the world can and will affect people in all other parts of the world. The impact of this shift is dramatic: radiation from Chernobyl pollutes vegetables grown in Sweden and then sold in Asia; the Internet frees

Chinese, North Korean, and Albanian citizens from the absolute control of their totalitarian governments; and so on. As the classic image from chaos theory explains, a butterfly flaps its wings and the air currents are changed two continents away. Although many political leaders appear not to have noticed, boundaries and borders have become all but meaningless (Adler, 1995). There is no longer a frontier or a foreign market in which what one does is either invisible or irrelevant to the rest of the world.

The Strategy of Peace: Global Unity Versus International Superiority

From the perspective of war and peace, the international, open-systems thinking of the twentieth century falsely allowed us to believe that wars in one part of the world would not affect people in other parts of the world. By contrast, peace in the global, closed system of the twenty-first century means seeking peace for everyone, not just for one country or one people.

In international, open systems, superiority defines peace. In the global, closed system, unity defines peace. Since there is no way to "win" a war through military superiority in a global, closed system, unifying strategies are the only viable option able to preclude world war.

WOMEN LEADERS AND WORLD PEACE

Does women's leadership center more on unifying strategies than men's leadership does? Beyond the asset of their lack of traditional, open-system military training and experience, what might women leaders bring to today's global, closed-system world? Women, it appears, tend to include the rest of the world in ways that have not been typical of most male leaders. Women leaders both symbolize unity (across time as well as within a territory) and, often, use distinctly unifying strategies. And perhaps, in the current transition to the twenty-first century, symbolism is more powerful than strategies.

First, today's women leaders, as a group, have a deeper and broader knowledge of the rest of the world than many of their male predecessors, and therefore they have a more profound understanding of others' points of view. Given the importance today of global understanding, it is noteworthy that two-thirds of today's women leaders were educated outside their home country. Moreover, perhaps because none of them planned to become president or prime minister, many have a breadth of education and experience that goes beyond more traditional leaders' narrow focus on economics, law, and political science. Perhaps Vigdís Finnbógadottir best symbolizes this cosmopolitan education: after finishing high school in her native Iceland she studied French literature and theater in France, theater in Denmark, French philosophy in Sweden, and, finally, English literature and education again in Iceland. Is it not more difficult to declare war on a people whose culture you know deeply and appreciate than it is to declare war on an unknown, objectified "enemy"? In the eloquent words of Burma's Aung San Suu Kyi (1995), "Without tolerance, the foundations for democracy and respect for human rights cannot be strengthened, and the achievements of peace will remain elusive. . . . It is not enough simply to 'live and let live': genuine tolerance requires an active effort to try to understand the point of view of others; it implies broadmindedness and vision, as well as confidence in one's own ability to meet new challenges without resorting to intransigence or violence."

Second, in addition to having a broader background, women leaders often symbolize unity for their nation. This has been particularly true of those women who came to office following the murder of a father or husband who had previously led the country. While most women leaders come to power without such family connections, a third have been strongly advantaged by membership—either by birth or through marriage—in highly prominent political families.[9] Nicaragua's Chamorro and the Philippines' Aquino both became symbols of national unity following their husbands' murders and were elected to lead reconciliation governments (Darling, 1996). Chamorro claimed to represent no ideology beyond national reconciliation (Benn, 1995). Of Chamorro's four adult children, two are prominent Sandanistas and two are equally prominent opponents of the Sandanistas—not an unusual split in war-torn Nicaragua. Chamorro's ability to bring all the members of her prominent family together for Sunday dinner each week has achieved nearly legendary status in Nicaragua. As "the grieving matriarch who can still hold the family together" (Saint-Germain, 1993, p. 80), Chamorro gives symbolic hope to the nation that it, too, can find peace based on unity. That this woman leader should find in family unity a symbol of national peace is neither surprising nor coincidental.

Ireland's Mary Robinson brings similar symbolism to her office. Robinson, a Catholic, is married to a Protestant, and their marriage symbolizes the possibility for unity, and therefore peace, in war-torn Northern Ireland. Again, it is neither surprising nor coincidental that this woman leader's family unity has become a symbol for national peace for her nation.

Following Prime Minister Levy Eshkol's death, Israel's Labor Party selected Golda Meir as the only person who could bring unity to the party and thus to the war-torn country. Likewise, Filipinos regarded Corazon Aquino as the only person who could credibly unify the people of the Philippines following the murder of her husband, slain opposition leader Benigno Aquino. During the campaign, when Aquino's opponent, Ferdinand Marcos, harped on Aquino's political inexperience, Aquino invariably answered, "Sure, I don't know anything about stealing or cheating, and definitely I don't know anything about killing my opponents" (Opfell, 1993, p. 135).

Some analysts have observed that women leaders use more inclusive strategies than their male counterparts (for example, Rosener, 1994), as noted previously. The most comprehensive review of the leadership styles of women and men at all organizational levels (Eagly and Johnson, 1990) found that "the strongest evidence . . . for a sex difference in leadership style occurred on the tendency for women to adopt a more democratic or participative style and for men to adopt a more autocratic or directive style." Of the 370 studies reviewed comparing male and female leaders' behavior, "92 percent of the comparisons went in the direction of more democratic behaviour from women than men" (cited in Vinnicombe and Colwill, 1995, p. 32). Although these studies have neither focused exclusively on elite levels of leadership nor included many non-Western women, some parallels among all women leaders are worth noting. Of the twenty-seven global women heads of state in Table 9.1, many appear to use more democratic approaches, including using more inclusive processes to build consensus and actively seeking both national and international unity.

Women tend to use broader strategies than men in coming to power, in part because the power structure frequently neither takes a woman's candidacy seriously nor supports her bid for office. Women therefore go directly to the people, using what could accurately be described as more broad-based, populist, and unifying strategies than those that men use (Adler, 1996).

In Ireland, for example, Mary Robinson visited more small communities than any other politician before her own party took her candidacy seriously. The opposition admits that by the time it recognized Mary Robinson as a serious presidential candidate, she was already unbeatable. In assessing her campaign, experts agreed that "by the time the other parties realised the strategic role being played by women, it was too late" (Finlay, 1990, p. 62). In Robinson's victory speech she stated that "there was nothing rational or reasonable about the campaign, which developed into a barnstorming, no-holds-barred battle between my ad hoc assembly of political activists, amateurs, idealists and romantic realists against the might, money and merciless onslaught of the greatest political party on this island. And we beat them!" (quoted in Finlay, 1990, p. 8).

Often a woman candidate's opposition will not take her seriously until late in the campaign, giving her a strategic advantage. And although a lack of support from their political parties would appear to work against women candidates, it gives women leaders more latitude to define their own agenda and therefore to introduce more substantive change.

The pattern of popular support preceding (and in some cases completely replacing) support from traditional political parties holds for women from political dynasties as well as for women from nonpolitical families. For example, Iceland's Finnbógadottir and Switzerland's Ruth Dreifuss both were elected with broad-based support from women. Pakistan's Benazir Bhutto, Israel's Golda Meir, and India's Indira Gandhi all transcended the hesitancy of their own political parties to gain broad-based support from both men and women prior to winning elections. In the Philippines, "Aquino insisted that she preferred not to be a candidate, but would relent in the face of popular demand. . . . When more than a million signatures were obtained . . . Aquino declared her candidacy" (Col, 1993, pp. 20–21). Following her decision to run for the presidency, she visited sixty-eight provinces (of seventy-three total) and held more than a thousand rallies. By contrast, her opponent visited only twenty-two provinces and held only thirty-four rallies. Filipinos refer to Aquino's victory as the "People's Revolution."

Even more important for peace is the fact that a disproportionate number of women leaders (as compared to men) use inclusive strategies to attempt to resolve civil wars and international conflicts. Although the media labeled the strategy naive and ineffective, Aquino invited both members of her own party and members of the opposition—including people deemed responsible for murdering her husband—into her cabinet. Similarly, Sri Lanka's Kumaratunga chose to meet with Tamil separatists in an attempt to work out a peaceful solution to Sri Lanka's civil war, looking beyond both past government policy and her own loss of her father and husband to the separatists. Likewise, even in the face of severe repression, Suu Kyi continues to advocate nonviolent meetings with Burma's military government.

This pattern of attempts at national consensus building is paralleled in most of the women leaders' approach to confrontational international situations. For example, without the support of many of her fellow Lithuanians, Prime Minister Prunskiene met directly with Mikhail Gorbachev following his demand that Lithuania rescind its declaration of independence. As Opfell (1993, p. 164) described it, Prunskiene "remained cool . . . and brushed away fears. 'Gorbachev is always saying that he and I are such good friends,' [Prunskiene] confided, with a smile, 'so I am writing a letter to my dear friend saying, "Mikhail Sergievich, will you attend to your dear Kazimiera Prunskiene with tanks?"'" Unfortunately, her strategy failed: Gorbachev sent in tanks. Perhaps we should not be surprised that twenty-first-century, consensus-based strategies for unity do not always work when one is confronted with the militaristic strategies of the last five thousand years.

THE FUTURE

In his speech accepting the Philadelphia Liberty Medal, Vaclav Havel, president of the Czech Republic, stated that "there are good reasons for suggesting that the modern age has ended. Many things indicate that we are going through a transitional period, when it seems that something is on the way out and something else is painfully being born. It is as if something were crumbling, decaying and exhausting itself, while something else, still indistinct, were arising from the rubble" (Havel, 1994, p. A27). Havel's appreciation of the transition that the world is now experiencing is certainly important to all of us as human beings. None of us can claim that the twentieth century is exiting on an impressive note, on a note imbued with wisdom. As we ask ourselves which of the twentieth century's legacies we wish to pass on to the children of the twenty-first century, we are humbled into shameful silence. Yes, we have advanced science and technology, but at the price of a polluted environment, cities infested with social chaos and physical decay, an increasingly skewed income distribution that condemns large proportions of the population to poverty (including people living in the world's most affluent societies), and rampant "limited wars" and isolated incidents that continue to claim lives. No, we are not exiting the twentieth century with pride. Unless we can learn to treat one another and our planet in a more civilized way, is it not blasphemy to continue to refer to ourselves as a civilization (Rechtschaffen, 1996)?

What would it take to bring civilization back into society? At a minimum, we need to escape our collective blindness. We need to reinterpret events within their broadest temporal, geographical, and cultural context. We need to take responsibility for creating a civilized future for ourselves and our children.

Returning to civilization requires escaping our collective blindness, literally changing perspective so we can begin to see once again. Returning to civilization requires seeing the present clearly by viewing it through non-twentieth-century lenses. It means escaping our collusive assumption that current reality is "OK," that it is as good as we can expect from ourselves. Perhaps our collective blindness is best exemplified by the "Teflon presidency" of former U.S. president Ronald Reagan. During Reagan's term, no matter what the evening news offered as evidence to the contrary, Americans continued to believe that the United States was number one and that the president could do no wrong.

The incessant parade of societal failures reported on the evening news is clearly not sufficient to let us either see or interpret the very messages they should be delivering to us. As Pirsig (1981, p. 63) observes, "What makes this world so hard to see clearly is not its strangeness, but its usualness." It is familiarity that blinds. Psychologist and futurist Jean Houston (1995) tells a wonderful story about her meeting with an Australian aboriginal woman at Uluuru (Ayers Rock). Houston comments to the aboriginal woman that she does not see how the aborigines can survive in such barren desert land. The aboriginal woman, after carefully pointing out the extensive variety of grasses, tuber plants, and other edible vegetation, sighs and responds to Houston, "I don't see how you people can survive when you see so little."

The science philosopher Thomas Kuhn (1962) helped us all to understand that even myriad individually disconfirming data cannot change our appreciation of reality. Only when disconfirming data are combined with a new lens, a new paradigm, are we able to see the fallacy and blindness inherent in our previous perspective. As management scholar Charles Hampden-Turner (1993, p. 12) observes, "You can only recognize that for which you have a pattern." Only when we use a new model of the possibilities for civilization will we begin to be able to see the world's current decay as a pattern rather than as multitudinous isolated events. And only once we can see will we be able to move on into a twenty-first century that does something more than replicate the degradations of the twentieth century.

What will allow us to see more and, more importantly, to see differently? One thing that will help is a vision, explicitly expressed, by a wise leader—a leader who offers an image of the future that is so markedly different from currently accepted interpretations of society that it allows us to see simultaneously the possibilities of the future and the decay of the present.

Jean Houston (1995) warns us that "As our means [have] become more perfected, our goals [have] become more confused." Twenty-first-century leaders escape the determinism of technique only by returning to the meaning of civilization. Perhaps having the courage to resurrect memories of peaceful civilizations that lived seven thousand years ago will help us reclaim the wisdom we need to create a twenty-first century that we can be proud of.

NOTES

1. The following section is drawn from Riane Eisler's insightful 1987 book *The Chalice and the Blade: Our History, Our Future.*
2. This and the following section draw on Adler 1996, which presents an in-depth background of twenty-five women leaders but does not focus on their relationship to war and peace.
3. There were no women political leaders in the 1950s. Three came to office in the 1960s, four in the 1970s, seven in the 1980s, and, by 1996, thirteen in the 1990s.
4. Whereas the focus of this chapter is on senior global political leaders, a similar number of women have emerged at the most senior levels of economic leadership. See, for example, "50 World-Class Executives," 1996.
5. To date only two women in the world (both currently in office) have ever followed another woman into office: Sri Lanka's current executive president and former prime minister, Chandrika Bandaranaike Kumaratunga (whose mother, Sirimavo Bandaranaike, was the modern world's first women prime minister), and Bangladesh's Hasina Wajed, who in 1997 followed Khaleda Zia into office as prime minister.
6. Bangladesh, Dominica, India, Israel, Lithuania, Netherlands-Antilles, Poland, Sri Lanka, and Yugoslavia.
7. Bangladesh, Central African Republic, Haiti, Ireland, Nicaragua, Pakistan, the Philippines, Portugal, and Rwanda.
8. Nobel Peace Prize recipient Aung San Suu Kyi led the political party that won Burma's 1990 election; however, the military prevented Suu Kyi from taking office and placed her under house arrest for more than six years. Whereas the military has renamed the country Myanmur, Suu Kyi still refers to it as Burma. Her keynote address to the 1995 Beijing Women's Conference was delivered on videotape, as Suu Kyi feared that the military would not let her return to Burma if she went to China to deliver the speech in person.
9. The nine women leaders in Table 9.1 who came from politically prominent families all led Asian or Latin American countries, where dynastic

policies are traditional for both men and women. They include Isabel Perón in Argentina, both Khaleda Zia and Hasina Wajid in Bangladesh, Indira Gandhi in India, Violetta Chamorro in Nicaragua, Benazir Bhutto in Pakistan, Corazon Aquino in the Philippines, and both Bandaranaike and Kumaratunga in Sri Lanka.

REFERENCES

Adler, N. J. "Competitive Frontiers: Cross-Cultural Management in the 21st Century." *International Journal of Intercultural Relations,* 1995, *19*(4), 523–537.

Adler, N. J. "Global Women Political Leaders: An Invisible History, an Increasingly Important Future." *Leadership Quarterly,* 1996, *7*(1), 133–161.

Aung San Suu Kyi. Keynote address, United Nations Conference on Women, Beijing, China, 1995.

Benn, M. "The Women Who Rule the World." *Cosmopolitan,* February 1995.

Blondel, J. *Political Leadership: Towards a General Analysis.* Thousand Oaks, Calif.: Sage, 1987.

Col, J. M. "Managing Softly in Turbulent Times: Corazon C. Aquino, President of the Philippines." In M. A. Genovese (ed.), *Women as National Leaders.* Thousand Oaks, Calif.: Sage, 1993.

Darling, J. "Nicaragua Voting Plagued by Snafus." *Montreal Gazette,* Oct. 21, 1996, p. B1.

Eagly, A. H., and Johnson, B. T. "Gender and Leadership Style: A Meta-analysis." *Psychological Bulletin,* 1990, *108*(2), 233–256.

Eisler, R. *The Chalice and the Blade: Our History, Our Future.* San Francisco: Harper San Francisco, 1987.

Fallaci, O. *Interviews with History.* Boston: Houghton Mifflin, 1976.

"50 Worldclass Executives." *Worldbusiness.* Mar.-Apr. 1996, pp. 21–31.

Finlay, F. *Mary Robinson: A President with a Purpose.* Dublin, Ireland: O'Brien Press, 1990.

Gimbutas, M. *The Civilization of the Goddess: The World of Old Europe.* San Francisco: Harper San Francisco, 1991.

Hampden-Turner, C. "The Structure of Entrapment: Dilemmas Standing in the Way of Women Managers and Strategies to Resolve Them." Paper presented at the Global Business Network conference "Women as a Driving Force in the Year 2010: A Window on Change," New York, Dec. 9–10, 1993.

Havel, V. "The New Measure of Man." *New York Times,* July 8, 1994, p. A27.

Houston, J. *Myths for the Future.* Boulder, Colo.: Sounds True Audio, 1995.

Kuhn, T. *The Structure of Scientific Revolutions.* Chicago: University of Chicago Press, 1962.

Lazerges, A. "Tansu Çiller" ["Turkish 'Mama'"]. *Diario 16,* June 15, 1993.

O'Neill, J. "Here's to You, Mrs. Robinson." *Montreal Gazette,* July 1994, p. B3.

Opfell, O. S. *Women Prime Ministers and Presidents.* Jefferson, N. C.: McFarland & Company, 1993.

Pirsig, R. M. *Zen and the Art of Motorcycle Maintenance: An Inquiry into Values.* New York: Bantam Books, 1981.

Rechtschaffen, S. *Timeshifting.* New York: Bantam Audio Publishing, 1996.

Rosener, J. B. "Ways Women Lead." In N. A. Nichols (ed.), *Reach for the Top.* Boston: Harvard Business School Press, 1994.

Saint-Germain, M. A. "Women in Power in Nicaragua: Myth and Reality." In M. A. Genovese (ed.), *Women as National Leaders.* Thousand Oaks, Calif.: Sage, 1993.

Vinnicombe, S., and Colwill, N. *The Essence of Women in Management.* Englewood Cliffs, N.J.: Prentice Hall, 1995.

10

DEVELOPING WISDOM AND COURAGE IN ORGANIZING AND SCIENCING

William R. Torbert

THIS CHAPTER, focusing on the health care industry, explores how the development of personal and organizational wisdom and courage can intersect. In health care, as in other industries, this transformation occurs not through objective research that leads to findings, then policies, and then actions undertaken to implement those policies. Rather, it can occur only through a process that is altogether unknown to most scholars and practitioners, though it has been known, partially and distortedly, by some ever since ancient times. This transformational process integrates personal, interpersonal, and wider organizational and social change through what I call first-, second-, and third-person research and practice.

What these involve is described more fully later. First, an illustration from health care offers an initial sense of what these terms mean. Later sections explore what kind of organizing structures and what type of social science encourage the integration of first-, second-, and third-person research and practice. But, for starters, these are the kinds of research that we adults can conduct in the midst of our daily activities of working, loving, and wondering.

THE U.S. HEALTH CARE INDUSTRY TODAY

As participants in it, we all know and feel that the U.S. health care industry—the nation's largest industry—is experiencing a tumultuous process of transformation (Fisher and Torbert, 1995). I myself have been engaged in second-person research and practice in relation to the industry for twenty years, initially simply as a member of a health management organization (HMO), later consulting to another HMO for five years, and still later serving on the board of the new, merged organization that combined these two organizations.

We all are relearning—though slowly, ambivalently, and inarticulately—the ancient wisdom that true health is preeminently an ongoing first-person research project or activity (though often more enthusiastically undertaken in association with others, as in the case of my father's daily water exercise class at age eighty-six). A general definition of health-enhancing first-person research and practice might include something like proactive, self-initiated exercise—whether mental (for example, meditation), emotional, or physical—engaged in with an ongoing sensitivity to the pace that best suits oneself (physically, such exercise usually reaches fruition in working up a sweat). By contrast, health is neither well conceived nor well maintained when treated as a taken-for-granted condition to be rectified by an occasional, technological fix based on third-person research.

Furthermore, we are beginning to learn that the daily character of our second-person research and practice—our associational activities at work, within our family, and at leisure—are critical to making our health and our life as a whole better or worse (Karasek and Theorell, 1991). Or as Sheila McNamee puts it in Chapter Five, "We must consider how to attend to the movement of conversations in and around our organizations. This is what gives life to an organization. The pulsing of realities in the making is the heart of organizational life."

Thus one can say that the primary issue in future health care research and practice—both medical and organizational—will be how to integrate third-person scientific research and institutional practice with first- and second-person research and practice. An example at the micro, or interpersonal, level is the relationship between a general practitioner and an ongoing patient. At its best this is an example of second-person research that encourages heightened first-person research and practice on the part of the patient (such as my father's water exercise) and simultaneously integrates a third-person research background into the patient's and physician's understanding of the case. Note, however, that at present medical schools strongly emphasize third-person research. They encourage the best students to become specialists who will focus on third-person research rather than generalists who will integrate first-, second-, and third-person research and practice (Howe, 1996). Note too, as will be discussed at greater length later, that modern science has tended to privilege third-person ("objective") research over first-person ("subjective") and second-person ("intersubjective") research. One wonders what kind of science can integrate first-, second-, and third-person research and practice, a question we will explore further.

But first back to health care. What is happening in health care today at the macro, industrywide, institutional scale? On the one hand, Columbia/HCA and other large, for-profit hospital chains are redefining the industry. Also, Kaiser Permanente and other multistate not-for-profit HMOs are rapidly merging. Such huge managed care organizations can threaten the traditional first-person independence of medical practitioners with third-person institutional controls—a frequent occurrence according to media reports. On the other hand, the new health management organizations can invent new standards of mutuality, interdisciplinarity, and peer review (Reason, 1994, 1995). By emphasizing the quality improvements to be gained through effective second-person research and practice among doctors and within individual practices, these new standards encourage an integration of first-person independence with second-person interdependence and third-person institutional challenge. This is more or less the story one hears from the executives of merging HMOs.

For example, Harvard Pilgrim Health Care, the largest New England HMO, is currently crafting a fifty-fifty "true not-for-profit partnership" with its Health Centers Division, which will make its current doctor-employees both more independent and more interdependent, rather than merely dependent on a third-person institution. It will offer them greater rewards for successful practice while at the same time requiring them to assume a greater share of the overall organizational risk and confronting them with hard questions about what constitutes excellent health care. Instead of vesting controlling power either in the parent organization or in the health centers themselves, the fifty-fifty partnership reminds both entities that maintaining a healthy (second-person research and practice) relationship is a key to the success of each. The intent is to structurally empower each partner equally, yet not vest either with enough power to act in an irresponsible way with respect to the other. How well this new (counterintuitive) ownership structure will work remains to be seen. Its skeletal outline, however, is an example of the kind of third-person organizational structure one would create with the aim of integrating first-person, second-person, and third-person research and practice.

FIRST-PERSON, SECOND-PERSON, AND THIRD-PERSON RESEARCH AND PRACTICE

Working from this initial, brief illustration of health care, let us explore what more generally constitutes each of the three types of research and practice and then what type of organizing and sciencing interweave first-person, second-person, and third-person research and practice. It should already be clear that this conceptualization of research and practice is about integrating courage and wisdom—experiments and tests of validity—in real-time interactions and that movement in this direction will transform our organizing, our sciencing, and our personal awareness.

Let us begin with first-person research and practice. In general this includes all of those forms of research and practice that one can do by oneself. This includes a variety of forms of writing—for example, journals or diaries, episodic or comprehensive memoirs or autobiographies, records of dreams or of daydreams of future scenarios (these can all become sources for second-person and third-person research and practice as well; see Torbert and Fisher, 1992; Fisher and Torbert, 1995). First-person research and practice also includes the varieties (and there are many) of meditation and prayer, either as distinct activities in a distinctive setting or in the midst of one's everyday activities. Furthermore, first-person research and practice can include chanting, asking questions of the *I Ching* (the ancient Chinese "book of changes") or tarot cards, dancing (for example, dervish whirling or Gurdjieffian movements), or otherwise physically exercising in an awareness-widening fashion. It can include craft or artistic work engaged in not primarily for the sake of the end product but for the experience of awareness and discovery felt during the activity itself.

To expand on just one of these first-person events, there is an immense, virtually unexplored challenge in trying to write autobiographically—first for oneself, second for feedback from trusted others ("second persons"), and third for feedback from strangers ("third persons"). Such autobiographical writing will not look much like the vast majority of published autobiographies. For in writing autobiographically as research and practice one seeks not to tell a predigested story or to construct a harmonious symphony that others will like but rather to record the less coherent quality of one's evolving life, in search of transforming ways of making meaning in one's ongoing relationships and projects. Insofar as such an autobiography is shared, it will first be shared with trusted others for the educational value of the subsequent conversation (and will thus become second-person research and practice). If shared publicly, the motive will be to initiate a wider conversation with the reader's life explorations.

Rousseau's *Confessions* come closer to this aim than St. Augustine's, since the latter offered the stock "reformed sinner" story. Closer still, it seems to me, are three contemporary books written in the middle of evolving lives: one by a Chinese woman in the Red Guard (Ang Min's *Red Azalea*, 1993), one by the poet Martha Ramsey (*Where I Stopped: Remembering Rape at Thirteen*, 1995), and one by our social scientist–consultant colleague Roger Harrison (1995). Ramsey's book, particularly, gives the reader a feel for how her much-later second-person research with other participants into the original events and trial described in the narrative reverberated back on her ongoing first-person search.

There has been a recent explosion of autobiographical sharing in our profession (Alderfer, 1988, 1989; Bateson, 1984; Bedeain, 1993; *Journal of Applied Behavioral Science*, 1989), but only rarely does a sense of suffering and learning from exploring previously undigested experiences and patterns show through (I would count as such Alderfer, 1989; Bateson, 1984; Harrison, 1995; the Starbuck and Weick chapters in Bedeain, 1993; and the autobiographical portion of Torbert, 1991). One requirement for doctoral dissertations in management from the Centre for Action Research in Professional Practice at the University of Bath is that they include a self-exploratory autobiographical essay. Even though we do not yet have clear standards of rigor in this domain, the very effort of self-criticism, self-theorizing, self-inquiry seems an ethical responsibility in a profession where each practitioner can wield significant power through his or her ideas, pedagogy, publications, or consultancies.

First-Person Research and Practice

Writing autobiographically is a highly imaginative, emotional, and reflective form of first-person research and practice. It should not be our only example of first-person research and practice, however, because it occurs too much within the current scholarly mode of reflecting and writing. Thus it may obscure the universes beyond contemporary social science that are implied by the notion of integrating research and practice, action and inquiry, courage and wisdom. To correct any such misdirection, let us explore briefly what kind of exercise—literal, physical, or dramatic—counts as first-person research and practice that can develop personal wisdom and courage.

Most forms of repetitive exercise that can be done absentmindedly do *not* count. If, however, without knowing just how I am going to move, I find myself taking and keeping, and breathing into and out from, the position of a Squatting Monkey,[1] I begin to feel more like a monkey. I hear birds outside as my monkey does. And my images—my hypotheses—multiply. I envision myself as having been a monkey in a former life. Yet when I try to taste the validity of that idea, I find that it is merely a distraction—a cowardly way out—from experiencing this strange feeling of my monkeyness now. Consequently I find the hypothesis that this is our one and only life more plausible than the many-lives hypothesis.

Put differently, even if it is not ultimately true that this is our one and only life, we ought to *act* as though it is. That means we should enter into our physical being as much as possible in order to feel the sensation of our presence here. So the exercise I need to try each morning is to begin to do that. Merely going out and running around the mile-and-a-half trail in the park near here doesn't necessarily accomplish that for me. It can be a tremendously inefficient way to accomplish this waking to my physical being. (I don't mean inefficient in the sense of wasting my time. My time out there is never wasted; the more time I spend running the better off I am. Instead I am referring to how quickly I can wake up to my physical presence, my sensations.)

You might try a physical exercise right now, as you are reading this, simply for the sake of experiencing and reexperiencing your bodily presence and thus becoming more present. If you are in a reclining chair, or whatever your posture, simply turn one of your wrists slightly and begin very slowly to exercise your fingers. Especially if you are slightly arthritic, as I am, this exercise can provide a tremendous thrill of reencountering a part of yourself that you deserve to know continually.

The kind of physical exercise I recommend as an aid in the search for wisdom and courage, for being present at all times and aware of the shape of one's current research and practice, is a kind of continual invention—for example, walking forward, then turning and walking backward for a time; skipping; twirling slowly first one way, then the other; raising your hands high above your head, then letting them hang at your sides. When I have great energy it can all be in the pantomime of a jester; ordinarily, however, I am so cowardly that neighbors passing me notice nothing extraordinary about my pace, since I adjust it to match their version of normality when I espy them, as I usually do well before they espy me. But again, my early-morning physical exercise is at best an analogue for the kind of physical exercise I can perform right now, as I compose on my word processor, and now, as I . . .

Such are two of the many flavors of first-person research. May this chapter invite you to explore this world of first-, second-, and third-person research and practice further for yourself, to seek out and participate in creating cooperative inquiries with colleagues and friends and to practice liberating disciplines (defined later in the chapter) within your family and other long-term communities of practice. May your sense of valid research and effective practice transform more than once during your remaining lifetime. And may you meet death itself inquiringly.

Second-Person Research and Practice

Second-person research and practice includes all the times we engage in supportive, self-disclosing, or confrontational acts with others in shared first-person research and practice. Another way of putting this is that second-person research and practice includes all conversations where those present share an intent to learn about themselves, about the others present, about a shared activity, or about the relationships that are forming, transforming, or dissolving. This can happen, but in empirical terms only rarely does happen in a therapeutic or consulting relationship; between friends or lovers; among team members at work, at school, or at play; in a theatrical production or improvisation; between a doctor, lawyer, or other professional and his or her client; and, of course, between a master-teacher and one or more apprentice-pupils. If such conversations are audiotaped or videotaped, then the resulting tapes can be used in further first-person research and practice, second-person research and practice, or third-person research and practice.

Second-person research and practice is characterized by alternations between rehearsal and performance, by periodic feedback among the participants about their perceptions of themselves and others present, and by periodic "feedforward" about what vision and strategies ought to guide continued action. At its best, second-person research and practice gradually transform hierarchical relationships into more peerlike arrangements (or else simply conclude them, if they are purely professional). This transformation toward an "I and Thou" partnership is the normative direction of second-person research and practice, because peers are those most empowered to challenge, support, balance, and understand one another—that is, to conduct valid research together (Buber, 1958; Cooperrider and Srivastva, 1987; Heron, 1996; Grudin, 1996; Jourard, 1968; Kramer, 1995; Rank, 1978; Reason, 1994, 1995; Rogers, 1961; Torbert, 1991). One of the characteristics of many interpersonal situations that keeps them from becoming more courageous and wise integrations of action and inquiry is that one or some or all of the parties act in ways that reinforce differences in unilateral power or hierarchical status, thus obstructing the development of mutuality.

As with first-person research and practice, the quality standards for second-person research and practice are little developed (outside of third-person research on psychotherapy; for example, see Truax and Carkhuff, 1967). Heron's *Cooperative Inquiry* (1996) is the most recent contribution to developing such standards, and one way of reading the subfield of "action science" (Argyris, Putnam, and Smith, 1985; Schön, 1983; Torbert, 1976, 1981) is as an early attempt to chart the territory of effective and valid second-person research and practice. But there is a long road to be traveled here. Determining which genre best communicates second-person research and practice in third-person publication venues is a little-discussed artistic and scientific dilemma. For example, although the *Journal of Management Inquiry* has developed a section on dialogue, it has in fact published no dialogues that exemplify second-person research and practice. Without a doubt the foremost and most sophisticated exemplars of second-person research and practice in a third-person publication venue remain, after nearly 2,500 years, Plato's dialogues. What is striking about the most sophisticated readings of Plato (for example, Bloom, 1967; Kaplan, 1997; Schmid, 1993) is that they re-present the dialogues as an exercise of second-person research and practice, not only in terms of the educational drama (the second-person research and practice) among the characters in the text but also in terms of the educational drama between the text and each reader, who accepts the invitation to engage in the inquiry (which is why the dialogues do not end with obvious "right answers"). A very different example of how a text can not only re-present dramatic first- and second-person research and practice that occurred in the past but also invite second-person research and practice between the reader and the text is Gurdjieff's *Life Is Real Only Then When 'I Am'* (1981).

Third-Person Research and Practice

Third-person research and practice can be of two very different sorts. The first sort, which is by far the most common, does not really qualify as research and practice at all, because it conceptually and operationally segregates research from practice. Whether as research or as practice, this third-person mode develops impersonal structures to which subordinate participants (whether research subjects or employees) are expected to conform. Furthermore, this third-person mode (whether in sciencing or in organizing) does not encourage ongoing first-person or second-person research and practice among participants, does not encourage challenges or transformation of the predetermined structures, and does not encourage transformation of the hierarchical power relationships at the outset into more peerlike relationships. Such is the nature of behaviorist research; of empirical-positivist research, more generally (see Table 10.1 and, in more detail, Exhibit 10.2 later in the chapter); of bureaucratic organizing (see "Systematic Productivity" in Stage V on Table 10.1); and of much of the actual practice of Total Quality Management and reengineering programs (practices that frequently correspond to systematic productivity, even though the rhetoric of collaborative inquiry is used).

The second, much more rare kind of third-person research and practice also begins by developing impersonal structures for persons initially unknown to the initiators of the organizing process. In all other respects, however, the aims of "true" third-person research and practice differ from those of bureaucratic organizing and positivist research. First and foremost, the actual tasks defined by true third-person research and practice structures *require* that participants engage in first- and second-person research and practice (expanding their awareness and exercising increasing creativity and choice) in order to accomplish the goals. Moreover, even though subordinate participants are initially expected to conform to the predefined structures, they are simultaneously encouraged and educated to confront them if they appear to be incongruous with the organizational mission. Put differently, true third-person research and practice structures create dilemmas and choices, not just constraints, for the participants. The resolution of these dilemmas demand leadership by the participants, along with increasing ability to translate the organization's or practice tradition's mission into strategies, actions, and outcomes that are increasingly congruent. Such organizational structures—and only such organizational structures—create the increasing mutuality that both

Table 10.1. Analogies Among Personal, Organizational, and Social-Scientific Developmental Paths.

Stage	Personal Development	Organizational Development	Social-Scientific Development
I.	Birth-Impulsive (0–6 years)	Conception	Anarchism (Feyerabend, 1975)

Multiple, distinctive impulses gradually resolve into a characteristic approach (for example, many fantasies resolve into a particular dream for a new organization).

Stage	Personal Development	Organizational Development	Social-Scientific Development
II.	Opportunist (7–12 years?)	Investment	Behaviorism

Dominant task: gain power (for example, by learning to ride a bike) to have desired effect on outside world.

Stage	Personal Development	Organizational Development	Social-Scientific Development
III.	Diplomatic (12 years–?)	Incorporation	Gestalt Sociologism

Looking glass self: understanding others' culture and expectations and molding one's own actions to succeed by their (for example, market) terms.

Stage	Personal Development	Organizational Development	Social-Scientific Development
IV.	Technician (16 years–?)	Experiments	Empirical Positivism

Intellectual mastery of outside systems such that actions equal experiments that confirm or disconfirm hypotheses and lead toward valid certainty.

Stage	Personal Development	Organizational Development	Social-Scientific Development
V.	Achiever (20? years–?)	Systematic Productivity	Multimethod Eclecticism

Pragmatic triangulation among plan and theory, operation and implementation, and outcome and evaluation in an incompletely predefined environment.

Stage	Personal Development	Organizational Development	Social-Scientific Development
VI.	Strategist (30? years–?)	Collaborative Inquiry	Postmodern Interpretivism

Self-conscious mission and philosophy, sense of timing and historicity, invitation to conversation among multiple voices and to reframe boundaries.

Stage	Personal Development	Organizational Development	Social-Scientific Development
VII.	Magician/Witch/Clown (40? years–?)	Foundational Community of Inquiry	Cooperative Inquiry

Life/science equals a mind/matter; love/death/transformation praxis among others, cultivating interplay and reattunement among inquiry, friendship, work, and material goods.

Table 10.1. (continued)

Stage	Personal Development	Organizational Development	Social-Scientific Development
		Liberating Disciplines	Developmental Action Inquiry
VIII.	Ironist (50? years–?)		

Full acceptance of multiparadigmatic nature of human consciousness and reality, including distances and alienation among paradigms, such that (1) few recognize paradigm differences as cause of wars, (2) few seek paradigm disconfirmation and transformation, and (3) few face the dilemma or paradox of "empowering leadership": that it must work indirectly through ironic words, gestures, and event-structures that create a moment-to-moment field of choice.

IX.

Behaviorism	Control of the other (through "operant conditioning")		
Gestalt Sociologism	Understanding of the other (better than that other's self-understanding)		
Empirical Positivism	Predictive certainty (valid certainty)		
Multimethod Eclecticism	Useful approximation (through triangulation)		
Postmodern Interpretivism	Re-presentation of perspectival pluralism (without privileging the writer's own perspective—"Ha ha!")		
Cooperative Inquiry	Creating transformational communities of inquiry (among mutually committed members with multiple perspectives)		
Developmental Action Inquiry	Enacting inquiry and liberating disciplines (across initially estranged cultures without shared purposes)		

supports and results from personal, group, organizational, and epistemological transformations (along the developmental paths shown in Table 10.1). Through this process, and through the initiating leaders' demonstrated willingness to clarify the mission and restructure where incongruities appear, the organizational structure becomes increasingly peer-centered. The leadership alertness and appropriate vulnerability required to be willing and able to generate such third-person research and practice is, of course, rare and can be generated only through long and continuing first- and second- person research and practice.

Such organizational structures, which I sketch in the next two sections, deserve the name "liberating disciplines" (see Stage VIII in Table 10.1; Torbert, 1974, 1978, 1991; Fisher and Torbert, 1995, for more detailed contextualization and illustration). As defined below, such organizational structures—and only such structures—will reliably develop increasing personal and organizational wisdom and courage among the participants.

SHORT ILLUSTRATIONS OF LIBERATING DISCIPLINES

The following heuristics and mini case studies of "ordinary" business situations in which the members gradually fashioned liberating disciplines (without ever calling them such or knowing the theory offered here) can introduce us to the "field" of liberating disciplines.

The simplest heuristic for creating a liberating discipline is first to list all the limiting conditions (such as lack of money, employees without the right skills, and so on) that prevent one from accomplishing some desired goal and then to set about inventing a structure that recognizes and even uses these limits to reach the goal. In principle this amounts to no more than the old saw, "turn problems into opportunities." But this cliche is as rarely enacted as it is regularly espoused, especially in the domain of creating social structures for doing tasks. For example, a strategic change team I was once part of, composed of faculty from different departments at a management school, decided that one of its limiting conditions was each member's propensity, as an academic, to argue and to need to be right. Faculty groups can easily argue themselves into terminal depression and withdrawal rather than agreeing to anything. Rather than attempting any number of complicated and covert means of overcoming this limiting condition, we simply recognized it and made a game of making fast decisions. Once several decisions had been made the limiting condition no longer existed, so the elaborate structure temporarily set in place to make fast decisions was no longer necessary. The group determined this through its own second-person research and practice.

A second simple heuristic for creating a liberating discipline, which the foregoing illustration also exemplifies, is to create a structure that, if it works, will become unnecessary. The most fundamental reason why liberating disciplines are necessary in the first place is that few human beings today exercise vulnerable, mutuality-enhancing, transforming power (Torbert, 1991). Few take full executive responsibility for the effects of their actions or treat others as true peers. The most fundamental aim of liberating disciplines, therefore, is to cultivate the development of subordinates and leaders toward the later stages through the transforming power of engaging them in first-, second-, and third-person research and practice. Hence, if liberating disciplines succeed, organizational members will increasingly take executive responsibility, increasingly treat one another as peers, render the original liberating discipline unnecessary, and increasingly create their own liberating disciplines.

A third simple heuristic for creating liberating disciplines is to ask oneself how to maximize both of two apparently opposite values, such as power and justice or inquiry and productivity. Usually we think we have to sacrifice one of these for the other or else compromise between the two. Totally new solutions to such dilemmas begin to suggest themselves, however, if we disdain our competitive assumptions and seek counterintuitive solutions. Thus the following, longer example shows how in one organization both the managers and the workers increased their ability to control discipline in the workplace, rather than empowering one party at the expense of the other.

The disciplinary procedure they instituted gradually developed at a company that had created autonomous production groups (Novelli and others, 1989). One value was the desire to be true to the vision of the autonomous groups and to have them be responsible for their own discipline problems. The opposing value was to centralize disciplinary decisions for efficiency, effectiveness, objectivity, and fairness (both within and across groups) in the decisions that were actually made. Although it was initially assumed that these work groups would manage their own disciplinary issues, no definite logistics were put in place for them to do so. Two difficulties arose.

First, the work teams often had difficulty disciplining themselves because to do so required confrontation and differentiation among group members (an example of moderately sophisticated second-person research and practice, which is not typically learned at school or in the workplace). Not only was this an uncustomary practice, it also seemed likely, to many team members, to hurt team spirit and working relations. Indeed, some teams began to ask senior management to handle their disciplinary problems for them.

Meanwhile, a whole class of unanticipated disciplinary problems arose (for example, stealing by workers in contexts unrelated to team activities). These seemed to require senior management action, but such centralized discipline seemed to many workers to violate the principle of work group–centered discipline.

Eventually, when faced with the need to reduce labor costs by a certain percentage during an economic downturn, the company (in response to workers' concerns) offered the work teams forty-eight hours to propose their own solutions to the problem. The teams offered a fully satisfactory set of proposals, which were implemented. But more important, the company realized it had invented a generalizable structure for resolving future disciplinary issues—what I would call a liberating discipline, since it both constrained and empowered participants and maximized two apparently opposing values, centralized direction and local options. Thereafter the work teams could choose either to deal with a given disciplinary issue within forty-eight hours or else let senior management deal with it. Senior management, in turn, could either accept the work team solution, if one were proposed, or impose its own solution. If a given work team were never to exercise self-discipline, or if senior management were never to accept a given team's recommendations, then such patterns would raise further questions and invite creative second-person and third-person research and practice. This way both parties possessed well-focused power and responsibility for action, and a breakdown in mutuality would be relatively easy to recognize.

A THEORY OF LIBERATING DISCIPLINES

The theory of liberating disciplines departs radically from all of our received notions of organizing—both top-down, constraining, bureaucratic, authoritarian, "Theory X" structures and bottom-up, participative, organic, democratic, "Theory Y" structures. Indeed, the theory of liberating discipline reverses the very definition of organization.

Listen to Katz and Kahn's definition (1978) in *The Social Psychology of Organizations*: "The organizational context is by definition a set of restrictions for focusing attention upon certain content areas and for narrowing the cognitive style to certain types of procedures. This is the inherent constraint. To call a social structure organized means that the degrees of freedom in the situation have been limited. Hence organizations often suffer from the failure to recognize the dilemma character of a situation and from blind persistence in sticking to terms of reference on the basis of which the problem is insoluble" (p. 277).

Let us attempt to create the mirror image opposite this definition of organizational structure, to define an organizing process that truly cultivates transforming research and practices through liberating disciplines. For the notion of a "constraining organizational structure," with its suggestion of an objective, external, social boundary superimposed on undisciplined, subjective persons, we can substitute the phrase "liberating social-psychological discipline." The word *liberating* mirrors the word *constraining*. And the term *social-psychological discipline* mirrors the term *organizational structure*, though less obviously so. In this mirror organization persons voluntarily take on new disciplines, based on internal commitment, rather than submitting and externally conforming to an external structure. The words *social-psychological* indicate that the social and the psychological penetrate each other, whereas the word *organization* suggests discontinuity between the personal (the psychological) and the social (the organizational).

But the phrase "liberating social-psychological discipline" is really too awkward to use. Let us shorten it, therefore, to "liberating disciplines"—a felicitous paradox that may open us to the mystery of effective organizing, stated in the plural to highlight the multiplicity of forms that the abstract definition will embrace. Now we have some of the reasoning that leads to the choice of the name "liberating disciplines" for this as yet rarely rediscovered form of organizing.

Continuing in this fashion to create a mirror image of the Katz and Kahn definition, with some poetic license we can produce the following initial definition of a liberating discipline on the left side of the page, with the Katz and Kahn conception on the right:

A liberating discipline	*An organizational context*
is by experience	*is by definition*
a set of challenges	*a set of restrictions*
for questioning (the quality of one's) attention	*for focusing one's attention*
and widening it	*and narrowing it*

and one's cognitive-emotional tracking to include the enacted task, process, and mission.

and one's cognitive style onto certain types of procedures.

This is the enacted dynamism.

This is the inherent constraint.

To call a social-psychological process liberating means that the degrees of freedom and discipline in the situation are expanding.

To call a social structure organized means that the degrees of freedom in the situation have been limited.

Hence organizations that cultivate transforming inquiry rarely suffer from the failure to recognize the dilemma character of a situation and from blind persistence in sticking to terms of reference on the basis of which the problem is insoluble.

Hence organizations often suffer from the failure

This definition means that a leadership intent on generating liberating disciplines will regard every organizational dilemma, directive, task, and encounter as an opportunity to challenge the attention of itself and others. The aim of each action, then, is never merely to accomplish a predetermined end but to widen the attention of participants, to get them to question and see whether the mission, strategy, present action, and outcome are congruous. At its most challenging such leadership action generates tasks that are incomprehensible and undoable without developing an ongoing awareness of the accompanying social-psychological processes and purposes (that is, without developing ongoing interplay among first-, second-, and third-person research and practice).

Liberating disciplines are inherently dynamic. Whatever structure is created at a given time is meant to evolve over time as the membership's overall awareness and initiative increases. Indeed, the leadership may initiate radical structural changes as much to heighten inquiry as to accomplish some predetermined end. Through liberating disciplines, both leaders and members can properly challenge the passive tendency to treat a given organizational structure as immutable and encourage instead a continuing search for a thread of meaning from the organization's mission or purpose, through cognitive structuring and restructuring, and through both passionate and dispassionate embodied action, resulting in visible events and products.

Two more corollaries about liberating disciplines follow directly from the foregoing comments. First, the appropriateness, legitimacy, or efficacy of a given organizational structure is in principle open to challenge by any organizational member at any time. Such challenges can function both to heighten members' vigilance and to better align organizational purposes, processes, practices, and profits. Incongruities among the organizational mission, strategies, operations, and outcomes are inevitable. But the leadership gains legitimacy and the organization as a whole gains confidence and efficacy by seeking out such incongruities and correcting them.

The second corollary points to the obverse condition: the leadership becomes vulnerable, in practice, to public discrediting if it acts inauthentically. That is, the leadership rapidly loses legitimacy if its tasks, processes, and purposes become incongruent with one another and it refuses to acknowledge and correct such incongruities. Thus in a very real sense the leadership of an organization that cultivates transforming inquiry puts itself in a highly vulnerable position. From the outset the leadership engages in a major calculated risk intended to generate increasing mutuality throughout the organization. It is no doubt their dim intuition that such is the case that keeps most organizational leaders from adopting this whole approach to organizing (and, of course, the fact that it cannot be adopted all at once in any event). However, we may predict that organizational leaders who have participated in liberating disciplines for a generation or more of their adulthood will actively seek out such conditions in order to keep themselves vigilant—in order to support their own first-person efforts to interweave moment-to-moment action and inquiry and to develop mutuality in their second-person research and practice. Moreover, they will understand that their social authenticity and mutuality with persons at all levels of conventional hierarchies, as well as their organizational transforming power, derive from their vulnerability.

At the same time, however, there is another side to this leadership vulnerability. When organizational members are young in their commitment to liberating disciplines, their attention is still predominantly restricted to what William Blake called single-visioned sleep (seeing the outside world as the only objective territory of experience, and not witnessing their own acting, thinking, and attending as equally real). As a result, their charges of leaderly or organizational incongruities may well be invalid and untrustworthy. Such charges may reflect their inability to apply Blake's "fourfold vision" (simultaneous awareness of purpose, process, action, and outcome) to themselves and their organization. An attentive leadership with such vision will turn conflicts into educational opportunities by challenging the charging members to retreat and taste and digest unexpected feedback. Indeed, the more adept the leadership is at interweaving action and inquiry, the more it will risk using all available forms of power to create a rich context for transforming inquiry, recognizing as it does so that no genuine personal or organizational transformation can be forced (Torbert, 1991).

All of the foregoing characteristics of liberating disciplines highlight the courage and wisdom required of a leadership to commit to such an organizing process in the first place, as well as the continual operation of this mode of organizing in developing courage and wisdom among all participants. Figure 10.1 offers a pictorial view of the dynamics of liberating disciplines and of the central role of free choice for all organizational participants at all times.

INTEGRATING FIRST-, SECOND-, AND THIRD-PERSON RESEARCH AND PRACTICE IN THE ORGANIZATIONAL SCIENCES

It is difficult to offer examples of scholars in our field who work at integrating first-, second-, and third-person research and practice. To do so requires working through a paradigmatic lens that is enormously different from empirical positivism, multimethod eclecticism, or even postmodern interpretivism—the three paradigmatic approaches that currently enjoy the greatest voice in the management academy and in management journals (see Exhibits 10.1 and 10.2). The paradigmatic approach that goes furthest at present in integrating first-, second-, and third-person research and practice (and that therefore corresponds to the just-described organizational approach of liberating disciplines) is what Table 10.1 and Exhibits 10.1 and 10.2 call developmental action inquiry. To my knowledge only two, little-known books are based on such an approach (Fisher and Torbert, 1995; Torbert, 1991). But let us examine briefly, by studying the table and exhibits in conjunction with the following paragraphs, how postmodern interpretivism points toward first-person research and practice, and the paradigmatic approach of cooperative inquiry toward second-person research and practice, in a process of paradigm transformation that moves toward integrating all three modes of research and practice.

Figure 10.1. Dynamic Model of the Operation of a Liberating Discipline.

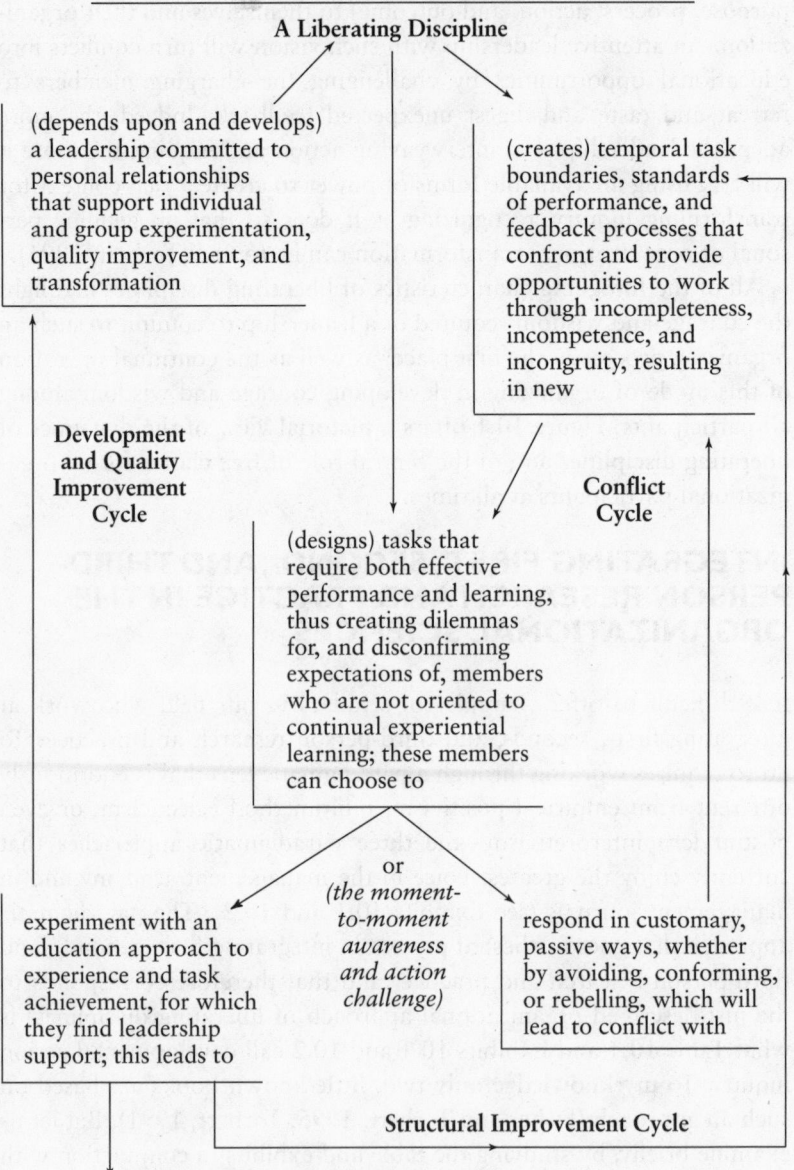

A Liberating Discipline

(depends upon and develops) a leadership committed to personal relationships that support individual and group experimentation, quality improvement, and transformation

(creates) temporal task boundaries, standards of performance, and feedback processes that confront and provide opportunities to work through incompleteness, incompetence, and incongruity, resulting in new

Development and Quality Improvement Cycle

Conflict Cycle

(designs) tasks that require both effective performance and learning, thus creating dilemmas for, and disconfirming expectations of, members who are not oriented to continual experiential learning; these members can choose to

or
(the moment-to-moment awareness and action challenge)

experiment with an education approach to experience and task achievement, for which they find leadership support; this leads to

respond in customary, passive ways, whether by avoiding, conforming, or rebelling, which will lead to conflict with

Structural Improvement Cycle

1. More effective task achievement, because system is increasingly self-correcting.
2. More learning and development by members, because experiments are supported and differences are confronted.
3. Increasing awareness of and responsibility for the relationship among organizational purposes, processes, and tasks, because the structure is increasingly perceived as empowering and just rather than repressive.

Exhibit 10.1. The Distinctive Aims of Seven Social-Scientific Paradigms.

Behaviorism	Control of the other (through "operant conditioning")
Gestalt Sociologism	Understanding of the other (better than that other's self-understanding)
Empirical Positivism	Predictive certainty (valid certainty)
Multimethod Eclecticism	Useful approximation (through triangulation)
Postmodern Interpretivism	Re-presentation of perspectival pluralism (without privileging the writer's own perspective—"Ha ha!")
Cooperative Inquiry	Creating transformational communities of inquiry (among mutually committed members with multiple perspectives)
Developmental Action Inquiry	Enacting inquiry and liberating disciplines (across initially estranged cultures without shared purposes)

Note: Each later paradigm dethrones the primacy of the previous aim, reinterprets its meaning, and addresses some of its incompleteness, by treating it as one strategic variable among others in the service of the new, qualitatively different aim. Each paradigm after Empirical Positivism becomes more inclusive of uncertain realities (rather than counting as reality only what one can be certain of) and also more inclusive of realities that are transformed by the very act of inquiring into them (for example, the researchers' own awareness and actions during the study).

David Boje seems to classify himself (and would likely be classified by others) as participating in the postmodern interpretivist paradigm (again, following Table 10.1 and Exhibits 10.1 and 10.2). Participants in this paradigmatic perspective generally espouse first-person research and practice in theory (that is, that one should write with a self-critical view of the fragmentary perspective one actually re-presents and with a deconstruction of one's own and others' hubristic and un-self-critical "grand narratives"). As often, however, these scholars stutter and duck first-person research in their practice (for example, in conversations in which the "postmodern" voice takes on a simultaneously defensive and dominating, totalizing tone). Moreover, the subjectivist, postmodern voice tends to overlook the possibility of second-person research and practice and to exercise rhetorical mystification in third-person writing (see, for example, Grudin's critique [1996] of Foucault). I apologize if I am currently throwing the very same jargon around in a similarly mystifying way; I mean to illuminate the stuttering start that this paradigmatic approach makes to integrating first-, second-, and third-person research and practice.

Although at a third-person distance one might be excused for taking instances of David Boje's rhetorical power, courage, and commitment as exemplars of the caricature of the postmodern interpretivist I have just briefly painted, my own second-person observations of and participation with David in practice persuade me that he wishes to integrate first-, second-, and third-person research and practice. He certainly means to move through his perspective to an ongoing existential search in the midst of his play/action/work, as witnessed by his proposal of marriage to his (now) wife in the midst of a session at an academic conference as well as by his current engagement in first-person, spiritual inquiry along with his third-person, administrative responsibilities.

A number of colleagues in our field, like Meryl Louis (1994) and Judi Marshall (1995), are experimenting with how to share their experiences with first- and second-person research and practices in a predominantly third-person mode. Peter Reason (1994) exemplifies the integration of first- and second-person research and practice in his own life, his professional and scholarly work, and in his writing; and in so doing he has probably ventured furthest toward enacting the cooperative inquiry paradigmatic mode (see also Heron, 1996).

Fisher and Torbert (1995) describe one experiment at integrating first-person, second-person, and third-person research and practice. We offer first-person accounts by managers of our efforts to exercise all three types of research and practice in our own companies. At the same time, we offer cases based on our own first-person, second-person, and third-person research and consulting with companies (this is not obvious, however, because the writing style ironically masks these cases as neutral, third-person accounts). Also, we do not explicitly discuss research methodology issues at all, since the book is aimed at encouraging the existential practice of action and inquiry. This ironic approach to conveying the possibility of integrating first-, second-, and third-person research and practice was adopted as a dialectical movement away from my earlier effort (Torbert, 1991) to write in an impersonal, third-person voice about third-person research and data. The 1995 book also speaks in an autobiographical voice, and as a reporter of real second-person research and practice dialogues in ongoing prac-

Exhibit 10.2. Brief Descriptions of Seven Social-Scientific Paradigms.

Behaviorism

Emanates from an *assertive, physical* quest for *reliable, unilateral control* through "operant conditioning" of an unapologetically *objectified and atomized external world*. Hence its preferred method of laboratory experiments (maximizing the scientist's unilateral control over variation); its nominalist presumption of iso-latable "stimuli" and "responses"; and its concentration on experimental sub-jects (such as rats and pigeons) that are unlikely to interpretively reframe the experiment and thus frustrate the scientist's goal. Behaviorism is particularly applicable to and successful with populations that share its assumptions about the world or inhabit total institutions (such as prisons, asylums, orphanages). Skinner (1953, 1971) was the archetypal behaviorist (see also Argyris, 1971). The special brilliance of the greatest behavioral lab experiments—such as the Asch experiments on conformity and the Milgram experiments on obedience to authority—is that they reveal the underlying lateral and hierarchical social pressures, structures, and presumptions through which this paradigm works in the human world, thereby raising the questions of whether, how, and when the human world works otherwise.

Gestalt Sociologism

Emanates from an *appreciative, emotional* quest to understand the *overall pattern* of subjective beliefs, values, and rituals of given "other" cultures. Hence its preferred method of *noninterventionist, ethnographic field observation;* its essentialist presump-tion of integrative ideas, norms, and selves (Cooley, 1956; Mead, 1934); and its concentration on ideographic case studies of human groups. The special brilliance of the greatest such studies (which have now become as controversial as they deserve to be), such as Mead's *Coming of Age in Samoa* (1960) and Whyte's *Street Corner Society* (1981), is that, by contrast to the alien culture they depict, they reveal the underlying mechanisms, categories, and presumptions through which our own encultured understanding works; and thereby, implicitly if not explicitly, they raise the question of whether our own assumptions are valid.

Empirical Positivism

Emanates from a *critical* (but not hermeneutically self-critical), *intellectual* quest for *valid certainty* about *deductively logical, universally generalizable, empirical propositions* (Cook and Campbell, 1979; Hunt, 1994). Not necessarily identified with a particular method, this paradigm privileges randomized samples; experi-mental, hypothesis-testing studies; and computer modeling of intelligence (because of the crisp and clear quantitative, binary certainty about distinctions between confirmation and disconfirmation). The special brilliance of the great-est studies in empirical positivism—such as Simon's theoretical and empirical demonstrations of the concept of bounded rationality (Simon, 1947, 1957, 1969, 1989, 1991; March and Simon, 1958; Turkle, 1991)—is that they show the limits of deductive rationality itself. The special danger of such work is that it

Exhibit 10.2.   (*continued*)

obscures the very possibility of a rationality that reaches beyond the inductive, the deductive, and the instrumental.

For example, the content of Simon's propositions about rationality may obscure the very type of constitutive rationality that Simon's work itself represents, as well as alternative constitutive rationalities (for example, those of each of the other developmental stages). The special "cleverness" of work like Simon's is that it uses the empirical positivist paradigm, its language and precision, to point to the triangulating, "satisficing" logic of multimethod eclecticism while simultaneously capturing, in the concept of "bounded rationality," the paradigmatic plight of all the developmentally early paradigms—which empirically include the psychology and methodology of well over 90 percent of all adults (Torbert, 1991).

Multimethod Eclecticism

Emanates from a *practical* quest *to increase* validity, understanding, applicability, and *percentage of the variance explained,* along with an aborning suspicion that different methods and measures may yield *incommensurable* results. Recommends *triangulation* among quantitative and qualitative methods, and is currently fashionable and in flower in the managerial disciplines (for example, see Eisenhardt, 1989; Dyer and Wilkins, 1991; Bartunek, Bobko, and Venkatraman, 1993). A brilliant example is Weick's early work in collaboration with Campbell, Dunnette, and Lawler (Campbell, Dunnette, Lawler, and Weick, 1970), *Managerial Behavior, Performance, and Effectiveness,* which is based on a "multitrait-multimethod matrix." "Disagreement between different observers," they say, "should not necessarily be viewed as a mark of unreliability . . . but should instead be viewed as a possibly valid indication that differing aspects of the manager's behavior are being accurately perceived and reported" (p. 115). Still another possibility is that disagreement among observers may result from their differing interpretive schemes, a possibility that opens us to the next paradigm, postmodern interpretivism.

Postmodern Interpretivism

Emanates from a *self-consciousness* in encountering the dilemmas of accounting for the *radical subjectivity and fragmentariness of perspective* that embraces every languaged perception and conception. No matter how validly and elegantly the strange, objecting reality at issue is clothed in the statistical, methodological, and theoretical constructions of the earlier, preparticipative social sciences, the postmodern interpretivist (for example, Denzin and Lincoln, 1994; Miller, 1994) wishes to deconstruct the implicit, presumedly neutral background of the objects foregrounded in the study, as well as that of the researcher and of the writing that makes up the critique (Fine, 1994, is an excellent brief exemplar). New types of validity are constructed, such as these:

1. Reflexive validity—a text's attempts to challenge its own validity claims (note the abstract, unillustrated voice of this "description," which is typical of postmodern interpretive writing).

2. Interpretation by the reader (such as your interpretation of this table of seven paradigms).

3. Rhizomatic validity—the text presents multiple voices that define situations differently. For example, prior to my inclusion of the italics in this description, Dal Fisher, a colleague, commented on this paragraph: "Can't help on this one, since I don't understand even a fragment of it. I guess I can suggest fewer terms (many fewer) and more illustration of actual works."

4. Situated validity—includes not just a disembodied voice but also an embodied, emotional, reflective voice (Lather, 1993) (for example, "I love Dal's and my differences").

Postmodern interpretivism strongly implies the need for a first-person research and practice (for example, Weick's *sense making*), but to date this requirement is more often stated in third-person, abstract terminology than practiced in first-person accounts interwoven with second- and third-person research.

Cooperative Inquiry

Emanates from a *commitment to creating communities that bridge subjectivities and differences of perspective and support transformation;* that is, *real-time communities of inquiry* (Spretnak, 1991; Torbert, 1976). (For example, the "family of inquiry," which includes Gregory Bateson (1972), Margaret Mead (1960), and their anthro-philosophico-autobiographical daughter, Mary Catherine Bateson, 1984, 1990.) Cooperative inquiry (Cooperrider and Srivastva, 1987; Heron, 1996; Reason, 1994) occurs in real time, with partners also committed to integrating action and inquiry (that is, to integrating first-, second-, and third-person research and practice). It recognizes that one does not first learn the truth and then act on it but rather that research itself and our lives as wholes are actions; thus we act before we deeply care about truth, we act as we seek truth (and as our sense of the truth that we seek transforms), and we seek truths that will inform not just a reflective concept of the world and future plans but our present awareness and action (MacMurray, 1953; Reason, 1995; Torbert, 1981).

The difficult and important questions come to be seen as how, in the midst of participating intersubjectively in specific situations, one can listen, experiment, and seek disconfirmation (Argyris, Putnam, and Smith, 1985) in a timely fashion (Torbert, 1991). Likewise, the primary question becomes not how to create an off-line community of inquiry among scientific writers and journal editors but how to create a real-time community of inquiry within one's family, at work, or within voluntary organizations to which one belongs. Fine (1994) points in this direction when she writes, "In the early 1990s, the whispers of a collective of activist researchers can be heard . . . seeking to work with, but not

Exhibit 10.2.   (*continued*)

romanticize, subjugated voices, searching for moments of social justice" (p. 81). Social constructivism is an epistemological interpretation consistent with this paradigmatic approach (Gergen, 1994).

Developmental Action Inquiry

Emanates from a growing appreciation that different persons, organizations, and cultures are complex, chaotic interweavings of the six prior paradigms (Pondy and Mitroff, 1979). No single one of these paradigms will win the paradigm war once and for all. Indeed, this very definition of the situation is illusory: it is not martial arts and paradigm wars but the arts of healing and interparadigmatic conversation and work that become a beckoning, shareable (but not *easily* shareable) purpose. An interweaving of first-, second-, and third-person research and practice makes such interparadigmatic conversation and work sustainable.

From the integrative developmental action inquiry perspective, each paradigmatic perspective is a positively powerful and beneficial analogue of the preeminent features of a situation at different moments and in recognized complementarity to the other approaches. By contrast, each paradigmatic perspective becomes demonic if it is asserted as the only legitimate kind of truth in all moments. "An active consciousness holds all ideas lightly" (Marshall, 1995).

Whereas each of the prior paradigms tends to emphasize its revolutionary dissimilarity from the paradigms before it, developmental action inquiry highlights the contrapuntal rhythms, interruptions, and interventions in developmental movement from one paradigm to another, whether in single conversations or in whole lives (Torbert, 1989). Fisher and Torbert (1995) provide an illustration of research in multiple modes, ranging from quantitative lab experiments using psychometric measures (empirical positivism) to multivoiced, qualitative culture studies (postmodern interpretivism) and cases of "observant participants" exercising real-time first-, second-, and third-person research and practice in their work.

All types of validity testing described in earlier paradigms are accepted as conditionally appropriate, depending on the degree to which one's current aims correspond with the purpose of truth seeking in that paradigm. Finally, however, in developmental action inquiry generalization is recognized as occurring one person at a time, and slowly within that person (over a lifetime) as she or he practices awareness-expanding action inquiry at more and more moments.

tice settings where we attempted to integrate first, second-, and third-person research and practice. Readers of Donald Schön's foreword to *The Reflective Practitioner* (1983) will recall that this early attempt at explicit ("naked") action inquiry led to strong charges of scientific impropriety ("blithe disregard for questions of validity and rigor" [p. xiii]): hence the dialectical choice to practice ironic masking in the 1995 book.

How to write in a coherent yet multi-genred manner that conveys to others the challenge, opportunity, and invitation to join the play in this type of research and practice is an ongoing question for me. This chapter is one more response. For my next, and last, major project I now imagine weaving together art, poetry, music, and video in a work of "social-science fiction" under a pseudonym (Mark O. Teufel in English, Signatûre deVil in French, and so on). But this choice is not taken with the belief that social-science fiction is the normative genre for developmental action inquiry. Rather it is taken as a next step in this scholar-practitioner's ongoing exploration of writing genres, research methods, and daily professional practice (that is, it is hopefully a liberating discipline for my work). What is clear in general is that all forms that aspire to integrating first-, second-, and third-person research and practice can generalize themselves only one person at a time, as you, or you, or you make an increasing commitment to integrating your research with your practice.

SEEKING, ALONE AND WITH OTHERS, TO INTEGRATE COURAGE AND WISDOM

I envisage the wisdom we seek through integrating first-, second-, and third-person research and practice as something embracing and hard to pin down—as having something to do with an awareness that integrates being, thinking, doing, and effectuating in our real-time relationships with others, as we create conditions for them to do so as well. How might you amend this characterization?

It seems to me that it takes courage to face and to suffer through our ongoing existential incongruities (for example, between what we meant, what we said, what we did, and the result we had) as we inquire toward wise integrity. Or is finding, properly conceptualizing, accepting, and transforming incongruities easy for you? or unimportant? or a disheartening way to guide practice?

It also seems to me that in a true moment-to-moment search (if we can even imagine such a commitment) there must surely be millions of such incongruous times—some minor, some major, some significant, some less so. Can you envision a true first-person search amid life that does not highlight the digestion of incongruities?

The closest I can come to envisioning the ultimate courage and the ultimate wisdom is as a taste for continually listening into the strum and scrape, the harmony and ache, of synesthetic, many-meaninged, dialogic experiencing (Grudin, 1996)—and as a taste for continually facing the creative dilemma of fashioning responsive, awakening thought and action in the present.

This listening and feeling with wonder; this vulnerability and suffering, without self-pity; this active attending can occur whether I am alone, with friends, or at work. Wise, courageous action does not so much alternate as dialogue with such continual listening. Are you at all familiar with such listening? Are you practicing it now as you read, listening simultaneously into yourself and into this writing? Does anything in you want to find someone or some tradition of practice that will challenge you to listen so more often, more deeply?

Those of us who are, or aspire to be, knowledgeable—such as those who participated in the conference at Case University that led to these chapters and this book—too easily substitute prefabricated rationalization and verbalization for the wonderful listening toward which wise courage continually resteers us. We who aspire to be "intellectuals" tend to equate knowledge and wisdom. But, in fact, my growing understanding is that wisdom is in essential, eternal tension with knowledge (as we ordinarily conceive knowledge). Hence Vaill's phrase, "the unspeakable texture of process wisdom" (Chapter Two).

Modern scientific knowledge is almost entirely the product of third-person, impersonal research conducted "off-line" (of course, the researcher is engaged in ongoing "on-line" experience throughout the research, but this quality of his or her experience is not attended to as part of the research). By contrast, the developmental action inquiry paradigm treats wisdom as the ongoing "on-line" integration of first-person research, second-person research, and third-person research conducted in the midst of action with others and in which the researcher recognizes himself or herself as an "observant participant" (Torbert, 1991, 1995).

Put differently again, wisdom has to do with integrating being, knowing, doing, and effecting *in a timely fashion;* by contrast, knowledge of local facts and generalizable theories almost never has anything to do with timing (and even when it does, as with developmental theory, thinking about the theory can substitute itself for attending to all the other layers of self and others in the present).

Modern science privileges as knowledge what we can be certain about at a distance. Because an embracing research and practice are a more significant proportion of reality, they guide our attention more to our present participation in the uncertain action of transformation that is occurring within each of us, as well as between ourselves and our family, friends, and colleagues and in the larger world. As we become increasingly wise, our attention parses itself out increasingly properly among what we know, where we are ignorant, and the overall interaction between what we can be more and less certain about. The wise woman's hammer does not bounce shy of the nail even as she wonders whether she will finish the shingling before the storm.

Again: knowledge "means" within paradigmatic limits; wisdom tests assumptions as well as theories, methods, and data, thus coming to "mean" across paradigms. And yet again: knowledge accumulates; wisdom empties (or dis-illusions, or reveals a deeper listening and a deeper rhythm). Educating the mind—as in modern science—generates mental dexterity and knowledge; educating the attention—as in an interweaving of first-person, second-person, and third-person research and practice amid our everyday living, loving, and working—generates conscious relatedness among mind, feeling, body, and nature and between motive and reach.

Educating the attention in the direction of ongoing inquiry amid acting (about the relationships among having, doing, knowing, and being), at an organizational level (about the relationships among outcomes, operations, strategies, and mission) and in science (about the relationships among data, methods, theories, and paradigmatic approaches)—such a repeatedly transformational research and practice generates wisdom. At least, that is the perspective elucidated here.

NOTE

1. I capitalize this term because, now that I have discovered it, the position seems a kind of ideal type to me—an eternal position that deserves to be experienced repeatedly so as to learn from attentively resting in it. This means it is not, for example, just an exercise to perform on a long flight because one has little room to do others.

REFERENCES

Alderfer, C. "Taking Ourselves Seriously as Researchers." In D. Berg and K. Smith (eds.), *The Self in Social Inquiry*. Thousand Oaks, Calif.: Sage, 1988.

Alderfer, C. "Theories Reflecting My Personal Experience and Life Development." *Journal of Applied Behavioral Science,* 1989, *25*(4), 351–364.

Argyris, C. [Review of B. F. Skinner's *Beyond Freedom and Dignity.*] Harvard Educational Review, 1971, *41*(4), 550–567.

Argyris, C., Putnam, R., and Smith, D. *Action Science: Concepts, Methods and Skills for Research and Intervention.* San Francisco: Jossey-Bass, 1985.

Bartunek, J., Bobko, P., and Venkatraman, N. "Toward Innovation and Diversity in Management Research Methods." *The Academy of Management Journal,* 1993, *36*(6), 1362–1373.

Bateson, G. "'Metalogues' and 'Theological Categories of Learning and Communication.'" In G. Bateson (ed.), *Steps to an Ecology of Mind.* Novato, Calif.: Chandler & Sharp, 1972.

Bateson, M. C. *With a Daughter's Eye: A Memoir of Margaret Mead and Gregory Bateson.* New York: HarperCollins, 1984.

Bateson, M. C. *Composing a Life.* New York: Penguin Books, 1990.

Bedeain, A. *Management Laureates: A Collection of Autobiographical Essays.* 3 vols. Greenwich, Conn.: JAI Press, 1993.

Bloom, A. *The Republic of Plato.* Chicago: University of Chicago Press, 1967.

Buber, M. *I and Thou.* New York: Scribner, 1958.

Campbell, D., Dunnette, M., Lawler, E., and Weick, K. *Managerial Behavior, Performance, and Effectiveness.* New York: McGraw-Hill, 1970.

Cook, T., and Campbell, D. *Quasi-Experimentation: Design and Analysis Issues for Field Settings.* Skokie, Ill.: Rand McNally, 1979.

Cooley, C. *Two Major Works: Social Organization. Human Nature and Social Order.* New York: Free Press, 1956.

Cooperrider, D., and Srivastva, S. "Appreciative Inquiry in Organizational Life." In R. Woodman and W. Pasmore (eds.), *Research on Organizational Change and Development.* Greenwich, Conn.: JAI Press, 1987.

Denzin, N., and Lincoln, Y. *Handbook of Qualitative Research.* Thousand Oaks, Calif.: Sage, 1994.

Dyer, W., and Wilkins, A. "Better Stories, Not Better Constructs, to Generate Better Theory: A Rejoinder to Eisenhardt." *Academy of Management Review,* 1991, *16*(3), 613–619.

Eisenhardt, K. "Building Theories from Case Study Research." *Academy of Management Review,* 1989, *14*(4), 532–550.

Feyerabend, P. K. *Against Method: Outline of an Anarchistic Theory of Knowledge.* Atlantic Highlands, N.J.: Humanities Press, 1975.

Fine, M. "Working the Hyphens: Reinventing Self and Other in Qualitative Research." In N. Denzin and Y. Lincoln (eds.), *Handbook of Qualitative Research.* Thousand Oaks, Calif.: Sage, 1994.

Fisher, D., and Torbert, W. *Personal and Organizational Transformations: The True Challenge of Continual Quality Improvement.* New York: McGraw-Hill, 1995.

Gergen, K. *Realities and Relationships: Soundings in Social Construction.* Cambridge, Mass.: Harvard University Press, 1994.

Grudin, R. *Undialogue: An Essay in Free Thought.* Boston: Houghton Mifflin, 1996.

Gurdjieff, G. *Life Is Real Only Then When 'I Am.'* New York: Triangle Press, 1981.

Harrison, R. *Consultant's Journey: A Dance of Work and Spirit.* San Francisco: Jossey-Bass, 1995.

Heron, J. *Cooperative Inquiry: Research into the Human Condition.* Thousand Oaks, Calif.: Sage, 1996.

Howe, P. "Medical Schools Faulted on Emphasis: Low Regard Found for Primary Care." *Boston Globe,* Sept. 4, 1996, p. A9.

Hunt, S. "On the Rhetoric of Qualitative Methods: Toward Historically Informed Argumentation in Management Inquiry." *Journal of Management Inquiry,* 1994, 3(3), 221–234.

Jourard, S. *Disclosing Man to Himself.* New York: Van Nostrand Reinhold, 1968.

Journal of Applied Behavioral Science, 25(4), 1989.

Kaplan, M. *Sexual Justice: Citizenship and the Politics of Desire.* New York: Routlege, 1997.

Karasek, R., and Theorell, T. *Healthy Work: Stress, Productivity, and the Reconstruction of Working Life.* New York: Basic Books, 1991.

Katz, J., and Kahn, R. *The Social Psychology of Organizations.* New York: Wiley, 1978.

Kegan, R. *The Evolving Self.* Cambridge, Mass.: Harvard University Press, 1982.

Kramer, R. "The Birth of Client-Centered Therapy: Carl Rogers, Otto Rank, and 'the Beyond.'" *Journal of Humanistic Psychology,* 1995, 35(4), 54–110.

Lather, P. "Fertile Obsession: Validity After Poststructuralism." *The Sociological Quarterly,* 1993, 34(4), 673–693.

Louis, M. "In the Manner of Friends: Learning from Quaker Practice for Organizational Renewal." *Journal of Organizational Change Management,* 1994, 7(1), 42–60.

MacMurray, J. *The Self as Agent and Persons in Relation.* Winchester, Mass.: Faber & Faber, 1953.

March, J., and Simon, H. *Organizations.* New York: Wiley, 1958.

Marshall, J. *Women Managers Moving On: Travelers in a Male World.* New York: Routledge, 1995.

Mead, G. *Mind, Self, and Society from the Standpoint of a Social Behaviorist.* Chicago: University of Chicago Press, 1934.

Mead, M. *Coming of Age in Samoa: A Psychological Study of Primitive Youth for Western Civilization.* New York: Mentor, 1960.

Miller, M. *Natural Thought and Transcendence in Adulthood: The Further Reaches of Adult Development.* Lanham, Md.: Rowman & Littlefield, 1994.

Min, A. *Red Azalea: Life and Love in China.* London: Victor Golancz, 1993.

Novelli, L., and others. "The Supervisor's Role in Self-Managed Work Teams: Four Alternative Perspectives Applied to a Case." Paper presented at an Academy of Management symposium, Washington D.C., 1989.

Pondy, L., and Mitroff, I. "Beyond Open-System Models of Organization." In B. M. Staw (ed.), *Research in Organizational Behavior.* Greenwich, Conn.: JAI Press, 1979.

Ramsey, M. *Where I Stopped: Remembering Rape at Thirteen.* New York: Putnam, 1995.

Rank, O. *Will Therapy: An Analysis of the Therapeutic Process in Terms of Relationship.* New York: Norton, 1978.

Reason, P. *Participation in Human Inquiry.* Thousand Oaks, Calif.: Sage, 1994.

Reason, P. "General Medical and Complementary Practitioners Working Together: The Epistemological Demands of Collaboration." Paper presented at the Symposium on Transforming Self, Work, and Scientific Inquiry, Academy of Management national meeting, Vancouver, 1995.

Rogers, C. *On Becoming a Person.* Boston: Houghton Mifflin, 1961.

Schmid, T. *Laches: A Dialogue on Manly Courage.* Ithaca, N.Y.: Cornell University Press, 1993.

Schön, D. *The Reflective Practitioner.* New York: Basic Books, 1983.

Simon, H. *Administrative Behavior.* Old Tappan, N.J.: Macmillan, 1947.

Simon, H. *Models of Man.* New York: Wiley, 1957.

Simon, H. *The Sciences of the Artificial.* Cambridge, Mass.: MIT Press, 1969.

Simon, H. *Models of Thought.* New Haven, Conn.: Yale University Press, 1989.

Simon, H. *Models of My Life.* New York: Basic Books, 1991.

Skinner, B. *Science and Human Behavior.* Old Tappan, N.J.: Macmillan, 1953.

Skinner, B. *Beyond Freedom and Dignity.* New York: Knopf, 1971.

Spretnak, C. *States of Grace: The Recovery of Meaning in the Postmodern Age.* New York: HarperCollins, 1991.

Torbert, W. "Doing Rawls' Justice." *Harvard Educational Review,* 1974, 44(4), 459–470.

Torbert, W. *Creating a Community of Inquiry.* New York: Wiley, 1976.

Torbert, W. "Educating Toward Shared Purpose, Self-Direction, and Quality Work: The Theory and Practice of Liberating Structure." *Journal of Higher Education,* 1978, 49(2), 109–135.

Torbert, W. "Why Educational Research Is So Uneducational: Toward A New Model of Social Science Based on Collaborative Inquiry." In P. Reason and J. Rowan (eds.), *Human Inquiry: A Sourcebook of New Paradigm Research*. New York: Wiley, 1981.

Torbert, W. "Leading Organizational Transformation." In R. Woodman and W. Pasmore (eds.), *Research in Organizational Change and Developments*. (9 vols.) Greenwich, Conn.: JAI Press, 1989.

Torbert, W. *The Power of Balance: Transforming Self, Society, and Scientific Inquiry*. Thousand Oaks, Calif.: Sage, 1991.

Torbert, W. "A Scientific Paradigm That Integrates Quantitative, Qualitative, and Action Research." Paper presented at the Symposium on Transforming Self, Work, and Scientific Inquiry, Academy of Management national meeting, Vancouver, 1995.

Torbert, W., and Fisher, D. "Autobiographical Awareness as a Catalyst for Managerial and Organizational Development." *Management Education and Development Journal*, 1992, 23(3), 184–198.

Truax, C., and Carkhuff, R. *Toward Effective Counseling and Psychotherapy*. Hawthorne, N.Y.: Aldine de Gruyter, 1967.

Turkle, S. "And Machines with Big Ideas: A Review of H. Simon's *Models of My Life*." *New York Times Book Review*, 1991.

Whyte, W. F. *Street Corner Society: The Social Structure of an Italian Slum*. (3rd ed.) Chicago: University of Chicago Press, 1981.

11

AN EPILOGUE: AN INVITATION
TO FUTURE DIALOGUE

Suresh Srivastva and Argun Saatçioğlu

THIS CHAPTER IS ABOUT a mode of understanding or knowing that relates to two fundamental human activities that are anything but new—imagining and engaging in dialogue. Imagination has always been at the service of humans, for creating cultures, civilizations, technologies, religions, altered pasts. It is often our connection to the novel and our way of dealing with the unknown. Dialogue has always been a principal way in which human beings relate to one another. Our natural tendency is to engage in dialogue with others—especially when, in Mikhail Bakhtin's words (1981), different standpoints expressing and enacting particular specificities come into contact, as in our day and age. Diversity of views and realities often makes what transpires between individuals more important than what they individually contain. From a wider perspective, imagination and dialogue come into view as tightly coupled human processes, supporting each other. As humans relate to each other dialogically, they create possibilities for mutual expansion of their thoughts and imaginations, which eventually propels them to new, original states of being and relating.

In our opinion, humans' ability to dialogue with one another in meaningful ways and to shape reality out of their imaginations is becoming increasingly essential for the future. These capabilities can enable us to make sense of the uncertainties and puzzles of our time as well as to actively construct shared, inspiring futures. In more elaborate terms, imagination and dialogue can become the primary means of generating knowledge about our complex realities, which can lay the ground for ever newer realities to be constructed. Knowledge is defined as a dialogic construct for the imaginative search for truth, and wisdom is defined as a virtue that promotes knowledge as such. Thus, achieving wisdom is testimony to embracing imagination and dialogue as a means of generating knowledge. Now, in view of that testimony, courage may be defined as an attitude that helps sustain wisdom. For wisdom is a moving target, because knowledge and truth are moving targets.

By promoting and sustaining imaginative and dialogic construction of knowledge, wisdom and courage can help organizations to survive and even thrive on the complexities and uncertainties of our day and age. Knowing can become a way of living in the present while creating new futures that reflect the originality of organization members' imagination and dialogues. The road to organizational wisdom is an organizational culture conducive to imagining and to relating dialogically. Given that imagination and dialogue are among the basic elements that shape human life, organizations need to assign them higher significance in determining how their organizational life evolves. What follows is our account of what this means and how it can be done.

In the first section following we describe how imagination can be brought explicitly to the service of understanding complex processes and phenomena. We also discuss some of the ways organizations can move away from the conventional to make their cultures more conducive to "imaginative knowing." The second section is about the dialogic origins of imagination and knowledge. It describes the characteristics of dialogue, provides a brief illustration of a dialogue, and elaborates on how organizations can make dialogue a relational norm. The chapter concludes by extending an open invitation to our readers to conceive alternative ways for imagination and dialogue to play a role in organizational life. The earlier chapters have provided cues and clues for the construction of a set of propositions that can serve as a source for continuing dialogue.

IMAGINATIVE KNOWING

Alfred North Whitehead (1938) believed that the perception of instability and actual instability constantly presuppose each other. For him, any claim of stability in any area of life constitutes a fallacy. "The essence of life," he wrote, "is to be found in the frustrations of the established order" (p. 87). By "order" he meant the relatively stable fragments of life, and by "frustrations," the constant movements from one such fragment to another. He implied that we can discover the unique aspects of life by interpreting instability and understanding the dynamics of how fragments of life interrelate.

This, as a matter of fact, is something we do every day, though perhaps with less rigor. When we try to make sense of our lives—or the lives of others, of nations, of cultures, or of organizations—we are interpreting the interrelations among fragments that make up meaningful wholes uniquely mapped out through time, rather than mere collections of isolated events or experiences. For instance, at times we take into account our childhood's impact on our adolescence, or our adolescence's impact on our adulthood, to make sense of our actions as adults. At other times we choose to fragment the past in different ways (for example, considering every ten years or each job we held) to make sense of the present. We rarely treat the fragments as isolated, unrelated segments. However, when we attempt to take our efforts to understand life further than usual and introduce some type of disciplined rigor into our questioning, we may feel pressured to pretend, at least temporarily, as if the fragments of life are disconnected. Rigor and precision by definition require "zoomed-in scrutiny" of the phenomena under investigation. Thus we concentrate on one fragment at a time, understand it to the best of our ability, and then try to make sense of how all the fragments interrelate. The trade-off involved in this rigorous procedure is that such a way of knowing can block our view of the whole and actually conceal certain interrelations among fragments that could potentially alter the meaning of the whole.

When we restrict our analyses to an aggregation of single fragments, we perceive relative stability and clarity but confine our interpretations and the dimensions of our knowledge to fragmental boundaries. On the other hand, when we concentrate on interrelations we observe instability and complexity, but our interpretations intensify and our knowledge of life potentially expands. Whitehead (1929) calls the act of knowledge generation, as such, "process thinking"—a holistic method of knowing life by making sense of the interrelations among its fragments.

Even though there is no one best way of knowing and understanding, process thinking is highly beneficial for organizations in meeting today's demands for knowledge and sensemaking. Things in and around organizations change so fast that to capture one fragment, isolate it, and scrutinize it with rigor usually lasts longer than the fragment itself. Therefore, concentrating on interrelations, by consciously employing process thinking, would prove to be more meaningful. The question then becomes, If fragments are short-lived, then how can organizations ever sufficiently understand the perplexing interrelations among them? The answer to this question brings forth what we call "imaginative knowing"—a way of knowing that couples process thinking with a proactive orientation. Imaginative knowing involves employing process thinking to understand the interrelations in which organizations participate proactively, rather than the ones they view as independent of them. Understanding interrelations that are shaped proactively is not only sensible but also more enriching than understanding those that are normally out of sight of our senses and intuition. The knowledge attained is a product of imagination, reflecting organizations' capacity to shape their lives and create their futures. A brief example of imaginative knowing will help illustrate the dynamics through which such a capacity is unleashed.

After accomplishing a challenging or puzzling task we are sometimes bewildered because we cannot recall all the steps we took to accomplish it. And if we ever do recall the whole process, the quality of our understanding depends heavily on our determining a meaningful relationality among our actions. Struggling to solve Rubik's Cube is a perfect illustration of this phenomenon. We patiently try out numerous sequences of moves until one sequence satisfies. In the end, the knowledge of the cube we attain by imaginative knowing is actually the knowledge of a sequence of interrelated moves that we shaped proactively. Having no predetermined script to rely on, we relied on our imagination to know the cube. Our *imagination* informed our process of shaping the cube, whereas our ability to understand that process revealed to us bits and pieces of the cube's endless unknowns.

Given the fact that the cube is, like life itself, an endless puzzle, our knowledge of it is, at best, imaginative and transformative—but never complete. Its real value lies in the fact that it can lead us to further imagining and thus new improvisations. New, untried sequences always await us: such is the outcome of imaginative knowing. It converges uncertainty, improvisation, change, and process thinking in such a way that the future is shaped by the knower but always consists of new unknowns, new starting points. As seen in Figure 11.1, when conceived in continuous, unfolding terms, each convergence becomes the starting point for the next. The primary constant is the imaginative nature of the knowledge attained. As illustrated in the figure, *imaginative knowing elicits knowledge inspired by uncertainty, preempted by instability (change), and grounded in improvisation.* Wisdom promotes imaginative knowing as a means of shaping the future. It is a virtue that bridges past, present, future, and knowing to locate new unknowns that can potentially keep our imagination vibrantly active in the service of the endless struggle to establish truth.

Given the outcome of imaginative knowing, two legitimate questions logically follow: To what extent is imaginative knowing applicable to organizations, and in which situations? After all, not everything we do in life is analogous to solving Rubik's Cube.

It is outside our cognitive and affective capabilities to analyze all actions in organizations to find patterns that explain why organizational behavior is the way it is "at present." Moreover, organizations do not always face or perceive uncertainty severe enough to motivate members to be proactive and improvisational. But these facts still do not undermine the significance of imaginative knowing. The issue here is not simply when organizations need imaginative knowing or whether or not they can engage in it, it is whether or not they prefer it. *Imaginative knowing is a preference.* There is no logical way to measure its applicability precisely or to determine optimal situations for it. Apart from our conviction that it is wiser to be able to be a proactive process thinker in our day and age, we can offer four observations that justify an organizational preference for imaginative knowing.

First of all, preferring imaginative knowing implies an appreciation of uncertainty. Members of an organization would hardly be passionate enough to proactively shape the interrelations in and around their work life if they did not enjoy the potential uncertainty involved in the process. Reliability and predictability are obscured. A conscious preference for imaginative knowing requires more than mere tolerance of uncertainty, however; it requires a view of uncertainty as a gift. One simply must "like" Rubik's Cube in order to be able to "know" it better.

Second, favoring imaginative knowing implies an intrinsic motivation to improvise. An organization that prefers imaginative knowing favors experiments, spontaneity, serendipity, and surprise. Members do not always think and act with a set of strictly predefined procedures or agendas before them. Rather, improvisation is a state of mind for them, one that can potentially create a reordered future.

Third, preferring imaginative knowing implies a view of change as opportunity. The imaginative organization thrives on change rather than reacting to it. Every recognized change is an opportunity to redefine and improve the organization. Members also deliberately

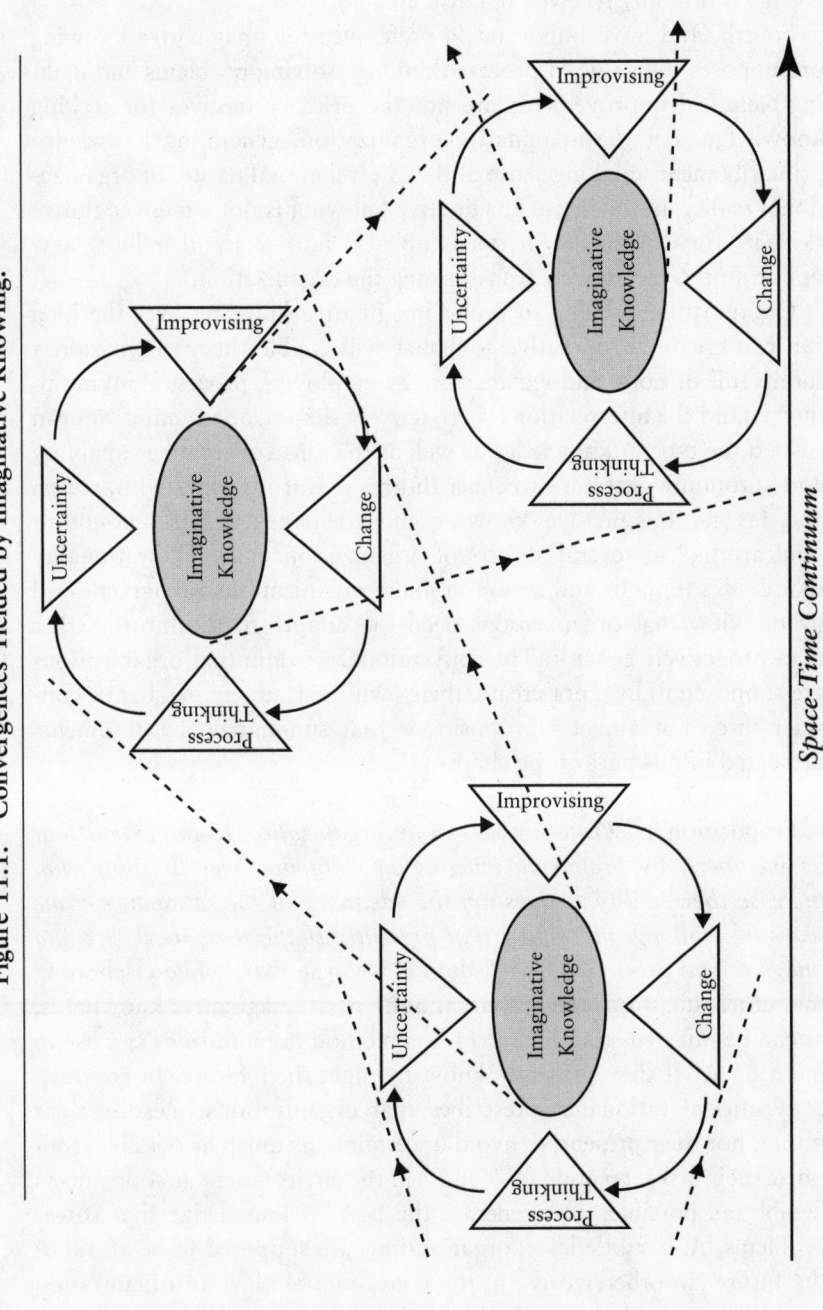

Figure 11.1. Convergences Yielded by Imaginative Knowing.

introduce instability into their work life, to reconfigure it. In this way change is not only received but also created.

Fourth, and most important, a preference for imaginative knowing presupposes the value of process thinking. Solving problems and making technical improvements are not the primary motives for seeking knowledge. For the imaginative organization, generating knowledge primarily means making sense of the interrelational nature of organizational reality. In this sense imaginative knowing is not a mere cognitive skill, it is a way of life. It opens up new horizons and induces new opportunities for actively transforming the organization.

Organizations willing to prefer imaginative knowing over the long run can create an operative soul that will enable them to envision a future full of hope and excitement. By employing process thinking to understand the interrelations it proactively shapes, an organization can sustain the type of knowledge as well as the sense of creative capability and autonomy necessary to enact futures that it identifies with, trusts, and favors. Imaginative knowing thus demands a fair amount of "unlearning" in several aspects of organizational life. The rationality that guides thought and action in many organizations is characterized by the view that organizations need to "adapt" to the future rather than proactively enact it. The conventional wisdom that organizations are supposed to live, not create, their own life is untenable. Let us consider three fundamental propositions that summarize the arguments presented in this part of the chapter.

Proposition 1: *Wisdom exists in an organization to the extent that its members, by preferring imaginative knowing over the long run, increase their ability to question the adequacy of the rational, routine ways of thinking and acting that presently shape their work life and imagine new ways to live.* Wisdom is a virtue that, while celebrating the future, questions the present and the past. Imaginative knowing is, as can be inferred from Figure 11.1, a method organizations can use to build on what they presently know to enact their future. In contrast, conventional rationality prescribes that organizations question their future, not their present, to avoid uncertainty as much as possible, routinize their tasks, respond to changes in the environment as soon and as flexibly as possible, and generate the type of knowledge that solves problems. At a subtle level, organizations are supposed to be afraid of the future. In other words, in the conventional view an organization needs to constantly secure certainty; refrain from spontaneous, improvisational ways of acting; react to rather than thrive on change; and generate or obtain the knowledge needed to maintain their present state rather than create their future. This paradigm is inconsistent with the assumptions of imaginative knowing.

The unfamiliarity of imaginative knowing to conventional rationality becomes even more clear when we test it against some of the key prevailing organizational doctrines and principles. In most formal organizations, for instance, rationality dictates that uncertainty and variation around core activities should be eliminated as much as possible (Thompson, 1967). Thus structures of organizations, and of parts of organizations, vary according to the types of uncertainties they confront (Stinchcombe, 1990), meaning that different parts of the organization function to "shield" it from different sources of uncertainty. The rationale for key organizational arrangements is to make sure that critical activities are not compromised by unexpected or uncontrollable factors. Improvisational motives and approaches are therefore especially avoided in core organizational activities—where imaginative knowing can make the biggest difference. Wisdom is minimized at the level where it can produce the highest benefit. Furthermore, organizations usually assess the quality of their structures, designs, and other arrangements in relation to the "demands of the environment" (Burns and Stalker, 1961; Emery and Trist, 1965; Lawrence and Lorsch, 1967; Mintzberg, 1979), not in relation to what proactive imagination can elicit. Organizational action, to a large extent, reflects members' perceptions of the environment (Chandler, 1962; Duncan, 1972; Milliken, 1987), not what the organization is actually capable of doing. Change is something the environment imposes on the organization, not a part *of* the organization. Hence basic motives for pursuing wisdom are conventionally not in place.

Organizational norms that reflect a fear of the future are evident even in less conventional genres of organizational thought and action that entertain the idea that organizations can and do shape their environments. For instance, a group of organizations may opt for a collective strategy to make their common environment more accommodating (Astley and Fombrun, 1983). They may choose, for example, to establish strategic relationships with one another to eliminate uncertainty in resource acquisition, competitive strategies, and political developments (Pfeffer and Salancik, 1978; Galaskiewicz, 1985). In such cases organizations do indeed act proactively to enact their future, but they are still aiming at *reducing uncertainty;* they rarely tap their members' imaginations to determine what they can do to shape *themselves,* rather than their environment. This type of proactivity does not lead to improvisation or imaginative knowledge. It is not a consequence of wisdom, it is merely "good strategy."

Examples abound of the incompatibility between conventional rationality and imaginative knowing. The origin of this incompatibility (and of the myth of the "fearful future") is rooted in the long-lasting *systems view* of organizations. The functionalist character of this view emphasizes the survival value of adapting to changes in the environment and of solving problems that compromise the "steady state" of organizations (Katz and Kahn, 1966). To an open system, uncertainty and instability are the worst of enemies. They are, in von Bertalannfy's (1968) words, "entropic" factors that threaten the system. In this respect, stamina, durability, and endurance are organizational needs more primary than imagination.

While the systems view has served organizations well as a conceptual tool for understanding and improving the maintenance of their life, progress in organizational life in a time of overabundant complexity and diversity seems to require organizations to move their focus beyond concerns for maintenance to concerns for imagination—or, beyond concerns for the present to concerns for the future. In a systems perspective, unquestioned concern for "adaptivity" and "equilibrium" chain organizational thought and action to the realities of the present or the past instead of the future. In other words, in times of uncertainty and change, the organization typically tries to stay how it is or go back to how it was before, rather than explore how it can be in the future. As a legend of modern functionalist sociology, Talcott Parsons (1951), puts it, how a social system maintains its present configuration is more primary than how it changes in terms of its health and survival. Imaginative knowing, on the other hand, runs on imagining the future, not on survival instincts. Wisdom in an organization that prefers imaginative knowing locates and enacts the future rather than the past or the present. In the long run, the proactive, improvisational introduction of instability to the organization is valued more than maintaining the status quo.

Due to its emphasis on the status quo, the systems view both necessitates and accommodates knowledge of the past and the present. This does not mean merely seeking out an understanding of history or explanations of today. Rather, it means that knowledge shaped by the systems view is meant to solve problems that began in the past and threaten the present state of the system. Therefore, conventional organizational knowledge is typically biased toward the present and the past and never oriented toward the future. Such is the case even when this knowledge is designed to be predictive of the future, because the agenda is still the maintenance of the status quo. Knowledge that seems to be irrelevant to the present or to predicted troubles are considered "strange" and "useless" by decision makers and organizational members in general (Mackenzie, 1994). "Good" knowledge is supposed to be the kind that helps the organization survive, not imagine; live, not create; adapt, not enact; and receive, not generate.

There is a critical connection between this conventional view of knowledge and the dimensions of knowledge that are usually generated in organizations. Problems that threaten the present state of the organizational system have traditionally been believed to be easier to both spot and understand in terms of the parts rather than the whole of the system. The thinking is that there is something wrong with a department, a machine, an employee, a task force, and so on, and due to that problem the overall system is presently compromised or might become compromised in the future. Hence, organizational knowledge that is past- or present-oriented is sought out with a heavy focus on the "troubled parts" of the system. The knowledge of the whole at any point in time is an aggregation of what is known of the parts. To put it another way, dimensions of organizational knowledge are traditionally confined to fragmental boundaries. Members are knowledgeable only about things that concern their work, not the work of others in the organization. How the fragments interrelate through time is a big, collective, forgotten mystery. Therefore, proactively shaping interrelations through time is a choice, a preference that is typically absent from the rational mind-set of the organized collective. Wisdom, by promoting imaginative knowledge, would enable such an organization to move beyond a fragmented view of itself and care primarily for the interrelations within its environment, structures, and life. The proactive motives that accompany this future-oriented, interrelational, holistic view enable an organization to develop a sense of what it *can* do and avoid being locked into what it *has* to do.

Coming back full circle, we can reinterpret imaginative knowing as a set of intentional, consecutive steps members of an organization can take while questioning the conventional, rational, systematic, fragmental views that shape their work lives. Appreciating uncertainty opens the doors to questioning what is already known and familiar and understanding new and initially strange things. Improvisation builds a sense of creative, imaginative capability and joy. Viewing change as opportunity maintains a proactive spirit. And imaginative knowing opens the doors to the celebrated, unknown territories of the future.

Proposition 2: *Wisdom exists in an organization to the extent that its members are free to question the adequacy of ways of thinking and acting in all areas of organizational activity and free to imagine without fear of bureaucratic control or pressure.* The bureaucratic, hierarchical culture in many organizations is not conducive to imaginative ways of living. Routines are not questioned unless there is sufficient evidence of a drop in efficiency and those doing the questioning have sufficient power to bring about change (Weber, 1947). One of the fundamental functions of bureaucracy is to control and predict organizational members' behavior. Impersonal role structures, spans of control, and authority relationships are created and routinized in the service of sustainable efficiency and organizational control. Bureaucratic optimization allocates a limited space for each individual and group, within which they have to think and operate. Each member is expected to learn and internalize ways of thinking and acting that concern only her or his individual task, responsibility, department, and so on. Knowledge of the rest of the organization is inaccessible at best. Thus, even if the members of a bureaucratic organization increase their ability to question the adequacy of the rational, routine ways of thinking and acting that shape their work life, the organization disapproves of their actually asking such questions. Organizational members are especially discouraged from questioning organizational inadequacies related to anything that falls outside their individual or departmental fragments. The point here is not whether members are informed about practices in parts of the organization other than theirs or even whether they can criticize them, it is whether or not they are aware of the patterns of thought and action that form the background of these practices. In most bureaucracies, differentiation of roles and power, both horizontally and vertically, is maintained by strict rules. Violating these rules usually elicits some form of reprimand, punishment, or negative reinforcement. Solid boundaries enforce a fragmented vision of organizational life. As mentioned earlier, fragmental awareness and concerns lead to fragmental knowledge. Therefore members in an organization need to be free to transcend bureaucratic barriers and realities to employ imaginative knowing and to understand the interrelations within their overall organization. Questioning and imagining limited by fragmental boundaries cannot propel an organization to attain and sustain the knowledge with which it can create its own future.

Imagining for the whole necessitates an awareness of the whole. Bureaucratic, hierarchical power structures may inhibit members' freedom to inquire in domains outside those over which they officially have influence. Limits on areas of inquiry imply limits on imagination. Therefore, to thrive on imaginative knowing over the long run, organizations need to create cultures that allow space for imagining over a wide spectrum, across all bureaucratic fragments. Wisdom should apply to everything about the organization. Perhaps organizations need to find ways to make it legitimate for every member to question and imagine the whole organization. This obviously means that those who hold more power than others will have to look at that power differently. They will need to use their power to empower others to question and imagine as wide an array of organizational thought and action as possible. Administrators would have to help create a culture, within their bureaucracy, where members of the organization can freely manifest questioning and imagining. The culture of the organization would need to breed optimism and value members' imagination. Bureaucracy would then function in the service of imagination. Higher value would be placed on adventure as well as the ability to learn, to change, and to promote new ideas. Political processes and reward systems would accommodate imagination. Innovation and imagination would have to be primary components of the cultural rhetoric rather than states of mind confined to a particular part, division, or group, from where they can have at best limited impact on organizational affairs. The following remarks (recorded by Morgan, 1988), offered by three different senior administrators whose organizations were struggling to become more flexible and innovative, speak to the difficulty in creating a culture where innovation and imagination are key elements of the mind set:

> The culture of my organization tends to block innovation because the dominant values are those of control.
>
> One of the real problems [in my organization] is to find ways of creating a cultural transition from a situation dominated by senior executives who have grown up with the business in a different context into the present era where we face vastly different problems. We now have more competition than ever ... and are going through a quantum change. One of our problems is to change our traditions and ways of operating ... so that we can engage in new battles.
>
> Organizations change over time, and you often end up with people who are stewards instead of builders. How do you change that [attitude] so they are not stewards [p. 71]?

These administrators expressed the challenge organizations may face in trying to move from a bureaucratic, conventional, rational, systematic, fragmental view of organizational life to one that embraces wisdom, imagination, proactivity, process thinking, and an orientation toward the future. By generating imaginative knowledge, organizations, regardless of how much they are bureaucratized, can know and understand their own creative strengths and capabilities. They can bring bureaucracy to their service. Even though it might be currently hard to find "ideal" examples of such organizations, it seems that the changing rhetoric of management and organization indicates that many organizations are willing to move in an imaginative direction. Below are three more examples of administrators, recorded by Morgan (1988), that reflect this movement. The first one has to do with brainstorming, creative thinking, and breaking bureaucratic barriers; the second, with questioning taken-for-granted ways of thinking and acting and with an orientation toward the future; and the third, with the power and implications of imagination.

> What we need to do in our organization is to generate and raise brainstorming to a more important activity. You need to get people in a room and say, "We will suspend critical judgement. You are not responsible for any foolish comments you make. For a couple of days, let's just hang it out!" This process needs to be made a part of everybody's job, [generating] a basket of ideas out of which the visionary can say: "Oh, yes, this is something that sounds [promising]."
>
> In my organization we legitimize self-questioning [and constructive debate]. We have discussions on our worst fears, our highest hopes, our strengths and our weaknesses. As you go through this process you make an assessment of reality. And you build from there. That helps legitimize the philosophy of "let's get it on the table": How do customers see us? What do our members think of us? What is the feedback? If you get all that stuff on the table, it legitimizes a process that can become constructive, because, at the bottom of it all is: "Okay, what are we going to do about this, this, this, and this? And where do we want to be three years from now?"
>
> Nirvana occurs when you can match your shadow, not what other people think . . . when you are nicely in sync with your own strengths [pp. 72–74].

In each of these three examples, the administrator refers to the whole organization—all the members. Questioning and imagining are acts they desire to see across all areas of their organization's activity. These administrators are prospective reshapers of bureaucracy as we have known it. Their ideas imply that they would minimize the traditional fear of bureaucratic control and pressure that members would normally have when they attempt to question and imagine ways of thinking and acting in areas that are outside their individual domain.

Proposition 3: *Wisdom is enhanced in an organization when all of its members maintain the courage to experience, equally, the possible discomfort that may result from imaginative knowing.* The fundamental issue organizations have to face to maintain an imaginative mode of life is the courage that is required to make effective use of questioning and imagining. Organizations must make it an organizational norm to question taken-for-granted ways of thinking and acting, on a wide scope. This will provide organizational members with the ability and freedom to question and imagine. Courage comes from being strong enough to maintain that ability and freedom across all levels of the organization over the long run. Imaginative knowing is not a troubleshooting tool, it is a mode of knowing and living. As such it may cause some or all organizational members to experience frustration, due to the constant, overarching search for an unknown, imagined future.

Overcoming resistance to change is the most critical factor in determining the success of a change effort. Effective change in collective thinking and action requires the minimization of resistance and "free riding," or taking unfair advantage of the contributions of others (Collins, 1992). In the case of imaginative knowing, organizational members are expected to feel discomfort in breaking their usual mode of life at a very fundamental level. They are encouraged to break with convention. Some members may choose to resist or do less because "others are doing enough." There is no way to minimize such problems but through culture. Given the potential influence of administrators on the cultural values of their organizations, they need to make sure that they themselves fully believe in the value of imaginative knowledge, they practice what they preach, and they are not discouraged by initial failures in employing imaginative knowing. Modeling and persistence are the most important tools an administrator has in cultivating a culture that truly embraces imaginative knowing over the long run. The following remarks from an administrator, also recorded by Morgan (1988), reflect the attitude we are talking about:

> I have tried to run [creativity sessions] with operations managers, and it's an impossible task. First, they focus on exactly what they have always done, unless you do ten [sessions] in a row. The tenth one [often] starts to be productive. [But] it is so discouraging for the first nine. You don't get anywhere. But the fact that it is not work-

ing shows that you may be on the right track. Because the more
resistance you get, the more likely it is that this is what you need to
be doing [p. 74].

Achieving the wisdom that helps sustain imaginative knowing over
the long run is a lengthy and challenging journey. It is difficult to precisely measure how well an organization does in achieving this wisdom. Due to the intangible nature of imagination, setting specific goals
against which an organization can "test its wisdom" represents a fallacy. As long as an organization believes that it does have wisdom, it
does not. Wisdom is not a quality an organization can have at one time
and not have at another—it is a mode of life. Given that process thinking implies continuity and that proactivity and imagination imply joyful ambiguity, any belief in the possession of wisdom in a fragment,
duration, or moment of time runs contrary to the nature of the wisdom
advocated here.

DIALOGIC CONSTRUCTION OF IMAGINATIVE KNOWLEDGE

An imaginative search for truth cannot be perpetuated by an individual
acting in isolation, for imaginative knowing has a reciprocal character:
it renders the "imaginer" (the knower) dependent on others to sustain
her or his act. Imagination is triggered and influenced by people, stories, movies, books, cultures, lectures, objects, and so on that the imaginer encounters. Every encounter invokes certain thoughts and feelings
that contribute to imagination. In the process of trying to solve Rubik's
Cube, for instance, our improvisations and imaginative thoughts come
as customized responses to the cube or to an extension of Mr. Rubik's
mind. The knowledge we attain in the end is, to a significant extent, a
product of our contact with the cube. In this sense we depend on our
encounter with the cube, or the mind behind it, in order to generate the
imaginative knowledge we attain. Thus interactions with others are the
primary sources of our thoughts, making our imagination and knowledge outcomes of our interactions as well.

Humans are the only beings in the world that have minds capable of
thinking, imagining, and knowing. These three processes are among
the most important ones that distinguish us from other creatures. What
may not be so obvious at first sight, however, is that these three faculties are also among the most important ones that distinguish us from
one another. All thinking, imagining, and knowing processes are

unique and distinctive. By employing these three faculties we acquire and manifest the unique aspects of our minds. Paradoxically, although we are born with preshaped minds or predetermined selves, we grow up and lead our lives in environments in which we acquire these things. Our encounters, relationships, and interactions with other people stretch and influence our minds. Throughout our lifetimes we build and maintain a sense of who we are, what we want, and where we would like to go through a process of mutual influence among ourselves and the others around us—parents, friends, spouses, children, colleagues, movie stars, politicians, neighbors, writers, and so on. Our minds derive their uniqueness from the eclectic totality of the conversations and interactions we have with others in the social space within which we exist. In Gregory Bateson's terms (1972), one's mind is not an individual possession boxed into one's brain but a property (with all the unique characteristics of a property) of the collective context. Thus one's ingenuity is determined by the diversity of beings with which one relates.

The process through which we allow others to influence and contribute to our minds is "dialogue." Dialogue is not mere physical conversation, it is a mode of relating. When we are in dialogue with another person, we allow her or his voice and thoughts to enter our minds, interrupt our thoughts, and provoke new ideas. This does not mean that we unconditionally surrender our thoughts or agree with her or him but that we let the other's mind influence our own. Difference of viewpoint is a prerequisite for true dialogue. Constant empathy and unquestioned isomorphism would gradually eliminate significant contributions from the mind of the other to ours, and vice versa. Mutuality and reciprocity are key norms for having a meaningful dialogue. In a dialogic interaction, each party contributes to the other and sees her or him as an active center of awareness capable of offering a rich perspective (Srivastva and Barrett, 1988). Without occasions for true dialogue, our minds lack the richness and diversity of experience potentially available to them, and our thoughts and knowledge gradually become thinner and unchanging.

Dialogue feeds our minds and therefore our imagination and knowledge. Our relationships are not always dialogic, however. Regardless of the number of people with whom we communicate, we do not allow the thoughts of just anybody to enter our minds and influence our thoughts. Prolonged isolation and monologic (nondialogic) patterns within our relationships lead our imaginations to become nondiverse and repetitive, making the new and the unknown absent from our imaginative repertoire. As a result we lack imagination, and our relationship to the future consists of simple forecasting. Since our thoughts, imagination, and knowledge are outcomes of our interactions with others, whether those interactions are dialogic or not makes a big difference in the nature of the thoughts, imagination, and knowledge we possess.

Monologic interactions are not conducive to imaginative knowing; they entail neither mutuality nor reciprocity. Hence wisdom promotes the dialogic construction of knowledge. The reciprocally and proactively shaped thoughts of dialogic partners are the authentic source of imaginative knowledge, not individual minds. Truly imaginative knowledge can only be constructed within a dialogue. It necessitates sincere interaction between minds rather than mere monologic communication.

The potential for dialogic relating between minds is an essential property of human relationships. It is testimony to the pervasive relationship between the origins of our thoughts and imagination and the reciprocal character of imaginative knowledge. Wisdom celebrates dialogic relating and reciprocity of imagination. Therefore wisdom cannot be a virtue of one; it can only be a virtue of many. In an interaction of two persons, for instance, if one invites and attempts to engage in dialogue but the other does not, their relationship would be monologic. It would lack both mutual contribution and expansion of minds. In any human interaction, the parties derive their energy to dialogue from one another's efforts to pursue wisdom. Unless both parties pursue wisdom, neither can remain in dialogue. Thus wisdom, as defined here, is not something individuals have; it is something relationships create. Dialogic relationships are both outcomes and contexts of wisdom. They are the interactive framework where minds come into contact, thoughts expand, imaginations emerge, and knowledge is coconstructed.

Participants in a dialogue experience change. Where they are during the dialogue and where they end up after it are different from where they start. The resulting imaginative knowledge transforms their past and constructs their future. In this respect their relationship is the source of what is to come. It is the origin not only of their minds but also of their futures.

Consider the following five-minute conversation and its aftermath:

John, Phillip, and Jenny are having lunch. John is a full-time graduate student in organizational behavior (OB). Phillip is a part-time graduate student in economics and a full-time financial analyst at a nationwide insurance company. Jenny is a high school teacher. Phillip and Jenny are married. John and Phillip are classmates in a group dynamics course Phillip is taking as an elective from John's department. They are engaged in a casual, friendly conversation. At one point Phillip starts sharing some of his plans for changing jobs in the near future, and John inquires as to why he is looking for another job.

JOHN: Why do you want to change jobs, Phillip? You don't enjoy what you do anymore or something?

PHILLIP: As a matter of fact, I want to change where I work rather than what I do. A lot of my friends at work feel the same way.

JOHN: Is there a problem with the company?

PHILLIP: Well, you might say that we've been lacking solid leadership. Nobody knows what the hell is going on. It seems like some of the big decisions are not being made fast enough at the top. People feel like there is no sense of future direction for the company. No investments, no new products, no new markets . . . no nothing. Some feel really pessimistic about the company's future.

JOHN: Do you have any idea as to why top management has not been doing something about this?

PHILLIP: I really don't know. We have a CEO who is known to be a competent and successful one. The vice presidents are also talented people. I can't really think of a specific reason, but I'd sure like to know.

JOHN: This situation brings to my mind a research study I'm currently involved in as part of a class I'm taking. Would you like to hear about it? It might be helpful to you in understanding what is going on in your company—who knows?

PHILLIP: Sure, but you may get tired. I may not understand it.

JOHN: Sure you can! Why do you think that way?

PHILLIP: I don't know. . . . There are times when I can't quite follow OB.

JOHN: Hmm. Are you one those people who think that OB is full of "touchy-feely" stuff?

PHILLIP: Touchy-feely? . . . I guess I am. I'm already having trouble understanding what is going on in the group dynamics class anyway.

JOHN: Well, this study is not that touchy-feely. Plus, don't underestimate yourself. You can understand anything, and you are doing fine in class—better than I am, at least. Besides, this research study is something closer to your "paradigm." It's an empirical study of the relationship between how much uncertainty managers experience at work and their attitudes toward change. I can tell you how we measure perceived uncertainty, and you can see whether or not it will be helpful to you in figuring out what is going on at work. It may be that top management is experiencing so much uncertainty that they are reluctant to make decisions that involve any significant future implication.

PHILLIP: It sounds interesting. Tell me more.

JENNY: Oh, come on, guys. I'll get bored if you start talking about research.

JOHN: It'll only take a few minutes. Plus, I'm sure you'll find it interesting too. If not, then let me know and I'll stop. We can talk about something else, and I can tell Phillip about my research later.

JENNY: All right, go ahead. I can take it for a few minutes.

JOHN: We use a questionnaire. It has twelve questions, grouped under three categories. One category measures the degree to which the respondent is satisfied with the amount of information available to him. The other measures the degree to which he can predict the outcomes of his decisions. And the third one measures the degree to which he can assign probabilities to alternative outcomes for his decisions.

PHILLIP: Hmm . . . Why do you ask those three groups of questions?

JOHN: What do you mean?

PHILLIP: I mean, can't you just go and simply ask people why they experience uncertainty?

JOHN: Well, it's because we found a prevalidated way to measure uncertainty. Somebody else used it before, and it works. That's always the better way to go.

PHILLIP: I get it. What were your categories again?

JOHN: Amount of information available for decision making, ability to predict outcomes, and ability to assign probabilities to alternative outcomes.

PHILLIP: Hmm. Actually, they sound really interesting.

JOHN: You know, maybe if you reword and casually ask these questions to people at work, you may get some interesting answers.

PHILLIP: Sounds like a good idea.

JENNY: Who are you giving this questionnaire to, John?

JOHN: In our sample we have people from several different organizations. Most of them are enrolled in the MBA program at the university. Some are high-level, some are mid-level, and some are lower-level employees.

JENNY: Are you asking the people around each respondent how much uncertainty they are experiencing?

JOHN: No. Why?

JENNY: Well, maybe their perceptions of uncertainty have an impact on that of the respondent.

JOHN: Hmm . . . interesting. How did you think of that?

JENNY: Well, at the school where I work we have a counseling program. We try to help seniors overcome their uncertainties about what they want to do in the future, develop some sort of direction, and think of a couple of alternatives about where they want to go. What we have discovered over the last few years is that the kids who seem to be uncertain about the future have friends who are also fairly uncertain. So we have been wondering about the degree to which the uncertainty students are experiencing is due to friends they have who feel the same way.

JOHN: Wow! That is a great question. I never thought of that.

PHILLIP: You know what? That makes me wonder, too. Maybe people at my company feel uncertain because everybody feels that way. I, for one, know that I got used to feeling uncertain because I frequently talked about it with friends at work.

JENNY: [To Phillip] Well, maybe you can try talking to people you rarely talk to, and see what happens. [To John] I'll share your research study with my friends at work. Maybe we can do something with it.

Following this exchange John gave a lot of thought to Jenny's idea and shared it with his fellow researchers, but they could not include it in their study, due to time constraints. He also shared it with some other graduate students he knew at other schools. The following year he found out that one of his friends at another school had taken Jenny's idea forward and conducted a study in which he looked at whether or not people who had similar perceptions of uncertainty had worked with one another and interacted frequently. His findings indicated that people's interactions with others have a huge impact on their perception of uncertainty in general. In certain cases this impact is greater than the impact of the availability of information and of their ability to predict the outcomes of decisions.

The participants in this interaction are in dialogue. They enter one another's universe, influence one another's thoughts, and coconstruct imaginative knowledge. Each plays a unique part in shaping the thoughts and knowledge that emerge from their relationship. Their dialogue transforms them, both as individuals and as a group, and redirects them toward a new future.

In summary, five fundamental ideas are illustrated in the preceding dialogue:

1. *Open invitations.* The parties extend open invitations for dialogue to one another. For example, after Phillip describes his situation at work, which has an impact on John's thoughts, John invites Phillip to join in a meaningful exchange. Also, Jenny invites John to dialogue after his research study has an impact on her thoughts. The open

nature of the invitations testify to the egalitarian nature of the conversation. After receiving her initial invitation, Jenny feels free to refuse, only to accept later on. True dialogue is a form of interaction based on freedom of entry and exit. Participants are free to both engage and disengage, without fear of jeopardizing the whole relationship. Coercing others to keep them participating in the dialogue (or, conversely, ignoring their feelings) would result in a false dialogue, or monologue.

2. *Internal dialogue.* Each party experiences and extends part of the overall dialogue internally (that is, pursues an internal dialogue) as the conversation goes on. Jenny, for instance, manifests her internal dialogue when she verbally engages the conversation at a later stage, to the surprise of both John and Phillip. She feels free to interrupt and redirect the thoughts of her dialogic partners because she has already been participating internally. We also see John's internal dialogue extending beyond his verbal conversation and leading to new thoughts and insights. This is a good example of how dialogue enhances imagination.

3. *Discovery of tacit knowledge.* One of the most important features of this dialogue is the way it brings the tacit knowledge of the parties out into the open. Tacit knowledge is that component of a person's knowledge that resides in an unarticulated form, beneath what the person explicitly "knows." It is a doing of his or her own, lacking the public, objective character of explicit knowledge (Polanyi, 1958). Individuals are not fully aware of their tacit knowledge because it is unformulated and cannot be clearly expressed. For example, even though Phillip has probably not heard any lectures or read any texts that explicitly stated that OB is full of "touchy-feely stuff," he "knows" that it is as a result of the unarticulated, unreasoned conclusions of his senses and feelings concerning OB. He just did not have the words to express that tacit knowledge until John gave him some. Discovery of one's tacit knowledge is the best indication that dialogue is taking place, because only a dialogic partner can reveal it. The surfacing and explaining of tacit knowledge are among the essential consequences of dialogue: the parties become informed about not only one another's but also their own assumptions.

Dissimilarity or contradictions between participants' tacit knowledge is a key prerequisite for meaningful dialogue. Dialogue is not a process in which initial assumptions have to be similar or standardized for the relationship to evolve. Rather, through dialogue mutual legitimacy and sensibility of participants' tacit knowledge are achieved. As mentioned earlier, isomorphism between conversing minds breeds monologues.

4. *Breaking the bounds of authority and expertise.* In this dialogue, even though each party belongs to a different profession, each values the others' contributions to her or his thoughts and knowledge regarding her or his area of expertise. John, for instance, does not let his authority and knowledge on his own research study keep Jenny's suggestion from influencing him. Jenny takes away a fresh perspective from John as well. In a dialogic exchange, participants relate at a level that reaches beyond the potential differences of authority or expertise among them. Remaining behind such differences rather than moving beyond them eliminates dialogue because it compromises true mutuality and reciprocity.

5. *Universalization of knowledge.* The knowledge that is dialogically constructed by the conversing parties does not belong to any one of them alone. They all possess it—or, more precisely, it belongs to their relationship. A key feature of a true dialogue is that the resulting knowledge is universalized, legitimated, and disseminated among the parties during the process of its construction—not after it, which is usually the case for knowledge that is not dialogically attained.

As John, Phillip, and Jenny engage in dialogue, their relationship becomes their way of knowing. In the process of relating to one another they engage in imaginative knowing. Every thought throughout their dialogue is interrelated with other thoughts. By briefly recalling the convergences that imaginative knowing yields (Figure 11.1), we can rephrase some key observations. Initially, John, Phillip, and Jenny are uncertain about where their conversation will take them. Appreciating this uncertainty, they start to share and form their thoughts in an unplanned yet coherent manner. Each improvises her or his responses to the other two, as all three engage and remain in dialogue. Their dialogue is an opportunity for them to contribute to and influence one another's minds in novel ways. Their powers of understanding process new, previously unknown linkages. It enriches their thoughts and inspires their imagination. In the end, they collectively pave the way to new knowledge. Within a dialogic framework, uncertainty, improvisation, change, and process thinking converge and elicit imaginative knowledge. John, Phillip, and Jenny *care more for the process than the product of their dialogue.* They all pursue wisdom.

The dialogue between John, Phillip, and Jenny is but one example among billions that support the idea that organizational members' relationships are the key forces that give life to an organization. How an organization's members interact or interrelate is a key factor in determining the nature of the thoughts, imagination, and knowledge that characterize life in and around the organization. Organizations are bodies of thought created by active thinkers (Weick, 1979). The existence of dialogic generation of thought within an organization is testimony to its wisdom. By fostering norms that legitimate and encourage dialogue, an organization can establish and maintain a relational context that imaginatively generates its own future. Through dialogue, organizational members can proactively enact change and make their relationships a source of the future that they favor. An imaginative search for truth via dialogue is an organization's way of constructing its future.

The conventional wisdom that bureaucracy fosters a monologic mode of relating to the extent that the organization dictates what thoughts, imaginations, and knowledge are legitimate and acceptable is constantly observable (Srivastva and Barrett, 1988). Role definitions and task specialization limit members to being expert only at what they are expected to know and do in the organization. Bureaucratic division of labor promulgates the view that each member's mind is an individual container, a fragment of thoughts and knowledge, that together with the other members' similarly constricted minds keeps the organization functioning as a whole. Thus members' encounters, interactions, and relationships are considered only in terms of members' coming together and functioning in systematically predetermined and controlled ways, as cogs in a machine. They are rarely considered sources of novel, imaginative thoughts, knowledge, and actions that can potentially capture and improve the whole of the organization.

Pursuing wisdom is a way for organizations to move beyond conventional genres of thought and action that limit dialogue. Wisdom implies seeing relationships as ways of thinking, imagining, and knowing. Let us now consider three fundamental propositions that summarize the arguments presented in this part of the chapter.

Proposition 4: *Wisdom exists in an organization to the extent that its members view as primary sources of knowledge not their individual minds but their relationships with one another.* For the members of an organization that pursues wisdom, what can be known by relating to others is more primary than what one knows individually. Relationships are celebrated as blueprints of collective knowing that can transform the whole organization. Viewing relationships as sources of new knowledge is analogous to both knowing the whole organization and relocating it to a new future. Organizations are collections of people with diverse perspectives who are brought together under a shared paradigm (Pfeffer, 1981). Dialogic relationships are social fields in which people, regardless of how diverse their perspectives are, can reciprocally "connect" and create novel paradigms. True dialogue, though, requires members to appreciate the differences in one another's thinking and to invite one another to contribute their different viewpoints to their relationships. Such appreciation and invitation can potentially enrich and broaden the collective mind of the organization. From fragmented, present- or past-oriented, self-centered levels of thought, knowledge, and action members can move to holistic, interrelated, future-oriented, pluralistic levels.

Proposition 5: *Wisdom exists in an organization to the extent that its members' dialogic relationships are as diverse as possible.* The more diverse the persons, groups, and levels represented in an organization's internal relationships, the greater the potential for creating unique futures and knowledge. Given the reciprocal character of imagining, the extent of the difference among the participants in a dialogic relationship contributes to the strength and novelty of the imaginative knowledge they coconstruct. Thus the more different the minds that relate, the more surprising and exciting the futures they imagine.

Differentiation and integration—of persons and groups—is an essential property of organizational life. Conventionally, differentiation and integration have been viewed as functional prerequisites that maintain an organization's equilibrium (Burns and Stalker, 1961; Lawrence and Lorsch, 1967). From a constructionist standpoint, they can also be viewed as dialogic prerequisites that ensure novel imaginations, knowledge, and futures. Differentiation refers to the diversity of views and concerns individuals bring into their dialogic relationships, which integrate them. Integration as such does not imply a functional aggregation of people or groups for purposes of organizational equilibrium but rather the formation and maintenance of "mindful" connections among members for imaginative knowing. The concept of organizational equilibrium changes meaning; it connotes an interpersonal complexity and instability generated by imagination and dialogue.

Dialogic integration of the diverse views and concerns of the persons, groups, and levels within an organization necessitates an unconventional view of power and freedom. A view of power as the ability to determine the topics, concerns, agendas, and rhetoric that characterize conversations among the parties in a relationship leads to monologues (Sampson, 1993). In a bureaucracy, those who have legitimate authority to determine the "faith" of the whole organization unilaterally specify which topics are legitimate for conversation as well as the degree to which those with less authority should contribute to or question such topics (Weber, 1947). The assumptions and tacit knowledge of the higher levels dominate the key aspects of organizational life. Such domination allows no space for true dialogue and discards the diversity of thought and knowledge available within the organization. Differences between minds can rarely be voiced, and diversity of views is treated as illegitimate or irrelevant. The minds and thoughts of those in charge are rarely interrupted or redirected. In fact, few are free even to engage in dialogue. The resulting monologic climate is not conducive to the discovery and articulation of tacit knowledge. Thus persons and groups at different levels independently acquire and maintain tacit knowledge that leads them to make inaccurate conclusions about others' lives and realities in the same organization. The only type of integration that occurs under such circumstances is when individuals "work together"; in such organizations integration never reflects the spirit that members "live together" and generate imaginative knowledge for the whole organization.

In a dialogic exchange participants relate at a level that reaches beyond the potential differences of authority and expertise among them. It follows that for genuine dialogue to occur in an organization, those with more authority and expertise than others need to apply their power so as to create dialogues rather than monologues. They need to help create an egalitarian culture that offers opportunities for everyone to relate to everyone else dialogically. In this way, instead of unilaterally determining the future of their organization, they will empower others to unleash their creativity and collectively imagine and enact new futures. From an administrative standpoint this calls for striking a balance between chaos and control. For instance, many administrators potentially face pressure to maintain functional, controlled integration when they encourage members to step beyond bureaucratic boundaries, relate to one another, and be creative. The following concerns (recorded by Morgan, 1988) of a high-level administrator speak to some aspects of this issue:

> There is a fine line between tough controls and chaos. You have to encourage creativity, so that people can contribute.... But there have to be some controls. How do you give people freedom yet have some control? How can you give a manager thousands of miles away the freedom to run an organization, yet have the proper controls that will give you the early warning systems if there are any problems? Striking that balance is a critical task of management [pp. 83–84].

The best ways that an administrator can overcome the ambiguity that might come with a culture that stresses relationships and creativity is to make herself or himself available for dialogue and to personally be a part of the organization-wide dialogue that generates imaginative knowledge. Staying detached is a monologic act that triggers control instincts. Fostering dialogue and imagination requires a dialogic mode of leadership, one that values different minds and the freedom to voice them.

Proposition 6: *Wisdom is enhanced in an organization when it encourages its members to celebrate the inconvenience of allocating time and effort to maintaining dialogues and when it allows them to experience the changes they live through as a result of dialogue.* For leaders and followers alike, dialogue is a mode of relating that necessitates dedication and commitment. The speed and rationality with which organizations are expected to function in our day are such that it may become easier and more convenient for members to switch to or remain in monologues rather than engage in dialogues. A true dialogue is not a "speedy" process but an all-encompassing and delicate one. The relating of minds, expansion of thought, emergence of imagination, and coconstruction of knowledge require not an efficient and rational approach but one that values the difficulties that accompany dialogue, for it is such difficulties that confirm dialogue.

Parties in a dialogue derive their energy to stay in the dialogue from their efforts to pursue wisdom. This implies minimization of free riding. Each member should be equally willing to experience the inconveniences that accompany dialogue. The elemental inconvenience is related to creating the time and effort for active dialogue. Interruption and redirection of one's streams of thought are basic inconveniences an individual must accept to engage in dialogue. Thus, creating a culture in which such inconveniences are legitimated and celebrated is a key organizational requirement for maintaining dialogue. Certain norms and events can encourage members to uphold a dialogic culture, increase their commitment to dialogue, and elevate their motivation to imagine. For example, setting aside specific time slots or setting up special activities in which members can come together and engage in dialogue to generate imaginative knowledge can help ensure that dialogue remains a part of an organization's life, despite its inconveniences. Such factors, as many people charged with fostering dialogue within an organization can confirm, can run into traditional, bureaucratic barriers and screening. The following observations of an administrator who tried to allocate some unstructured time for dialogue and creativity (also recorded by Morgan, 1988) exemplify some of the potential problems one may face:

> The problem is that people are taking time off, and if something goes wrong, they will be seen as "goofing off.". . . Companies don't believe that their employees are committed to their organizations, and that's why they don't want to give them time to do things that are not productive in a concrete way. The way you get ahead [nowadays] is by going from one organization to another and cutting a better deal. That makes senior management unhappy about being loose with people's time, because they don't believe that they are going to put that time to work for the organization over a long career. I am not just talking about senior people not allowing their juniors to do this. I am talking about senior people not allowing themselves to do it [p. 76].

Another basic instance of learning associated with dialogue is the personal transformation participants of dialogue can and do experience. The personal change that occurs from engaging in dialogue is different from, yet an integral part of, change in the form of new organizational futures. It refers to the change an individual can potentially experience within herself or himself. The discovery and articulation of tacit knowledge is the source of the personal change that dialogue elicits. As parties experience one another's tacit knowledge and attempt to articulate their own, they unravel and impact their assumptions about one another, about other people, and, depending on the topic and range of their dialogue, several key organizational issues. In an organization in which dialogue is the primary mode of relating, members view the discovery and articulation of their tacit knowledge as an indication that they are generating imaginative knowledge and enacting new futures. Their orientation concerning the future and the inconveniences that will come with it are what transform them as well as their organization.

CONCLUSION

Organizational science has only recently opened up to the idea that wisdom plays a key role in organizational life. But modeled as it is on the empirical sciences, organizational science runs the risk of relying too much on its dominant methods in shaping alternative notions and definitions of wisdom in organizational life. We believe that this runs counter to the nature of wisdom as a quality that can always outgrow itself. In other words, there always is (and must be) the possibility to become wiser. Wisdom, therefore, can never be measured for certain. In our opinion it is more important to enrich the meaning of wisdom and to look for its sources than it is to measure it.

In this chapter we have defined wisdom in association with imagination and dialogue because we believe that organizational wisdom lies somewhere in between a vibrant conception of the future and a respect for interaction. Organizations can pursue wisdom by altering their dominant way of knowing. In the social sphere, knowledge represents reality. As we assign our imagination and dialogues primary roles in generating knowledge, we socially construct the reality of the future. It is in such processes that we truly pursue wisdom. Given the common-sense conception of wisdom in many cultures as a quality that is extremely difficult to attain, it seems ironic that engaging in dialogue with one another, giving voice to our imagination, and never believing that our knowledge is ever sufficient are enough to pursue wisdom.

From this perspective the organizational setting, by nature, provides its members the most necessary prerequisites for wisdom—fellow members, an organizational future that can depend on members' imaginations, and endless needs and opportunities to improve and expand organizational knowledge. The first step to pursuing organizational wisdom is simply to become aware of these prerequisites. Novel organizational realities and futures are created as members capitalize on these prerequisites as a means of pursuing wisdom.

The definitions, arguments, and propositions put forth in this chapter are an attempt to provide a kaleidoscopic way of seeing knowledge, which can make organizational wisdom visible to the eyes of many others. They are also what we have to contribute to the dialogue about wisdom.

REFERENCES

Astley, G. W., and Fombrun, C. J. "Collective Strategy: Social Ecology of Organizational Environments." *Academy of Management Review,* 1983, *8,* 576–587.

Bakhtin, M. M. *The Dialogic Imagination.* Austin: University of Texas Press, 1981.

Bateson, G. *Steps to an Ecology of Mind.* New York: Ballentine, 1972.

Burns, T., and Stalker, G. M. *The Management of Innovation.* New York: Tavistock, 1961.

Chandler, A. D. *Strategy and Structure.* Cambridge, Mass.: MIT Press, 1962.

Collins, R. *Sociological Insight: An Introduction to Non-obvious Sociology.* New York: Oxford University Press, 1992.

Duncan, R. B. "Characteristics of Organizational Environments and Perceived

Environmental Uncertainty." *Administrative Science Quarterly,* 1972, *17,* 313–327.

Emery, F. E., and Trist, E. L. "The Causal Texture of Organizational Environments." *Human Relations,* 1965, *18,* 21–32.

Galaskiewicz, J. "Interorganizational Relations." In *Annual Review of Sociology* (no. 11). Palo Alto, Calif.: Annual Reviews, 1985.

Katz, D., and Kahn, R. L. *The Social Psychology of Organizations.* New York: Wiley, 1966.

Lawrence, P. R., and Lorsch, J. W. *Organization and Environment.* Boston: Harvard Business School Press, 1967.

Mackenzie, K. D. "Some Real-World Adventures of a Bench Scientist." In R. H. Killmann and Associates (eds.), *Producing Useful Knowledge for Organizations.* San Francisco: Jossey-Bass, 1994.

Milliken, F. J. "Three Types of Perceived Uncertainty About the Environment: State, Effect, and Response." *Academy of Management Review,* 1987, *12,* 133–143.

Mintzberg, H. *The Structuring of Organizations.* Englewood Cliffs, N.J.: Prentice Hall, 1979.

Morgan, G. *Riding the Waves of Change: Developing Managerial Competencies for a Turbulent World.* San Francisco: Jossey-Bass, 1988.

Parsons, T. *The Social System.* New York: Free Press, 1951.

Pfeffer, J. "Management as Symbolic Action." In L. L. Cummings and B. M. Staw (eds.), *Research in Organizational Behavior.* Greenwich, Conn.: JAI Press, 1981.

Pfeffer, J., and Salancik, G. R. *The External Control of Organizations: A Resource Dependence Perspective.* New York: HarperCollins, 1978.

Polanyi, M. *The Study of Man.* New York: Routledge, 1958.

Sampson, E. E. *Celebrating the Other: A Dialogic Account of Human Nature.* Boulder, Colo.: Westview Press, 1993.

Srivastva, S., and Barrett, F. J. "Foundations for Executive Integrity: Dialogue, Diversity, Development." In S. Srivastva and Associates (eds.), *Executive Integrity: The Search for High Human Values in Organizational Life.* San Francisco: Jossey-Bass, 1988.

Stinchcombe, A. L. *Information and Organizations.* Berkeley: University of California Press, 1990.

Thompson, J. D. *Organizations in Action: Social Science Bases of Administrative Theory.* New York: McGraw-Hill, 1967.

von Bertalannfy, L. *General Systems Theory.* New York: Braziller, 1968.

Weber, M. *Theory of Social and Economic Organization.* New York: Free Press, 1947.

Weick, K. "Cognitive Processes in Organizations." In B. M. Staw (ed.), *Research in Organizational Behavior.* Greenwich, Conn.: JAI Press, 1979.

Whitehead, A. N. *Process and Reality.* New York: Free Press, 1929.

Whitehead, A. N. *Modes of Thought.* New York: Free Press, 1938.

NAME INDEX

A

Adler, N. J., 206, 207, 213, 215
Ahiauzu, A., 160
Aktouf, O., 185
Alderfer, C., 226
Alexander, S., 183
Alvesson, M., 184, 185
Ammons, A. R., 35
Anzaldua, G., 136
Aquino, C., 18, 215–216, 220
Aram, J., 170, 182
Argyris, C., 185, 229, 243, 245
Astley, G. W., 261
Aung San Suu Kyi, 210, 211, 214, 216, 219
Aupperle, K., 171

B

Bakhtin, M. M., 130, 254
Bamforth, K., 186
Barnard, C. I., 7, 33, 34
Barrett, F. J., 269, 277
Bartunek, J., 244
Bateson, G., 110, 269
Bateson, M. C., 226, 245
Beatty, R. W., 85
Bedain, A., 226
Beetz, S., 148
Bellah, R. H., 139
Benn, M., 214
Bennis, W., 161
Berkowitz, L., 184
Berle, A., 157, 170
Berliner, P. .F., 57
Beyer, J. M., 65, 68, 73, 74, 77, 80, 81, 94
Bhandarkar, A., 161
Bhasin, M., 174

Bhatt, K., 160
Bhutto, B., 216, 220
Bibeault, D., 159
Bigelow, J., 66
Billings, P., 90
Blanshard, B., 41, 42, 68
Block, P., 185, 186, 190
Blondel, J., 207
Bloom, A., 229
Bobko, P., 244
Bohan, J. S., 143
Boje, D. M., 149
Bollier, D., 3, 16
Bowers, D., 161
Bowie, N., 68
Bracker, J., 160
Brandenberger, A. M., 148
Brief, A., 184
Brockner, J., 84
Brown, D., 175
Brown, L., 175
Browning, D., 25
Bruce, R., 87
Buber, M., 229
Burke, J. E., 3–4
Burleigh, M., 124
Burnham, D., 178
Burns, T., 261, 263, 278
Burrell, G., 157, 185

C

Caldwell, D. F., 66
Cameron, K. S., 84, 85
Camillus, J., 163
Campbell, D., 243, 244
Campbell, O. T., 60, 61
Carkhuff, R., 229
Carroll, A., 170, 171

SUBJECT INDEX

A

Absolute, preoccupation with, 38
Action, 8, 48, 52
Action science, 229
Alacrity Foundation, 180–181
Altruism: basis of, 183; case examples of, 184; defined, 183; prosocial organizational behavior and, 183–184
Ambivalence: attitude of wisdom and, 60–61; firefighting and, 61–62; LCES system and, 62
Art: heroism and, 142; management as, 34
Assimilation, 50–51
Attachment, 50
Attitude of wisdom: ambivalence and, 60–61; assimilation and, 49–51; attachment and, 50; attentiveness and, 8, 52; caution and, 54–57; caution-confidence balance and, 7–8, 54–56; conceptual slack and, 52; confidence and, 49–54; defined, 7, 40; doubt and, 50–52, 54, 56; failing to notice and, 54; firefighting and, 40, 47; ignorance and, 52–53; improvisation and, 8, 57–59; limitations of, 48; older truths and, 49; overcaution and, 7–8, 46–47; rarity of, 49, 52; refinements in, 47–48; successful simultaneity and, 8, 48; theme of, 46–47; wise physician example of, 53
Autobiographical accounts, 225–226

B

Balance: of confidence/overcaution, 7–8, 46–47, 57; improvisation and, 57, 59; of knowledge/doubt, 58–59
Barings Bank, 82–83
Behaviorism, 241, 243
Ben & Jerry's, 17, 172–173
Bhagavad Gita, 1–2, 186
Bharat Heavy Electricals, Ltd. (BHEL), 17, 174–175
British Steel, 170
Bureaucratization, 264–265

C

Cascades, Inc., 185
Çatal Höyük, 17, 205
Caution: balancing confidence and, 7–8, 57–59; conversion to wisdom of, 56; information processing and, 55
Centrality, fallacy of, 51
Challenger space shuttle, 83–84
Change: consistency and, 88; dysfunctional organization and, 87; honoring past and, 87–88; imaginative knowing and, 267; management culture and, 88–89; managerial wisdom/courage and, 89–91, 94; as opportunity, 258–239, 263; permanent whitewater analogy and, 37; philosophy of temporality and, 37; proactivity and, 261–263; punctuated equilibrium model of, 86; radical, 86, 88–89; reengineering